CONTROVERSIES IN MISSION

D1114167

OTHER BOOKS IN THE EMS SERIES

ABOUT EMS

www.emsweb.org

The Evangelical Missiological Society is a professional organization with more than 400 members comprised of missiologists, mission administrators, reflective mission practitioners, teachers, pastors with strategic missiological interests, and students of missiology. EMS exists to advance the cause of world evangelization. We do this through study and evaluation of mission concepts and strategies from a biblical perspective with a view to commending sound mission theory and practice to churches, mission agencies, and schools of missionary training around the world. We hold an annual national conference and eight regional meetings in the United States and Canada.

Evangelical
Missiological
Society
Series

no. **24**

CONTROVERSIES IN MISSION

THEOLOGY, PEOPLE, AND PRACTICE OF MISSION IN THE 21ST CENTURY

ROCHELLE CATHCART SCHEUERMANN AND EDWARD L. SMITHER | **EDITORS**

WILLIAM CAREY
LIBRARY

Controversies in Mission: Theology, People, and Practice of Mission in the 21st Century

Copyright © 2016 by Evangelical Missiological Society

All rights reserved.

No part of this book may be reproduced, stored in a retrieval system, or transmitted in any form or by any means—electronic, mechanical, photocopy, recording, or otherwise—without prior written permission of the publisher, except brief quotations used in connection with reviews in magazines or newspapers.

Unless otherwise noted, Scripture quotations are from The Holy Bible, New International Version, NIVR Copyright © 1973, 1978, 1984, 2011 by Biblica, Inc. Used by permission of Zondervan. All rights reserved worldwide.

Scripture quotations marked "NASB" are taken from the New American Standard Bible®, Copyright © 1960, 1962, 1963, 1968, 1971, 1972, 1973, 1975, 1977, 1995 by The Lockman Foundation. Used by permission. (www.Lockman.org)

Scripture quotations marked "NRSV" are taken from the New Revised Standard Version Bible, copyright 1989, Division of Christian Education of the National Council of the Churches of Christ in the United States of America. Used by permission. All rights reserved.

Scripture quotations marked "NAS" are taken from the NEW AMERICAN STANDARD BIBLE®, Copyright © 1960,1962,1963,1968,1971,1972,1973,1975,1977,1995 by The Lockman Foundation. Used by permission.

Published by William Carey Library

1605 E. Elizabeth St.

Pasadena, CA 91104 | www.missionbooks.org

Melissa Hicks, copyeditor

Josie Leung, graphic design

William Carey Library is a ministry of

Frontier Ventures | www.frontierventures.org

Printed in the United States of America

20 19 18 17 16   5 4 3 2 1 BP

Library of Congress Cataloging-in-Publication Data

Names: Scheuermann, Rochelle Cathcart, editor.

Title: Controversies in mission : theology, people, and practice of mission
   in the 21st century / Rochelle Cathcart Scheuermann and Edward L. Smither, editors.

Description: Pasadena, CA : William Carey Library, 2016. | Series: Evangelical Missiological Society
   series ; 24 | Includes bibliographical references and index. | Description based on print version
   record and CIP data provided by publisher; resource not viewed.

Identifiers: LCCN 2016018913 (print) | LCCN 2016018069 (ebook) | ISBN
   9780878088928 (eBook) | ISBN 9780878080540 (pbk.) | ISBN 0878080546 (pbk.)

Subjects: LCSH: Missions--History--21st century.

Classification: LCC BV2120 (print) | LCC BV2120 .C65 2016 (ebook) | DDC
   266.009/05--dc23

LC record available at https://lccn.loc.gov/2016018913

CONTENTS

CONTRIBUTORS

Miriam Adeney (PhD, Washington State University) is a missiologist, a professor at Seattle Pacific University, and an author. Her books include *Kingdom Without Borders* (on global Christianity); *Wealth, Women, and God* (on the Arabian Gulf); *Daughters of Islam* (on building bridges with Muslims); *How to Write: A Christian Writer's Guide;* and *God's Foreign Policy: Practical Ways to Help the World's Poor.* Miriam has worked on six continents, but her special focus is Southeast Asia.

David Beine (PhD, Washington State University) is currently a professor of intercultural studies at Moody Bible Institute-Spokane, WA. He has also served with Wycliffe Bible Translators and SIL International since 1987 in a variety of capacities including language survey specialist (1987–1991), branch anthropology consultant (1994–2004), literacy project coordinator (1998–2013), training school director (2002–2008), and senior international anthropology consultant (2008–2015).

Larry W. Caldwell (PhD, Fuller Theological Seminary) taught missions and Bible interpretation courses in Asia for thirty years, mostly at Asian Theological Seminary in Manila, Philippines. He is currently chief academic officer and dean of Sioux Falls Seminary, as well as director of training and strategy for the international ministries division of Converge Worldwide.

David R. Dunaetz (PhD, Claremont Graduate University) teaches organizational psychology at Azusa Pacific University. His research program focuses on conflict processes in Christian organizations. He was a church planter in France for seventeen years with WorldVenture.

Mark Hausfeld (DMin, Northern Baptist Theological Seminary) is president and professor of urban and Islamic studies at the Assemblies of God Theological Seminary. Previously, he served Assemblies of God World Missions as international director of Global Initiative: Reaching Muslim Peoples; an area director for Central Eurasia missionaries; missionary in Pakistan; and urban church planter and pastor in the city of Chicago.

David J. Hesselgrave (PhD, University of Minnesota) was a missionary to Japan with the Evangelical Free Church of America from 1950 to 1962 and professor of mission at Trinity Evangelical Divinity School from 1965 until his retirement in 1991. He is the author of many monographs and the author of a number of books including *Communicating Christ Cross-Culturally, Planting Churches Cross-Culturally,* and *Paradigms in Conflict.*

Kevin Higgins (PhD, Fuller Theological Seminary) is international director of Global Teams. He and his wife have served for over twenty-five years in the Muslim world, in direct disciple making and in training and coaching other workers.

Eunice Hong (PhD, Biola University) has served as the English Ministry pastor at Glory Church of Jesus Christ since 2002. Her doctoral dissertation focused on the cultural and generational differences between first-generation Koreans and second-generation Korean Americans in the Korean American church.

Jerry M. Ireland (PhD, Liberty University) has served as a missionary with the Assemblies of God since 2006, and lives in Lomé, Togo. He is passionate about developing approaches to compassionate missions that focus on strengthening the capacity of local churches. He is also the author of *Evangelism and Social Concern in the Theology of Carl F. H. Henry*.

Christopher R. Little (PhD, Fuller Theological Seminary) is professor of intercultural studies at Columbia International University and has served in Europe, Africa, and the Middle East. He is the author of *The Revelation of God Among the Unevangelized: An Evangelical Appraisal and Missiological Contribution to the Debate*, *Mission in the Way of Paul: Biblical Mission for the Church in the Twenty-First Century*, and *Polemic Missiology for the 21st Century: In Memoriam of Roland Allen*, as well as numerous articles on mission in various journals.

Greg Mathias (PhD, Southeastern Baptist Theological Seminary) is assistant professor of global studies and associate director of the Center for Great Commission Studies at Southeastern Baptist Theological Seminary. He is a former missionary with the International Mission Board (SBC) and now mentors international church planting students serving around the world.

Mark Naylor (ThD, University of South Africa) ministered among Sindhi Muslims in the province of Sindh Pakistan from 1985 to 1999, including serving on the Sindhi Bible translation team, a project of the Pakistan Bible Society. He continues to serve as supervisor and primary exegete of the project, travelling to Pakistan twice a year. Mark is also on the faculty of Northwest Baptist Seminary (Langley, BC) and is employed by Fellowship International (Guelph, ON) as the coordinator of international leadership development.

Kenneth R. Nehrbass (PhD, Biola University) is an assistant professor and program director of the PhD in intercultural studies at Cook School of Intercultural Studies at Biola University. As members of Wycliffe Bible Translators, he and his wife worked with a team of nationals to translate the New Testament in the Southwest Tanna language of Vanuatu. He continues to volunteer as a translation and anthropology consultant with Wycliffe/SIL and the Seed Company.

Robert J. Priest (PhD, University of California, Berkeley) is G. W. Aldeen professor of international studies and professor of mission and anthropology at Trinity Evangelical Divinity School. He is the current president of the Evangelical Missiological Society, and former president of the American Society of Missiology. He grew up in Bolivia among the Siriono Indians with whom his parents served as Wycliffe missionaries, and later carried out research in Peru with the Aguaruna Indians. His publications have focused on a wide variety of missiological topics, from short-term missions to witchcraft accusations.

Rochelle Cathcart Scheuermann (PhD, Trinity Evangelical Divinity School) is director and assistant professor of intercultural studies at Lincoln Christian University. She has served as associate pastor at a church plant (Salt Lake City, UT), taught overseas (Thailand, Cambodia, and Kenya), and since 2012 has served as the North Central Regional vice-president of the Evangelical Missiological Society. She has written several articles that have focused on contextualization, preaching and culture, and mission theology and is the co-author of the textbook, *Preaching in the Contemporary World*.

Edward L. Smither (PhD, University of Wales-Trinity St. David; PhD, University of Pretoria) is associate professor and dean of intercultural studies at Columbia International University. He served for fourteen years in intercultural ministry in North Africa, Europe, and the USA and his books include *Mission in the Early Church* and *Brazilian Evangelical Missions in the Arab World*.

ACKNOWLEDGMENTS

This project is the outcome of the hard work of many active participants in the Evangelical Missiological Society in 2015. In particular we would like to express our gratitude to:

- The eight regional Vice Presidents of EMS who coordinated regional meetings and suggested the papers that were read at the annual meeting in Dallas.
- The cadre of missiologists who presented their work in these regional meetings and also at the annual conference.
- The peer review team who offered invaluable feedback on each article in this volume.
- Bill Harris and the staff at the Graduate Institute of Applied Linguistics in Dallas who served as incredible servants and great hosts for the annual EMS meeting.
- EMS President Robert Priest for his vision, leadership, and encouragement in the process of putting together this book.
- The editorial team of William Carey Library, especially Jeff Minard and Melissa Hicks, for their expertise.

Finally, as editors we would like to thank our families. Rochelle would like thank her husband Barrett for his unfailing love, support, and encouragement. Edward is grateful to his wife Shawn for her continual encouragement and support.

INTRODUCTION

Rochelle Cathcart Scheuermann

Given the diversity in the global body of Christ today—different theological and church traditions, varying temperaments of missionaries, and the increased cultural diversity of the global church on mission—controversy should really come as no surprise. However, with the ease of communication and travel in the twenty-first century, we are, perhaps, more aware of controversies than ever before. It is not that controversies have not existed in the past, or that there are more controversies in the present day, but rather globalization has given us the tools to become more aware of our surroundings and to interact with others in ways unprecedented in history.

Globalization, itself, is a double-edged sword. We can thank globalization for the ability to communicate with ease; however, ease has not always been coupled with prudence. Social media has changed the ways in which we disseminate and take in information and our interactions are often in short sound bites that reflect the new expectation that we should immediately have an opinion and make judgments about statements and events for which we often lack vital facts. We can also thank globalization for the ability to travel and cross cultural boundaries; however, access to new people and places has not always been coupled with humility, hospitality, or cultural awareness. We are challenged today in how we think about and engage cultural and social "others." How do we understand the local people of other cultures who receive us as missionaries (both short-term and long-term), and how do they understand us? How do we respond to diaspora groups, refugees, and the exploited coming to our own culture?

This book is one attempt to hit the pause button on this rapid-paced world and to reflect on how we do mission, especially in light of the new layers of complexity that globalization brings. It is said that there is nothing new under the sun, and while many of these chapters will engage in new aspects of mission and cultural encounter unique to the twenty-first century, the underlying issues of each chapter are age-old topics that have reared their heads at various times throughout history: priorities in mission, power struggles, perspectives on cultural others, and contextualization.

Part One examines theological issues that arise in mission. In an adaptation of his presidential address from the 2015 national EMS meeting in Dallas, TX, Robert Priest calls us to consider how we engage social others as we do mission. Looking at the issues of Paul's cultural encounter with Gentiles that became the bedrock of controversy in the early church, Priest argues that mission requires deep cultural understanding and humility.

Christopher Little and Jerry Ireland continue the examination of mission theology by pushing the discussion on mission priorities forward. Little recognizes that this is an old debate; however, he argues that it is one that is still necessary to address, in part, because of the new giving patterns of evangelicals (favoring humanitarian works over traditional missions) and the redefinition of gospel and mission in contemporary discussions. In view of the biblical, historical and contemporary arenas, Little urges us to consider the priority of evangelization as the key task and goal of mission(s). Little and Ireland both recognize that the split between social concerns and evangelism has been long and deep; however, Ireland is hopeful that an evangelical consensus on this issue is possible. Based on the theology of Carl F. H. Henry, Ireland suggests that we discard the terms prioritism and holism—which have entirely too much baggage and polarization—and adopt new terminology that, based on Henry's regenerational model of theology, makes evangelism the macro priority which includes the necessary nature of social concern.

The final chapter of Part One highlights a neglected aspect of contemporary mission theology: the role of ethics within missiological practice. Greg Mathias notes that modern ethics has experienced a shift in its metaphysical grounding which has subsequently altered the understandings of progress, power, and success. Applying this to missiological practice, Mathias questions whether or not we have allowed task completion to override the moral richness of our Great Commission and focuses our attention on the ideas of managerial missiology, the Church Growth Movement, and contemporary marketing strategies applied to missions to illustrate his concerns. In the end, he calls for missiology to better connect ethics to missions through the realm of virtue.

Part Two shifts our view from the biblical and theological grounding of mission to the people mission involves. Eunice Hong and David Dunaetz consider the tensions that arise between people. Based on interviews with second-generation Korean American pastors, Hong uncovers the factors that contribute to church splits within multigenerational Korean American churches. She suggests that the desire for control, a strong sense of cultural ambiguity on the part of the first-generation pastors, and the lacking sense of ownership on the part of the second-generation pastors have contributed to a power struggle within multi-generational Korean American churches and the ensuing interpersonal tensions and conflicts. As a way forward, Hong suggests church leaders engage in a dialogue on servant leadership in order to resolve differences.

With conflict between missionaries remaining a top reason for missionary attrition, Dunaetz revisits how mission organizations approach conflict management. Comparing, contrasting and critiquing submission and cooperation models, he concludes that missionaries and organizations are best served when they engage in the mutuality and compassion of the Cooperation Paradigm.

Both Kenneth Nehrbass and Dave Beine look at the roles of missionaries. Nehrbass examines the "ugly American" image and whether or not it applies to missionaries from the United States. With the insight from interviews, he considers how international opinions of U.S. American missionaries help or hinder mission work and affect those who host missionaries as well as the missionaries themselves. Beine looks at the western missionary role more specifically, to evaluate the local and national translator model being adopted by groups like Wycliffe Global Alliance and to answer the question: Is there still a place for the western translator? He recognizes the benefits and correctives of the translation shift at play, but cautions that the pendulum might be swinging too far. Beine calls for a middle ground that will preserve the quality of Bible translation through the unique insights of a collaborative translation endeavor that includes outsiders (western translators) and insiders (local translators).

Ending our discussion on the people of mission, Miriam Adeney, in a moving narrative, shifts our focus to one of the more polarizing topics of our day: immigrants. Through three tales (Chinese, Sri Lankan, and Laotian), Adeney addresses the challenging issues of law and gospel and the ways in which God is using the response of Christians in the United States to expand the Kingdom globally.

Part Three engages the practice of mission with a look at one of the most controversial topics of our modern day: translation. The first three essays all consider aspects of divine familial terms in the translation of the Bible among Muslims. In a charitable dialogue, Mark Hausfeld et al. argue for the necessary retention of Father and Son terminology and Kevin Higgins presents a dissenting perspective that challenges the report from the World Evangelical Alliance Global Review Panel. Adding a new voice to the discussion, Mark Naylor considers the effect that the "Son of God" controversy has had on other Bible translation efforts not associated with the larger translation organizations like Wycliffe, SIL, or CanIL.

Closing out the section, Larry Caldwell challenges the ways hermeneutics is taught in intercultural contexts. He contends that we have only given lip service to *sola Scriptura* and the priesthood of all believers by generally teaching students *about* Bible interpretation (with a reliance on extra-biblical tools and aides) rather than how to interpret the Bible using nothing but the text. He questions whether such an approach to biblical interpretation is relevant for all contexts, especially those where such tools and aides are not available. As an alternative, Caldwell suggests it is possible to interpret the Bible without such aids and he concludes with suggestions for implementing a "Bible only" hermeneutic.

As a conclusion to this book, in Part Four, the distinguished missionary statesman, David Hesselgrave, surveys the historical trajectory of evangelical missions (along with its controversies and divisions) and considers what the future will be. Hesselgrave nuances the issues of the past with particular insight that leads him to consider the current state of evangelical missions and to issue a warning about our future.

Crossing social, cultural, and religious barriers and making disciples of all nations has probably never been without some level of controversy. Addressing these hot issues affords us moments of pause and needed reflection. It is our hope that the chapters you are about the read will help all of us to (1) carefully consider issues causing tension and contention within current mission thought, practice and strategy and then (2) engage in serious but charitable dialogue for the sake of God's mission and the salvation of all peoples.

PART ONE

Biblical Perspectives and Theology of Mission

CHAPTER 1

CONTROVERSY ON PAUL'S FIRST MISSIONARY JOURNEY
Lessons for Today
Robert J. Priest

In Acts 13 the Holy Spirit instructed the church of Antioch to set aside Barnabas and Saul for an unspecified work. At the end of their journey, Paul and Barnabas returned to Antioch and specified what their Spirit-given work had involved, *an opening of a door of faith to the Gentiles* (Acts 14:27). Saul had understood more than a decade earlier that he was to be an apostle to the Gentiles, so whatever occurred on this journey was not completely discontinuous from what had come before. Moreover, while followers of Jesus were largely Jewish, they were not exclusively so. Cornelius had already walked through a door of faith. In Antioch, there were not only Gentile proselytes but God-fearing Gentiles that had never become fully Jewish who now followed Jesus. And yet the Antioch mission in those early days, according to Richard Longnecker (1971, 38) was probably "carried out exclusively in terms of the synagogue and as an adjunct to the ministry to Jews, without consideration being given to whether it was proper to appeal more widely and directly to Gentiles" (see also Stott 1990, 202–203). It is to this audience that Paul and Barnabas announce that something new has just taken place in terms of opening a door of faith to the Gentiles.

While early Jewish believers did accept Cornelius, they nonetheless had a difficult time trying to understand the import of his conversion for missiological practice. Moreover, the issues they faced were not entirely different from challenges Christians through history have faced as they struggle with how to engage social others with the gospel.

My parents were Wycliffe missionaries in Bolivia. As a child, I lived across wide cultural-linguistic divides between Siriono Indians,

Spanish-speaking Bolivians, and North American missionaries. Through primary socialization, members of each group had acquired—within their group—shared language, musical aesthetics, notions of clean and unclean food, and rules of emotional display or moral judgment. Even people's names signaled their community: such as Rafael, Guillermo, Jorge, and Ana-Maria, or Perry, Bill, Cliff, Helen, Marion, or Echobii, Equataya, Jeje, Eanta. My parents' colleagues and supporters knew my father as Perry Priest, but no Siriono could pronounce that name. So they gave him a Siriono name: Taitaeoko. If a reporter today wished to interview Siriono about Perry Priest, she might conclude that Perry Priest was an American urban legend; that he had never lived with the Siriono. However, if she asked about the missionary Taitaeoko, every Siriono could tell stories, and would doubtless point to some young Siriono named after the esteemed missionary Taitaeoko.

In Acts 13 we encounter a similar name change, from Saul to Paul. Christians have often mischaracterized this name change as marking conversion, as in one book I saw in the Wheaton College library that illustrated this with a pre-conversion picture of a dark and swarthy Saul followed by a post-conversion portrait of a radiant and glowing Paul. Our Bible story books for children routinely teach that the Saul-to-Paul name change marked conversion (Berenstain and Berenstain 2013, 254; Bostrom 2004, 38–39; Elkins and O'Connor 2003, 377; Florea and Whiting 2014, 9; Reimann 2014, 15; Strobel and Florea 2015, 97). Scholars also occasionally affirm this idea (Apostolos-Cappadona 2014, 336; Paloutzian 2014, 211; Rambo and Farhadian 2014, 3), as do pastors and devotional writers (Matte 2015, 156–157; Hunt 1995, 119). However, the name shift in the biblical text occurred over a decade after his conversion. Paul, as we will see, like Taitaeoko, is the name of a missionary, not the name of a convert.

Our pastors teach us to think of names in terms of etymology—but this is not particularly helpful here. Saul means "asked for/ prayed for." It is a good name acknowledging God as the giver of this life. Paul means "shorty, stumpy, squirt, little"—hardly a better name etymologically.

It is not because of etymology that, as Johnny Cash reminds us, "Life ain't easy for a boy named Sue," but because names identify us with things like gender or ethnic identity. Sokpyo Hong, Hae-Won Kim, Jinsuk Byun disclose a different ethnic identity than Guillermo Cruz, Rafael Sanchez, Jaime Mendoza, Ana-Maria Lopez. Of course, while we are alert to nuances and distinctions in our contemporary context, nuances and distinctions that would have been obvious to people in the book of Acts may totally escape us 2000 years later. Barnabas, Joseph, and Saul are good Jewish names. Cornelius, Apollos, Silas, and Paul are not. Paul is a Greek name, and also a Roman cognomen. While, as a Roman citizen, Saul would have also had a Roman cognomen—which most biblical scholars believe was Paul, it was the name Saul rather than Paul which he utilized in this initial phase of ministry.

As Barnabas and Saul commence their first missionary journey they initially preach only to Jews within synagogues. Barnabas, the original leader of the missionary band, was a respected Levite, already well-known among Jews in Cyprus where he was from. However, how did Saul introduce himself? Based on the evidence of his pattern elsewhere, he doubtless identified himself as a Jew from Tarsus, a Hebrew of the Hebrews, trained under Gamaliel, named after the first great Jewish king, King Saul, and like King Saul also from the tribe of Benjamin. In the context of ministry to Jews, Saul was a trusted insider name, an important signal of shared Jewish identity.

However, while Barnabas and Saul's ministry on Cyprus was not oriented to reaching Gentiles, it was on Cyprus that they had their first Gentile convert. Moreover, the initial encounter came about not through an intentional missiological strategy on their part, but purely at the initiative of the Gentile. A Roman official, with a Roman name Paul, exercised his political power to demand an accounting from them. This proconsul was not a God-fearing "worshipper at the gate," not already tied into the Jewish religious system. He was simply a Gentile living his life as a Gentile. Moreover, in responding to the Roman Proconsul it is not the older Levite Barnabas who steps to the fore, but his younger partner who had been called as an apostle to the Gentiles over a decade earlier. Furthermore, his partner does not introduce himself as Saul, a Benjaminite, Hebrew of the Hebrews, a Pharisee, but rather as Paul. Our English translations fail to make clear that our apostle, himself a Roman citizen, introduces himself with the same name as the man he is addressing. Paul is speaking to Paul.

In Latin America, there is a word, *tocayo,* by which any two people with the same name can claim a special relationship with each other. If I introduce myself as Roberto, not uncommonly Bolivians or Peruvians with that name have exclaimed, "Ah, that's my name too–we're *tocayos!*" Paul would have made a good Latin American, closing the social distance between himself and the Roman Proconsul, he introduces himself, not with his Jewish name Saul, but with his Roman name Paul. And then he preaches the gospel. Moreover, the Roman Proconsul Paul, his *tocayo,* a Gentile with no prior affinity for Judaism, becomes a believer. This appears to have been an incredible and catalytic event—crystallizing an emergent missiology for Gentile outreach (Longnecker 1995, 215–216; Stott 1990, 220)—a shift that, as we will see, proved highly disturbing to some Jewish followers of Jesus.

The author of Acts marks the significance of this event in several ways. First, it is here that the author of Acts drops all usage of the Jewish name Saul, and permanently shifts to Paul—a shift doubtless reflecting Paul's own shifting usage as he transitioned to a self-conscious focus on Gentiles as his audience (Keener 2013, 2021; Lenski 2008, 503; Witherington 1998, 401; Gonzalez 2003, 72; Horsley 1987, 8). As N. T. Wright explains:

> The name "Saul" didn't play well in the wider non-Jewish world. Its Greek form, "Saulos," was an adjective that described someone walking or behaving in an effeminate way: "mincing" might be our closest equivalent . . . So, like many Jews going out into the Greek world, Paul used a regular Greek name, whether because it was another name he had had all along, which is quite possible, or because it was close

to his own real name, just as some immigrants change
their names into something more recognizable in the
new country. One thing was certain. Paul was serious about getting the message out to the wider world.
When you even change your own name, you show
that you really mean business. (2008, 6–7)

Like Perry Priest, well-known to Siriono, but only as Taitaeoko,
so our missionary in Acts would become famous not under the Jewish
name Saul, but rather Paul, apostle to the Gentiles. Only briefly in
Acts 22, while speaking to a Jewish crowd in Hebrew, does Paul again
refer to himself as Saul. Otherwise, he is known as Paul from here on.
It is exclusively as Paul that he identifies in all his writings. For this
man, who had been "extremely zealous" for his "ancestral tradition"
(Gal 1:14), and who took pride in his ethnic identity (Phil 3:7)—one
marker of which was his name Saul, this shift should be understood
as no small matter.

A second way that Luke marks the significance of the catalytic
event is by signaling a shift in leadership. Before this event, the name
Barnabas comes first, Barnabas and Saul—presumably marking Barnabas as leader of the missionary band. However, after the conversion
of the Roman Proconsul, Paul's name comes first. It is now Paul and
Barnabas. Moreover, in case this is too subtle for us, the first time the
team is referenced after the catalytic event, Barnabas' name is dropped
altogether, and we are simply told, "Paul and his companions" (Acts
13:13) traveled on. After that, it is "Paul and Barnabas," "Paul and
Barnabas."

Luke does not intend us to understand the shift in leadership to be
the result of a power struggle, but rather that this was a natural shift
given the emerging focus on Gentile mission. While the older Levite,
Barnabas, exercised natural leadership in a ministry focused on Jews,
the actual encounter with the Roman Proconsul made clear that it
was Paul who had exceptional strengths in relating to a Gentile world.
Thus, such a shift in leadership was a natural accompaniment to the
emerging focus on Gentile mission, with Paul moving into his central

calling, announced over a decade earlier, as an apostle to the Gentiles. Barnabas, from every indication, was fully supportive of such a shift.

A third way in which Luke marks the catalytic nature of this event with the Roman Proconsul is by giving us a lengthy exposition of what their message and ministry looked like in their very next place of ministry—Pisidian Antioch. Here Paul preaches in a synagogue explicitly acknowledging the Gentiles who are present. He announces that his message of salvation is for both Jews and Gentiles and that, through Jesus, forgiveness of sins is offered to "everyone who believes," an offer, he indicates, not contingent on following Jewish law. The Gentiles, who are present, subsequently tell their friends to come and listen to a message directed to them as Gentiles unlike any they have heard before. Moreover, the following week, a whole city of Gentiles gathers in excitement to listen to a message inviting them into a saving relationship with God by faith in Jesus, a salvation not contingent on first adopting Jewish identity and practice. Under this new message, synagogue leaders were not to function as gatekeepers enforcing the claim that access to God depends on aligning with Jewish identity and practice.

Gentiles as Gentiles were invited into a community of faith in Jesus. Not surprisingly synagogue leaders, jealously protective of their gatekeeper role and the centrality of Jewish identity and practice, vigorously opposed this message. At this point, Paul and Barnabas declare that "we now turn to the Gentiles" (Acts 13:46). The Gentiles, who heard them, were glad, and many believed, and the word of the Lord spread. From this point onward this was their pattern of ministry. At the end of their journey, they reported back in Antioch all that God had done through them on this trip and how through them God had opened a door of faith to the Gentiles.

Two thousand years later, in a conference with people who have eaten bacon for breakfast, and where nobody knows whether the man sitting next to you is circumcised or not, and where, in any case, no one conceptualizes Christian faith in terms of adherence to Jewish circumcision or dietary law, it is hard for us to appreciate the profundity of the shift or the difficulty that this shift posed for many early Jewish believers in Jesus.

You might think that the dramatic conversion of a powerful Roman Proconsul who had no prior connection to synagogue life, with all the possibilities that this conversion hinted at for a new missiological paradigm of successful Gentile outreach—you might think that this moment would have been a peak experience of unity and enthusiastic excitement for the missionary team. However, you would be wrong. One member of the missionary team chose to signal his unhappiness with what was happening in the strongest terms possible—by abandoning the team altogether, and heading back, not to Antioch that had approved their mission, but to the mother church in Jerusalem. As with any missionary that prematurely leaves the field, back in Jerusalem John Mark would have wished to justify his abandonment of the mission team, and many Jerusalem believers would have been deeply sympathetic to any verbalized disquiet over the new mission approach. With news of the new approach conveyed by John Mark, and perhaps by other travelers, it was not long until a band of Jewish Christians from Jerusalem organized their own mission team to follow after Paul and Barnabas and to insist that all Gentile converts must Judaize to be genuine followers of Jesus.

In the book of Galatians that Paul wrote in response to these developments, we get a snapshot of just how hard it was for early Jewish believers to make the transition to a Gentile mission that was not Judaizing. In Galatians, we learn that even Peter and Barnabas at times failed to grasp the implications of what was at stake.

Paul later temporarily expressed unwillingness to readmit John Mark to the mission team. This was perhaps less because he was an old-fashioned missionary who did not like quitters when the response was discouraging, than because of distrust for someone who, when response had been very encouraging, demonstrated by his departure a lack of support for the new missiological model of Gentile mission (Longnecker 1971, 43). Indeed, John Mark may well have contributed to the very Judaizing crisis that had so jeopardized the significant gospel headway Paul and Barnabas had made on this first missionary journey, thus explaining the depth of feeling behind Paul's refusal to readmit him to the missionary band (Longnecker 1971, 43). Of course, later on Paul would come to acknowledge Mark as a wonderful partner in Gentile mission.

Paul was a remarkable missionary. His primary socialization had taught him to reject all Gentile offers of food as unclean, a rejection that quite naturally created great social distance. However he underwent a profound paradigm shift, coming to affirm that no food "is unclean of itself" (Rom 14:14). He advised Jewish believers to eat what Gentile hosts set before them, asking no questions for conscience sake (1 Cor 10:25, 27). He modeled this in his own life. With fellow Jews, Paul ate like a Jew, to win Jews. However, with Gentiles, Paul ate whatever they set before him. He writes, "I have become all things to all people that I may by all means save some" (1 Cor 9:22). As a missionary to the Gentiles, Saul became Paul. Moreover, like my father, whose reputation among the Siriono was earned under the name Taitaeoko, rather than Perry Priest, so our apostle to the Gentiles achieved renown as a missionary, not under his Jewish name Saul, but under a Gentile name Paul.

You might think that initial ethnocentrism in gospel witness was a past problem uniquely faced by Jewish believers, but, of course, this has been a common and ongoing challenge for cross-cultural witness throughout Christian history. All of us are naturally ethnocentric. You might think that with the example and teaching of Paul that the rest of us would "get it." However, throughout much of Christian history we misread even the significance of the shift from Saul to Paul in the biblical narrative, misreading this as a marker of conversion rather than as missiological strategic adjustment. Paul, I argue, was not the name of a convert, but of a missionary entering into the cultural world of his audience. And yet, through much of Christian history, missionaries took this name change as a template not for themselves to make adjustments as missionaries, but as a model for them to require that converts make cultural adjustments and adopt convert names.

Under the Catholic "Christendom" model, the idea of a specified pool of "Christian names" evolved. John Calvin insisted that Protestant babies be given Bible names, not "Catholic" names like "Claude" (Naphy 1995). New England Pilgrims and Puritans not only used Bible names, but gave their children names like "Inasmuch" or "Increase"—sometimes derived from the practice of closing one's eyes, pointing in the Bible, and naming one's child whatever was pointed to. Protestants, however, were never able to arrive at a consensus on what constituted "Christian names" comparable to the Catholic consensus based on their list of saints.

Catholic missions insisted on a name change at conversion. As recently as the 1950s, their fund drives sometimes allowed donors to submit a name (such as of a deceased parent or grandparent), along with the designated amount per baptism. Missionary priests then received funds with lists of names attached and were expected to baptize Africans with names from this list.

Protestant missionaries sometimes also required that converts adopt Christian names, which they sometimes stressed should be Bible names. From Congo to India or Java, missionaries insisted that the names given by parents were pagan names, unclean names that must be repudiated and replaced by Christian names. A Javanese convert, Ajisaka needed a Christian name like Peter or Hendrick. A Ugandan convert, Nzuzi needed a Christian name like Paul, or Charles, or William. Since missionaries came from communities that had never consistently adhered to the "Bible name" requirement, they themselves often had names like Helen, Charles or Hendrik. Their names frequently entered the repertoire of "Christian names" in the new setting.

One result of such a name change requirement was that what was designed to be a marker of religious identity was also a marker of social location. When names flow from Europeans to Africans, and when traditional names linking one to one's own African heritage and ancestry are disavowed as pagan, the name shift confuses religious conversion and cultural conversion. Christian identity is defined against ethnic identity. One is asked to choose between being Christian and being African, between being Christian or being Indian.

The name change requirement sends the signal that the prior name is associated with something bad, something unchristian. Moreover, if even indigenous names are unclean of themselves, how much more indigenous music and drums, and dance, and dress, and architecture. That is, the name change requirement typically signaled a whole paradigm of missiological engagement that was diametrically opposite to that modeled and taught by Paul.

It is also worth keeping in mind that this name change paradigm is implicated in issues of power. Adam's naming of the animals was linked to the exercise of dominion. When Babylonian officials gave Daniel a new name Belteshazzar, and similarly renamed his three friends, this was an exercise of dominion, of assimilating them to the Baylonian colonial hegemony. When Robinson Crusoe saved the life of a man, he did not ask, "What is your name?" Rather, he said, "I made him know his name should be Friday." Mythically, Crusoe and many colonialists acted as if they were a second Adam facing an unnamed world that needed naming. Not, "What is your name?" Or, "What is the name of this place?" But "I so name you (or this place)!" The power to name is the power to exercise dominion. So Crusoe says, "I . . . taught him to say Master, and then let him know that was to be my name." The story, of course, is fiction. But it is a Christian story, where Crusoe shares the gospel with Friday, and where Friday voluntarily places his neck under the foot of Crusoe. That is, here we see European fantasies of missionary evangelization merging with fantasies of power and cultural or racial superiority.

When a Genevan father brought his son for baptism to one of Calvin's French ministers, desiring to name his son Claude after himself, the minister unilaterally baptized the child "Abraham." This was experienced as a usurpation of a father's right to name. Indeed so resentful, and on occasion violent, did Genevans become at this usurpation of parental naming prerogatives, that Calvin wondered if an armed guard would not need to be posted at every baptism

(Naphy 1995, 89, 92). In mission settings when missionaries or church officials declare that the name given by a loving parent is bad, wrong, unchristian and needs to be replaced with one acceptable to them, this is an act of intrusive power. When a missionary school only admits students with "Christian names" (Aluko 1993, 28), this, too, is hegemonic.

It would be one thing if this carried biblical backing. In fact, this is directly opposite to the Pauline model. Paul did not confuse markers of social and ethnic identity with internal relationship to God. Rather than requiring cultural accommodation on the part of Gentile converts, Saul himself, as Paul, accommodated the culture and identity of his audience. He called for no change based on human convention or ethnic tradition. To do so would be an act of hegemonic disrespect. Paul vigorously rebuked Peter, who did not treat Jewish customs as binding on himself, but nonetheless "compelled the Gentiles to live like Jews" (Gal 2:14). Similarly, many missionaries came from Christian communities with no such "Christian name" requirement for themselves, but nonetheless imposed the norm on converts in a process that compelled converts to adopt markers from the missionaries' home culture.

On the island of Java, more than 100 years ago, Coolen, the son of a Russian immigrant father and a Javanese mother, led in the growth of an early Christian movement (Hefner 1993). As Javanese became Christians, Coolen told them not to renounce the names their parents had given them. They learned to worship using musical aesthetics that were Javanese. Their church architecture was Javanese. Their dress and haircuts were Javanese. They used shadow plays to tell the stories of the Bible. They used religious vocabulary from their own language, not loan words from other languages, to share the gospel. And there emerged the beginnings of a significant movement of believers. However Dutch colonial Christians insisted they were less than fully converted – that a convert like Ajisaka needed a Christian name like Hendrik, that they needed to use Christian music (European, not Javanese), that they needed Christian church architecture, and clothing, and haircuts. We say in English, "a rose by any other name would smell as sweet." However, that is not true. Names themselves have great power. When, within a Dutch colonial order, Ajisaka is forced to renounce his name for a new name Hendrik, he now smelled less sweet, more foreign. As Hendrik, Ajisaka loses identifying links to family, heritage, ethnic group—and adds identifying ties with the Dutch colonial order. We say, "Sticks and stone will break my bones, but names will never hurt me!" However, we are wrong. Names do have the power to harm. Names that unnecessarily sever ties to family are harmful. Names that honor a foreign culture and stigmatize one's own, are harmful. Names that force a choice between being Christian and being Javanese are harmful. The aroma of Hendrick's life and witness did not smell as sweet to other Javanese as the aroma of Ajisaka's had. The new (Dutch) Christian music did not feel as aesthetically compelling and resonant. Moreover, the emerging movement turning to Christ was stopped in its tracks (see Hefner 1993). This is precisely the sort of thing Paul had fought against in his battle with Judaizers.

To the extent that missionaries fostered the name change requirement with such consequences (and many missionaries did not), they did so without biblical warrant and against the model of that first missionary, the Apostle Paul. Such practices arose not from fidelity to the biblical model, but out of failure to read our Bibles carefully.

Saul did not demand that Gentile converts change their names, even if they had names with pagan religious overtones like Apollos, Hermes, Narcissus, Olympas, or Silvanus. Rather, as a Jewish missionary to Gentiles, he made the adjustment, publically identifying himself with a Gentile name Paul. As he engaged Gentile cultural patterns related to such things as food, he insisted "nothing is unclean of itself," and called on all believers to imitate him, for example, to graciously accept the food served to them by unbelievers. It was in large part through Paul's ministry that the gospel successfully entered Gentile cultural worlds. We are the beneficiaries.

At the time of his conversion Saul learned that he was a "chosen *skeuos*, a chosen vessel" to proclaim Jesus name to the Gentiles.

Forever after, Paul was to express amazement that the light of the knowledge of the glory of God was to be transmitted through *skeues-in*, vessels of clay—which he insists we all are.

We are finite and weak. We are human. We are linguistically and culturally particular, having acquired through socialization culturally shaped categories, intuitions, and criteria of judgment that underpin and enhance our communication and positive relations with those who are culturally like us—but that also turns out to be ethnocentric and problematic when engaging social others. If God's purposes through us extended only to people just like us, we could intuitively apply our understandings acquired through primary socialization. Early Jewish believers in Jesus intuitively understood other Jews and how best to relate to them when they shared their faith. However, understanding and appropriately engaging a Gentile audience was something altogether different.

And yet, God, the Creator of the universe, indwelling us with his Spirit, desires to accomplish his purposes on earth in and through us, vessels of clay though we are. He calls us not to a hegemonic use of power, but to the missionary witness of vessels of clay. God accomplishes his missionary ends, in part, by calling certain individuals to a unique and specialized vocation—missionaries in the tradition of the apostle Paul, with specialized intercultural and linguistic skills and understandings and commitments. Some reading this paper have such a specialized calling.

Missionaries have always been confronted with the challenges of effective communication cross-culturally. Consider the case of an American evangelist in India, preaching a sermon he has preached in his own country many times, but this time to high caste Brahmans—the story of the prodigal son. The audience is very responsive to this story of a wayward son and loving father—until the evangelist tells of a fatted calf being killed and eaten. His audience turns cold and hostile. "The cow is like our mother," they say, "it gives us milk. You do not kill and eat your mother."

Americans can appreciate the impact of the story if they imagine a foreign evangelist in America telling a wonderful story, but where at the end of the story, the hero inexplicably kills, barbecues and eats the family's Golden Retriever. Such a foreign evangelist would have failed to understand the American "sacred dog" complex, failed to understand the dog stories that American children grow up with (stories of Toto, Old Yeller, and Lassie), and failed to understand the American proverb that a "dog is a man's best friend!"—that Americans like dogs in our homes, that we let them lick our faces and sleep in our beds, that we have dog doctors, dog hotels, and dog cemeteries. In the United States, you can sometimes mistreat people and get away with it, but mistreat a dog and even a professional football player will go to jail. While Hollywood movies relentlessly feature people being killed in bloody ways, such movies carefully respect taboos on violence towards dogs. Years ago my then eleven-year-old daughter Shelly asked me to see the movie "Dante's Peak" with her. The story features a volcano, a family, a dog, and a mother-in-law. As the volcano erupts, and the family has to flee, the dog cannot be found. The family has to leave without the dog. My daughter, a dog-lover, was in tears. I turned to her, "Shelly, this is an American movie. That dog will not die. I promise!" And sure enough, by the end of the movie, the dog is alive, and the mother-in-law is dead, and it is a great American movie!

People around the world are human in variable ways, shaped by variable cultural narratives, confronting diverse realities. And while missionaries have often confronted this diversity at deep levels, it is also true that every single reader of this paper will live and work in a globalized and culturally diverse world. We are all in relations with people whose primary socialization was quite different from our own. The model of Paul, who desires to become all things to all persons, to enter into their social worlds, applies not just to professional missionaries, but to all contemporary believers.

Sometimes it is harder to make small cultural adjustments than large ones. I remember Dr. Robertson McQuilkin, president of Columbia International University (CIU), commenting that when CIU

recruited missions faculty who grew up in the North of the USA—
faculty who had made amazing adjustments to cultures around the
world, and asked them to live and teach in the American South, that
they found it much less easy to adjust. They could adapt to everybody else, and show respect, but were not able to love and respect
white southerners. As a college student, I asked my aunt, Muriel Mc-
Quilkin, for advice on dating, courtship, and marriage. She told me
that the most important thing if I was to be a missionary, is that I
marry someone that can love other people across all differences and
boundaries. Moreover, she pointed to a young lady, Kersten Bayt, that
she said was an awesome example of this. A few years later, as we
prepared to get married, I invited Kersten Bayt to a family Christmas
with my relatives in Mississippi. I had some anxieties. My southern
relatives knew that "Yankees" were prejudiced towards southerners,
and so they sometimes returned the favor. And Kersten was not only a
Yankee, she was from California. She grew up near Berkeley, wearing
blue jeans, not dresses. She grew up vegetarian and had never used
make-up before going to college in the South. So here was the test.
Was Kersten the kind of person my Aunt Muriel said she was? This
was the year that women were all talking about the "four season color
analysis," to be used in figuring out what colors look best on each
person. And my relatives all started talking about this. To my mother,
who lived her whole life as a missionary with the poorest of the poor
in Bolivia and Nigeria, this discussion seemed worldly and superficial.
However, Kersten, a good relativist in the tradition of Paul, believing
that the important thing was her relationship with these women and
showing love to them, jumped right into the conversation. She had
a background in art and was soon helping my cousins and aunts figure out what colors looked best on them. Then one aunt mentioned
that she had a friend who did facials and painted fingernails. Kersten
enthusiastically joined in. My male cousins with their hunting dogs
and hunting stories wanted to get to know Kersten. She had grown
up shaped by the values of John Muir. You were supposed to appreciate Bambi, not shoot him. However, Greg and Stan were people

to be loved, and Kersten expressed all the right levels of interest and appreciation, oohing and aahing as they told their stories of hunting, and of the blood rituals involved. All kinds of things become the occasion either for boundaries and barriers or for alignments where we enter into other peoples' world. My relatives loved Kersten. When she spoke about spiritual matters, my relatives were happy to listen with affection and respect.

A while back I struck up a conversation on an airplane, disclosing that I was a seminary professor and that my PhD was in anthropology. My seatmate was astonished. Why in the world would a seminary hire an anthropologist? The straightforward answer is that Trinity Evangelical Divinity School believes that God is a missionary God. God uses finite vessels of clay, who need to be trained not only to understand and communicate the Scriptures but to understand those to whom we minister—people often quite different from ourselves. We must consider how to enter their social worlds, and what ministry to them should involve. Proverbs 19:2 tells us, "It is not good to have zeal, without knowledge, nor to be hasty and miss the way." It is not good for air traffic controllers to have zeal without knowledge, nor surgeons. It was not good for first century ethnocentric Jewish believers to have zeal for Gentile conversion married to misunderstandings of what the gospel ought to mean for them. It is not good for Christians, of any sort, to have zeal in relation to Muslim or Buddhist neighbors, but with complete ignorance and misunderstandings of Buddhism or Islam. It is not good to engage social others with complete ignorance of the sorts of things that missiologists can help us understand.

The Apostle Paul exemplified an incredible ability to make cultural adjustments. However, it is also true that he called on believers to resist other social influences. That is, the adjustments he calls for are not without accompanying concerns for faithful orthodoxy and orthopraxy. In the remainder of this book, authors are engaging difficult issues. These matters are truly difficult. The following are a few implications of what we have considered that should be kept in mind as one approaches these discussions.

1. The simple missionary activity of transmitting the gospel across cultural and ethnic divides triggers profound difficulties and questions that are not easy to resolve. Thus, missiology is a field that naturally raises deeply difficult issues.

2. Christians who are not bicultural and who lack cultural or missiological training, but who nonetheless attempt ministry across cultural and religious lines will naturally and ethnocentrically tend, like the Judaizers before them, to treat cultural elements from their own culture as normative for others. This is a problem.

3. When Christian missionaries are ethnocentric, and also operate from positions of socio-economic strength, this becomes doubly problematic. It is vital that our missiological reflection be attentive to dimensions of power and neocolonialism.

4. In most mission settings, there has already been a long history of missionary engagement often exemplifying the same patterns the apostle Paul critiqued. That is, such history has often involved both ethnocentrism and power dynamics. Sometimes missionaries demanded that converts adopt new names from missionary host countries. Sometimes they required Hindu converts to eat beef or Muslim converts to eat pork, or insisted that the church use musical aesthetics birthed in Europe or North America, for example. This prior history has often contributed to problematic Christian patterns and identities, posing profound difficulties for new or potential believers, and for those attempting to encourage a reframing of missional engagement in more Pauline ways.

5. When missionaries and missiologists wish to make adjustments that will reduce inappropriate barriers to the

gospel, they are fully in the train and lineage of Paul, and should not simply be labeled postmodern relativists.

6. However, this does not mean that every adjustment is a good one. Critical judgment, both theological and missiological, needs to be brought to bear on the issues involved. Healthy forms of contextualization must be pursued. However, inappropriate syncretism must be guarded against.

7. The best people to exercise critical review of such new proposals should be Christians who are missiologically trained, and who are not culturally and linguistically distant from the settings where the issues at stake are located.

8. However, we do need forums for engaging the issues, just as the Jerusalem Council provided. Missiology conferences, and peer-reviewed publications such as this one, are ideal venues comprising an ideal community for testing and evaluating the ideas involved. That is, a community of those who are deeply knowledgeable about the cultural, linguistic, and religious contexts in view, as well as of Bible and theology, and who have advanced missiological training, are ideally positioned to help the body of Christ consider the issues. This book provides one such forum for us to examine and evaluate the issues at stake, as we endeavor faithfully and appropriately to follow in the missionary lineage of Paul.

REFERENCES

Aluko, Taiye. 1993. "Naming Ceremony in African Independent Churches: A Cultural Revolution." *The Indian Journal of Theology* 35: 20–32.

Apostolos-Cappadona, Diane. 2014. "Seeing Religious Conversion through the Arts." In *The Oxford Handbook of Religious Conversion*, edited by Lewis R. Rambo and Charles E. Farhadian, 327–342. New York: Oxford University Press.

Arnold, Clinton. 2002. *Acts*. Grand Rapids, MI: Zondervan.

Berenstain, Jan, and Mark Berenstain. 2013. *The Berenstain Bears Storybook Bible*. Grand Rapids, MI: Zondervan.

Bostrom, Kathleen Long. 2004. *Paul's Call: How Saul Became a Christian*. Louisville, KY: Westminster John Knox Press.

Elkins, Stephen, and Tim O'Connor. 2003. *The Word and Song Bible: The Bible for Young Believers*. Nashville, TN: Broadman and Holman Publishers.

Florea, Jesse, and Karen Whiting. 2014. *The One-Year Devotions for Active Boys*. Carol Stream, IL: Tyndale House Publishers.

Gonzalez, Justo. 2003. *Three Months with the Spirit*. Nashville, TN: Abingdon Press.

Griggs, Donald, and Paul Walasky. 2014. *Acts from Scratch*. Louisville, KY: Westminster John Knox Press.

Harrill, J. Albert. 2012. *Paul the Apostle: His Life and Legacy in their Roman Context*. New York: Cambridge University Press.

Hefner, Robert W. 1993. "Of Faith and Commitment: Christian Conversion in Muslim Java." In *Conversion to Christianity: Historical and Anthropological Perspectives on a Great Transformation*, edited by Robert W. Hefner, 99–127. Berkeley: University of California Press.

Horsley, G. H. R. 1987. "Name Change as an Indication of Religious Conversion in Antiquity." *Numen* 34, no. 1: 1–17.

Hunt, T. W. 1995. *The Mind of Christ: The Transforming Power of Thinking His Thoughts*. USA: T. W. Hunt.

Keener, Craig S. 2013. *Acts: An Exegetical Commentary, Volume 2*. Grand Rapids, MI: Baker Academic.

Lenski, R. C. H. 2008. *The Interpretation of The Acts of the Apostles 1–14*. Minneapolis, MN: Augsburg Press.

Longnecker, Richard. 1971. *The Ministry and Message of Paul*. Grand Rapids, MI: Zondervan.

———. 1990. *Galatians*. Waco, TX: Word, Inc.

———. 1995 *Acts*. Grand Rapids, MI: Zondervan.

Matte, Gregg. 2015. *Unstoppable Gospel: Living Out the World-Changing Vision of Jesus' First Followers*. Grand Rapids, MI: Baker Books.

Naphy, W. G. 1995. "Baptisms, Church Riots and Social Unrest in Calvin's Geneva." *Sixteenth Century Journal* 26: 87–97.

Paloutzian, Raymond F. 2014. "Psychology of Religious Conversion and Spiritual Transformation." In *The Oxford Handbook of Religious Conversion*, edited by Lewis R. Rambo and Charles E. Farhadian, 209–239. New York, NY: Oxford University Press.

Rambo, Lewis R., and Charles E. Farhadian. 2014. "Introduction." In *The Oxford Handbook of Religious Conversion*, edited by Lewis R. Rambo and Charles E. Farhadian, 1–22. New York, NY: Oxford University Press.

Reimann, Jim. 2014. *Saul is Born Again: The Conversion of the Apostle Paul*. Nofit, Israel: Intelecty, Ltd.

Schenck, Kenneth. 2009. *God's Plan Fulfilled: A Guide for Understanding the New Testament*. Marion, IN: Triangle Publishing.

Smith, W. Michael. 1984. "An Eye-opener for the Rural Javanese." In *Unto the Uttermost: Missions in the Christian Churches/Churches of Christ*, edited by Doug Priest, Jr., 216–228. Pasadena, CA: William Carey Library.

Stott, John. 1990. *The Message of Acts: The Spirit, the Church & the World*. Downers Grove, IL: Intervarsity Press.

Strobel, Lee, and Jesse Florea. 2015. *The Case for Grace for Kids*. Grand Rapids, MI: Zondervan.

Witherington, Ben. 1998. *The Acts of the Apostles: A Socio-Rhetorical Commentary*. Grand Rapids, MI: William B. Eerdmans.

Wright, N. T. 2008. *Acts for Everyone, Part 2*. Louisville, KY: Westminster John Knox Press.

CHAPTER 2

THE CASE FOR PRIORITISM

Christopher R. Little

The temptation to drift in mission is real. Jesus faced it when he was tempted by the devil (Matt 4:1–11). Peter experienced it when Simon offered money for the power of the Spirit (Acts 8:18–24). Paul confronted it when he refused to compromise his stance on circumcision (Gal 5:11). It is the subject of a recent book, *Mission Drift* (2014), by Peter Greer and Chris Horst, in which Chris Crane, CEO of Edify, is quoted as saying, "It's the exception that an organization stays true to its mission . . . The natural course—the unfortunate natural evolution of many originally Christ-centered missions—is to drift" (19). As a contemporary witness to this phenomenon, Andy Crouch, executive editor of *Christianity Today,* observes, "These days I do not often meet Christians so passionate about evangelism that they question the need for doing justice. I am much more likely to meet Christians so passionate about justice that they question the need for evangelism . . . In short, working for justice is cool. Proclaiming the gospel is not" (2013, 82).

This state of affairs did not happen by accident. It is the result of very successful steps toward promoting a more holistic or integral framework for mission as expressed, among other places, in the Iguassu Affirmation (1999), the Micah Declaration (2001), and the Cape Town Commitment (2010). Those who advance evangelism as the priority in the mission of the church are now in the clear minority among self-described evangelicals.[1] For some, the issue is settled with no need to rehash old ground (cf. Padilla 2007, 162). Others, like

---

1. *Evangelical Missions Quarterly* (2012, 264–271) recently published a "Symposium" and asked five different leaders to articulate their views regarding

A. Scott Moreau, surmise that "the next generation of evangelical missionaries—and perhaps missiologists—will *assume* holism as the appropriate biblical picture rather than explore the text to discover whether it is" and he is "convinced that the question of the scope of the ministry of the church among evangelicals is not fully settled" (2012, 318).

AN OLD DEBATE STILL NECESSARY

The debate has, in fact, been going on for a long time. So why not just agree to disagree and move forward? Simply because the stakes are too high to overlook, set aside, or not contest. These include, first and foremost, the eternal destiny of the unevangelized. Since they are the ones who have the most to lose, their concerns should be front and center. Second, generous Christians in the West, in revealing their commitments, are now giving more to humanitarian causes than to what traditionally has been known as missions. Recent statistics show that evangelicals are donating more than $1.9 billion to relief and development but only $1.3 billion to foreign missions (Olsen 2013, 11). Third, the way in which such terms as gospel, Kingdom, and mission are being redefined is unprecedented and calls for redress. Last, given the largely unchallenged shifts transpiring in missions today, it is essential to equip the church, both locally and globally, to reflect, communicate, and act in a more missiologically-informed manner.

It is entirely possible that non-western Christians will dismiss this whole discussion as irrelevant since it stems from the unique history in western quarters related to the fundamentalism/modernism controversy at the beginning of the twentieth century, developments within the World Council of Churches (WCC) subsequent to WWII, and the formation of the Lausanne Movement. That would be unfortunate because wherever and whenever God's people have had to contend

---

the relationship between proclamation and social action, and only one presented a view approximating the prioritistic position.

with issues such as theological liberalism; the Hocking Report; the decline and then abandonment of world evangelization in the Student Volunteer Movement, the YM/WCA, and in mainline Protestant denominations—as the western church has had to—there are opportunities for non-western Christians to learn how to handle the same issues if and when they arise in their own contexts.

CONTRASTING PRIORITISM AND HOLISM

The most classic statement on prioritism in print comes from Donald McGavran:

> A multitude of excellent enterprises lie around us. So great is the number and so urgent the calls, that Christians can easily lose their way among them, seeing them all equally as mission. But in doing the good, they can fail of the best. In winning the preliminaries, they can lose the main game. They can be treating a troublesome itch, while the patient dies of cholera. The question of priorities cannot be avoided . . .

Among other desires of God-in-Christ, He beyond question wills that persons be found—that is, be reconciled to Himself. Most cordially admitting that God has other purposes, we should remember that we serve a God *Who Finds Persons*. He has an overriding concern that men should be redeemed. However we understand the word, biblical witness is clear that men are "lost." The Finding God wants them *found*—that is, brought into a redemptive relationship to Jesus Christ where, baptized in His Name, they become part of His Household. (1980, 24)

Other well-known figures within evangelicalism who are self-described prioritists include: Carl Henry, Arthur Glasser, Ralph Winter, George Peters, Robertson McQuilkin, David Hesselgrave, John Piper, Ajith Fernando, Andreas Köstenberger, and Eckhard Schnabel.

C. René Padilla, who more than anyone else should be credited with convincing evangelicalism of the need to embrace a holistic approach to mission over the past several decades, states:

> Holistic mission is mission oriented towards the meeting of basic human needs, including the need of God, but also the need of food, love, housing, clothes, physical and mental health, and a sense of human dignity. Furthermore, this approach takes into account that people are spiritual, social and bodily beings, made to live in relationship with God, with their neighbors, and with God's creation. Consequently, it presupposes that it is not enough to take care of the spiritual well-being of an individual without any regard for his or her personal relationships and position in society and in the world. As Jesus saw it, love for God is inseparable from love for neighbor (Matt 22:40). (2007, 158)

Respected figures within evangelicalism who are self-described holists include: Samuel Escobar, J. Andrew Kirk, Ron Sider, Chris Wright, Tetsunao Yamamori, Bryant Myers, James Nkansah-Obrempong, Richard Stearns, Gary Haugen, and Dean Flemming.

A careful review of the literature on both sides of the debate uncovers further contrasts between the two views as depicted in the chart on the following page.[2]

Several points of explanation are in order. First, this chart builds upon the one by Hesselgrave (2005, 120–122), but equates holism with revisionist holism and folds restrained holism into prioritism since making a distinction between these views—both of which affirm the priority of proclamation—is somewhat arbitrary.

---

2. Of course, not all prioritists and holists would affirm each point in their represented columns, yet the evidence shows that these distinctions generally hold up.

PRIORITISM		HOLISM
Evangelism/disciple-making/church planting are more important than other ancillary activities		Evangelism/disciple-making/church planting are equally as important as other ancillary activities
Emphasizes apostles and early church as models for mission (Representationalism)		Emphasizes Jesus as model for mission (Incarnationalism)*
Kingdom of God in the church through conversion		Kingdom of God in church and society through socio-economic, political action
Social activity as means to the end of conversion		Social activity as means to the end of improving society
Focuses on what Christ has done for the church		Focuses on what the church can do for society
Gospel is what Christ has done for the church		Gospel is what the church does for others
Gospel communicated only through word		Gospel communicated and demonstrated through word and deed
Theological hierarchy of proclamation over ancillary activities (word > deed)		Theological equality between proclamation and ancillary activities (word = deed)
Committed more to the lost than to the poor		Committed more to the poor than the lost or equally committed to both
Aims at getting people on earth to heaven		Aims at getting heaven to people on earth
More emphasis given to the NT than the OT		More emphasis given to the OT than the NT or equal weight given to both
Criticizes holism for being so earthly minded that it does no heavenly good		Criticizes prioritism for being so heavenly minded that it does no earthly good
Mission as specific task		Mission as everything the church does
Analogy: Mission is rescuing people from a burning building		Analogy: Mission is rescuing a burning building with people inside

Column labels (left to right): FUNDAMENTALISM | ON THE FENCE | LIBERALISM

*For an explanation of these terms, see Hesselgrave (2005, 141ff)

Second, it seeks to illustrate that prioritism is not fundamentalist in the sense that it rejects social action, and holism is not universalistic in the sense it repudiates gospel proclamation. What distinguishes prioritism from holism is a qualitative difference between word and deed, evangelism and social action, and proclamation and demonstration. Prioritism believes that "the primary deed of love that one can do for a fallen world is to share the gospel with that world" (Witherington 2009, 25–26). Holism, on the other hand, engages the world "without concern for which is most important" (Gordon 2010, 108).[3]

Third, given the widespread assumption today that dichotomies are conceptually unhelpful, the chart opens itself to criticism. However, what is being stipulated here is not a *dichotomy* between word and deed but rather a *hierarchy* of word over deed. Moreover, it is important to note that whereas dichotomies are intrinsic to a Christian worldview (e.g., Creator/creation, invisible/visible, life/death, heaven/hell, saved/lost, light/darkness, holy/unholy, etc.), holism was originally fashioned in accordance with a "unitary and monistic conception of the universe" in which all ontological hierarchies were dismissed outright (Smuts 1926, 108–109, 335–336). As such, there is a fundamental worldview clash between the theocentric categories of biblical revelation and the Neoplatonic ones of holism (cf. Groothuis 2011, 327).

Last, it is entirely possible that some will refuse being drawn to one side of the debate and remain on the fence by affirming something akin to holistic prioritism or prioritistic holism. But, if the principle of non-contradiction holds true (A ≠ non-A), such a position is untenable. One cannot logically affirm at the same time the statements "there are priorities in mission" and "there are no priorities in mission" as true. One must be true and the other false; there are no other options. Hence, a choice must be made.

---

3. This aspect of holism is confirmed by Vinoth Ramachandra: "as a church we have no liberty to 'prioritize'" (2006, 54).

WHY NOT HOLISM?

There is no question that holists are some of the most respected, intelligent, self-sacrificing, and Christ-honoring people involved in God's mission among the nations today. But holism, as presently conceived, cannot bear the weight of expectations placed upon it as a viable paradigm for mission. This is demonstrable in the following ways.

Kerygmatic Issues

The gospel from a holistic perspective is now being characterized as something the church is (Stearns 2009, 3), lives (LTWG 2010), embodies (LTWG 2010), and demonstrates (Micah Network 2001), and evangelism as "all actions" (Burris and Douglas 2012, 3), which the church performs in inviting people "through word, deed, and example . . . to follow Christ" (Flemming 2013, 18). Apparently, the terms "gospel" and "evangelism" have no limits, and if they do, they have no meaning. But the "gospel is not infinitely malleable, and cannot without fatal loss be reduced to whatever constitutes good news in a given culture" (Ferdinando 2007, 140–141) and "evangelism needs to be defined carefully so that its special task is not lost within the wider demands of mission" (Peace 2007, 115). Toward this end, Scot McKnight (2011, 46) suggests the contemporary church must return to "the earliest days of the church" and consider the *apostolic gospel tradition*" as revealed in 1 Corinthians 15:1–8: *"that Christ died, that Christ was buried, that Christ was raised, and that Christ appeared."* This framework points to "something at the grassroots level: the word *gospel* was used in the world of Jews at the time of the apostles to *announce* something, to *declare* something as good news—the word *euangelion* always means good news. 'To gospel' is to herald, to proclaim, and to declare something about something" (McKnight 2011, 27). Thus, McKnight rightly deduces, "the gospel is to announce good news about key events in the life of Jesus Christ" (2011, 46, 49–50). What this means is that "the gospel itself is always an external word that comes to me announcing that someone else in history has accomplished my salvation for me" (Horton 2009a, 48), which thereby implies, "[w]e are not the Good News, but its recipients and heralds; not the newsmakers, just the reporters" (Horton 2009b, 127). As such, "the biblical gospel is inherently a *verbal* thing [which] cannot be preached by our deeds" (Litfin 2012, 36, 45). "Social action and caring for the poor," on the other hand, "is not . . . the gospel [but] implications" (Bird 2013, 53) or "entailments" (Carson, 2013, 353) of it. "Evangelism," then, "is the act of the giving verbal witness to the good news, confident that its power does not fluctuate with the strengths or weaknesses of the messenger" (Litfin 2012, 55). If, in relation to the mission of the church, "we want to be New Testament Christians," then "this gospel must once again become our gospel" (McKnight, 2011, 133).

Basileia Issues

At the beginning of the twenty-first century, the Kingdom of God was heralded by evangelicals as the means to "break the impasse between evangelism and social action" (Glasser 2003, 12). But unfortunately, instead of clarifying the mission of God, this effort confounded it. For example, "Kingdom missiology" is now being advanced to encourage the church to perform "faithfully the whole work of the Kingdom of God to the whole world" (Burris and Douglas 2012, 1) which evidently involves "more than simply winning men and women to Christ" (Swanson and Williams 2010, 81). Rather, Kingdom work strives "for the redemption of people, their social systems, and the environment that sustains their life" (Myers 2002, 49), using "the current trends toward capitalism and economic development to [raise] the standard of living . . . for all" (Eldred 2005, 48, 71). This surprisingly results in "something permanent, something that will not be displaced in the world to come . . . When a well is dug, a school is built or an orphanage opens its gates, the dream of God [i.e., the Kingdom] becomes actualized in our time" (Moore 2012, 152).

To speak in such terms is of course nothing new as even Sider held to the views above. However, upon further reflection he later modified his view of the Kingdom, saying, "It is important to note that *absolutely none* of the scores of New Testament texts on the Kingdom of God speak of the presence of the Kingdom apart from the conscious confession of Christ . . . There seems to be no warrant in the New Testament for talking about the coming of the Kingdom of God via societal change apart from confession of Christ" (Sider and Parker 1985, 104; cf. Sider 1975, 258, 262ff). On the meaning of the Kingdom, George Ladd states, "[t]he church cannot build the Kingdom or become the Kingdom, but the church witnesses to God's Kingdom—to God's redeeming acts in Christ both past and future" (1974, 265–266). Glasser observes, "[t]o preach [the Kingdom] is to issue a call to conversion" for "apart from the new birth one cannot see, much less enter, the Kingdom of God" (2003 358, 246). I. Howard Marshall notes, "[t]he Kingdom consists of those who respond to the message in repentance and faith and thereby enter into the sphere of God's salvation and life" (2004, 80). Accordingly, Christians should "be wary of making over-ambitious claims for particular manifestations of the [Kingdom's] presence" (Kirk 2006, 94), "not call social change the coming of the Kingdom" (Chester 2013, 90), realize that "Kingdom mission is church mission . . . because . . . Kingdom mission is first and foremost about a redemptive reality of living under King Jesus" (McKnight 2014, 157), and recognize that "efforts to make the world a better place do not inherently qualify as Kingdom work" since non-Christians can "work to make the world a better place, but they are not, in doing so, building *Christ's* Kingdom" (Liftin 2012, 121). Thus, "[t]he phrase 'Kingdom work' is confusing and nonbiblical and . . . should be jettisoned" (DeYoung and Gilbert 2011, 112) in favor of describing the church's socio-economic engagement with the world as "good works . . . in the public sector for the common good" (McKnight 2014, 118).

Missiological Issues

Without question, the most disturbing trend within evangelical missiology today, one which confirms that the greatest challenges facing this academic field are not "methodological [but] theological"

(Hesselgrave 2001, 3), is the wholesale attempt to renegotiate the boundary on which mission occurs. Mission, among self-declared evangelicals, now includes: "caring for the environment" (Bliss 2013, 17), "creating jobs and wealth" (Johnson 2009, 42), "giving to fellow believers in need" (Flemming 2013, 192), "political action, in fighting social injustice" (Woolnough 2010, 6), and "anti-trafficking work, care for AIDS and malaria patients, food for the hungry, clothing for the naked, release for the prisoners" (Moore 2012, 159). This expansive definition of mission justifies Carl Braaten's concern that "holistic mission has contributed to such a great inflation in the meaning of mission, including everything the church is doing, that there is the danger that evangelism, which is the heart of mission, will become buried in an avalanche of church activism" (1985, 11).

In the middle of the last century, Stephen Neill (1959) faced the same situation with the World Council of Churches (WCC) when it began to label every praiseworthy work of the church as mission. As a corrective, he set forth his now famous dictum: "If mission is everything, mission is nothing. If everything that the church does is to be classed as 'mission,' we shall have to find another term for the church's particular responsibility for 'the heathen,' those who have never yet heard the name of Christ" (1959, 81). He later expounded upon this statement by defining mission as *the intentional crossing of barriers from church to non-church in word and deed for the sake of the proclamation of the gospel*" (quoted in Van Engen 1991, 28). However, David Bosch interjected a contravening viewpoint when he stated, "Whoever we are, we are tempted to incarcerate the *missio Dei* in the narrow confines of our own predilections, thereby of necessity reverting to one-sidedness and reductionism. We should beware of any attempt at delineating mission too sharply" (1991, 512). In similar fashion, Wright, working within the framework of a biblical theology of redemption for the entire cosmos, believes, in contradiction to Neill's statement, that "It would seem more biblical to say, 'If everything is mission . . . everything is mission. .'. . [E]verything a Christian and a Christian church is, says and does should be missional in its conscious participation in the mission of God in God's world" (2010, 26). As such, the evangelical church is now faced with a situation where, according to Timothy Tennent, "the word [mission] has been [so] broadened . . . to mean 'everything the church should be doing,'" that it has lost "any distinctive emphasis or character" (2010, 54).

In light of this predicament, missiology needs to reconsider the question: what is and what is not mission? In other words, is the church responsible for both world evangelization and world reparation? Robertson McQuilkin points in the right direction when he deems "the question of final destiny [to be] *the* theological issue for missions" (2006, 42). Consequently, if the church has to choose among competing agendas, if it has to accept its limitations, if it has to grope for the narrow way, then it should chart its course in mission with reference to those who have the most to lose (and gain) in the debate—the not-yet evangelized. Hence, Neill's viewpoint should trump Bosch's and Wright's, and the church should embrace "lostness" as the only non-negotiable boundary for mission and "final destiny" as the leading theological impetus for all its interactions with the world (McQuilkin 2006, 42). Accordingly, "[n]othing can be called mission in the biblical sense which is not . . . directed toward conversion" (Walter Freytag quoted in Beyerhaus 1971, 101). "There is but one acid test that should be applied to all activities that claim to represent obedience in mission," Glasser argues, "Do they . . . produce disciples of Jesus Christ?" (1974, 8). Rightly defined, "'Mission' is not simply . . . 'everything that the church does,' but the deliberate activity of a community of faith that . . . [seeks] to win other people for the content of faith and the way of life espoused by that community" (Schnabel, 2012, 563). In terms of impetus, "the only valid motive and purpose of missions is . . . to call men and peoples to confront themselves with God's acts of revelation and salvation for man. . . . If [other things] usurp the place of the apostolic motive, which is the alone valid and tenable one, they transform the Christian church into a goodwill agency for the diffusion of refined and cultured idealism" and lose "all intrinsic relation with the central apostolic consciousness that we are to be witnesses to God and His revelational dealing with man and the world" (Kraemer, 1963, 292–293).

WHY PRIORITISM?

Prioritists would do well to continue to listen to and learn from holists as all "see in a mirror dimly" and "know [only] in part" (1 Cor 13:12). However, more persuasive arguments will need to be articulated by holists for prioritists to compromise any of the following convictions.

Almost two millennia ago, Augustine of Hippo, while referencing the Great Commandment, shed light on the nature of mission by commenting that the:

> Divine Master inculcates two precepts—the love of God and the love of our neighbor—and as in these precepts a man finds three things he has to love—God, himself, and his neighbor—and that he who loves God loves himself thereby, it follows that he must endeavor to get his neighbor to love God, since he is ordered to love his neighbor as himself. (1950, 692)

Augustine says two things here which must not go unnoticed: 1) the way to loving oneself is to love God; and 2) the way to loving one's neighbor is to encourage him to love God as well. Thus, although there are many ways to express the Great Commandment, its purest manifestation comes when God's people persuade others to love God. This is the highest display of love a person can ever show because, as Piper notes, "our greatest satisfaction" (2010, 130) and "our greatest good, comes to us *in* God" (2004, 40). Therefore, when it comes to the lost, the best way to obey the Great Commandment is to implement the Great Commission.

This point leads to the next. In the face of horrendous injustices in the economic, social, political, and environmental spheres of present-day human existence, there is one injustice which far surpasses them all. As Orthodox mission theologian Anastasios Yannoulatos rightly contends, the Christian:

> Believes that for every human being there is no treasure more precious than the truth that was revealed by the word of God. Therefore, he feels that the people who suffer injustice most in our time are those who have been deprived of the Word, not because they themselves refuse to listen, but for the simple reason that those who have known it for centuries have not been interested in passing it on. (2010, 59)

The most recent statistics indicate that those subjected to this predicament amount to over 2.1 billion unevangelized people (cf. Johnson 2015, 29). Surely this is the most currently pervasive and eternally consequential injustice confronting the mission of the church. This is not to excuse or minimize human suffering in any way since "Christians are rightly concerned about the grievous imbalances of wealth and food and freedom in the world" (Moffett 2009, 599–600). But Christians must go beyond the horizontal dimension to the vertical one and press the question, "What about the most devastating imbalance of all: the unequal distribution of the light of the knowledge of God in Jesus Christ?" (Moffett 2009, 600). This is what the early church as well as the church during the modern missionary era focused on, and which the contemporary church must do so again.[4]

In addition, Jesus and Paul on mission have much to interject into this discussion. Rather than painting a contrasting picture between these two, which prioritism has sometimes inadvertently done as a result of allowing holism to define the terms (cf. Hesselgrave 2005, 144ff), there is clear continuity between the Son of God and his apostle to the Gentiles regarding mission. Luke 4:18–19 has been described by holists as the "mission statement" for Jesus' life

---

4.   Robert Woodberry observes that although colonial missionaries "perceived societal reform as a natural extension of their faith," they "viewed conversion as their primary goal" (2012, 254–255).

which combines "faith with action to overcome injustice and oppression" (Engel and Dyrness 2000, 23). But a closer look at the passage shows that:

> of the four infinitives from Isaiah that show the purpose of the Spirit's anointing and sending of Jesus, three involve preaching. The poor are evangelized (*euangelizomai*); the prisoners have release and the blind have recovery of sight proclaimed (*kērussō*) to them; the year of the Lord's favor, the Jubilee year, is proclaimed (*kērussō*). The other purpose is to send the oppressed away in freedom. Luke, then, regards the primary activity of Jesus' ministry as preaching. (Larkin 1998, 158)

Moreover, at the end of Luke 4, one encounters the statement: "I must preach the Kingdom of God to the other cities also, for I was sent for this purpose" (v. 43; cf. Mark 1:38). Hence, a careful reading of this chapter shows that the "mission statement" of the Messiah centers on proclamation. In conformity to Jesus' mission, Paul testifies:

> For this purpose I [Jesus] have appeared to you, to appoint you . . . a witness . . . rescuing you from the *Jewish* people and from the Gentiles, to whom I am sending you, to open their eyes so that they may turn from darkness to light and from the dominion of Satan to God, that they may receive forgiveness of sins and an inheritance among those who have been sanctified by faith in Me. (Acts 26:16–18)

Elsewhere, he is even more specific, "For Christ did not send me to baptize, but to preach the gospel, not in cleverness of speech, so that the cross of Christ would not be made void" (1 Cor 1:17). Thus, if such an orientation marked out the two greatest missionary exemplars of the New Testament, one needs to come up with a legitimate reason why it does not hold true for who desire to follow in their footsteps today.

Another vital subject which is rarely, if ever, considered in this discussion is the ministry of the Spirit of God in the church's witness. According to Harry Boer, "there is a surprising and unanimous testimony in the New Testament to the relationship between the Spirit poured out at Pentecost and the witness of the church" (1961, 112). The evidence he presents in support of this thesis is at least threefold: 1) several versions of the Great Commission show "the inescapable correlation" between the witness of the church and the work of the Spirit (cf. Matt 28:20; Mark 16:20; Luke 24:47–48; Acts 1:8), signifying that "the Spirit who indwells the church and constitutes her life is a Spirit of witness"; 2) the terms associated with the activity of the promised Paraclete as described in John 14 to 16 include *"teach, remind, guide, show, convict, witness"* and thereby indicate that the Spirit is "Christ's witness in and through men to the church and to the world"; and 3) the apostles in general being "filled with the Holy Spirit and [speaking] with other tongues, as the Spirit was giving them utterance" and Peter in particular proclaiming the truth about the life, death, and resurrection of Jesus (Acts 2:14ff), "establish that the central task of the church is to witness to the great works of God in the power of the Spirit" (1961, 101ff). In light of this, Boer concludes: "If the Holy Spirit given at Pentecost is so centrally the origin and the undergirding, informing and empowering principle of the missionary witness of the church, it would seem reasonable to expect that he should also have the greatest significance for the *concrete manner* in which the actual missionary work of the church is performed" (1961, 205).

WORD OVER DEED

If there is one remaining task for prioritism to clarify it is this: in what sense can evangelism be considered the priority in relation to all other ancillary activities in the mission of the church?

There is first of all a *theological* priority. It is disappointing that in some of the major contemporary works on holistic/integral mission the reality of hell is given either scant recognition or ignored altogether.[5] The explanation for this may be the need to address the physical aspects of humanity over against the spiritual in an effort to rectify the supposed dualistic tendencies of prioritism in which the spirit takes precedence over the flesh. But what prioritism asserts is not that the spirit is more important than the flesh, but that eternal realities always outweigh temporal ones. As Tim Chester explains:

> To say that physical and spiritual belong together is very different from saying that the temporal is as important as the eternal. The Bible consistently says we should make the eternal future our priority. In Matthew 10:28 we read: "Do not fear those who kill the body but cannot kill the soul." Is that dualism? Is this saying that the soul is more important than the body? If it is, then it is Jesus who says it. But in fact Jesus goes on: "Rather fear him who can destroy both soul and body in hell" (Matt 10:28). The issue is not whether the soul is more important than the body . . . The issue is that our eternal fate is more important than what happens to us in this life . . . [T]he priority of the eternal future means that the greatest need for all of us is to be reconciled to God and so escape his wrath . . . Time and again this has proved the greatest challenge facing Christian social involvement—to

---

5. E.g., it is mentioned once in Wright (2006, 306), Wright (2010, 100), and Douglas (2012, 195), but not at all in the Micah Network Declaration on Integral Mission (Micah Network, 2001), the Lausanne Occasional Paper on Holistic Mission (Padilla, 2005), Myers (2002), or Flemming (2013). For more on this subject, see Hesselgrave, "The Eclipse of the Eternal in Contemporary Missiology" (2008, 53ff).

keep in view the greatest gift we have to offer a needy world: the words of eternal life. (2013, 58–60)

Indeed, "Placing that which is temporal and unsatisfying alongside that which is eternal and teleologically final as special components of a life of service presents a mystifying incongruity. 'Labor not for the bread that perishes but for that which endures to eternal life' [John 6:27]" (Nettles 1990, 6). One can only hope that those who affirm "*the nonultimacy of death*" will eventually come around to advocating the primacy of evangelism (Wright 2006, 439).

Second, there is an *abiding* priority. John Stott believed that the:

Distinction between evangelism and social action is often artificial. Although some individual Christians are called to specialist ministries (some as evangelists, others as social workers, and so forth), the Christian community as a whole should not have to choose, any more than Jesus did. In many missionary situations such a choice would be inconceivable. The evangelist could not with integrity proclaim the good news to the victims of flood or famine while ignoring their physical plight. (1979, 34)

In sympathy to this view, Wright maintains:

The language of the "priority of evangelism" implies that the only proper starting point must always be evangelistic proclamation. *Priority* means it is the most important, most urgent, thing to be done first, and everything else must take second, third or fourth place. But the difficulty with this is that (1) it is not always possible or desirable to the immediate situation, and (2) it does not even reflect the actual practice of Jesus." (2006, 318)

What is implied in these statements is that the existential context should be allowed to dictate the terms of mission. This same sentiment was expressed at the WCC's Uppsala assembly (1968) in the catchphrase "the world sets the agenda" (Yates 1994, 197). However, not the context, the world, or anything else other than divine revelation can be allowed to establish the missionary impulse of the church. In reality, "if we wish to reflect on 'biblical foundations for mission,' our point of departure should not be the contemporary enterprise we seek to justify, but the biblical sense of what being sent into the world signifies" (Bosch 1993, 177). The reason why this is critically important is because "If . . . social advance is put first in time . . . it is obvious that faith in Christ is not the foundation but the coping stone of social and moral progress [and consequently] we have, by deeds which speak louder than words, taught men to seek 'all these things' first [rather than] the Kingdom of God and His righteousness" (Allen 1962, 83). Jesus and Paul, both of whom launched their ministries with proclamation (Mark 1:14–15; Acts 9:19–20), avoided this pitfall in mission in direct contradiction to the holistic mandate. In John 6, when the hungry multitudes sought the blessings of the Kingdom apart from submission to the King, Jesus redirected their attention to this truth: "I am the bread of life; he who comes to Me will not hunger, and he who believes in Me will never thirst" (John 6:35). Also, even though Paul's church planting efforts negatively impacted the business ventures and livelihoods of people (Acts 16:16–21; 19:19, 23–27), he refused to shift his priorities. By implication, what this shows is that: 1) there can be mission without social action, but the same cannot be said for proclamation; 2) the *missio Dei* determines the *missio hominum*, not vice versa; and 3) the personal aspirations of God's servants are not what define the *missio ecclesiae*, but rather the divine obligations placed upon it with regard to the lost (cf. Luke 19:10; John 5:30; 1 Cor 9:19–22; 10:32–33). As such, those involved in social work must remember that while "evangelism and social action are partners in many situations, it is inadequate to think of them as corresponding activities of equal impact [because] the greatest need of the poor, as it is for all people, is to be reconciled with God" (Chester 2013, 73). Thus, even while arranging a tourniquet for a lost person bleeding to death, the good news of how to avoid the wrath of God by believing in Jesus Christ must still be shared (cf. John 3:36; Eph 5:6).

Third, there is a *strategic* priority to word over deed. Lesslie Newbigin is well-known for saying that "to set word and deed, preaching and action, against each other is absurd . . . The words explain the deeds, and the deeds validate the words" (1989, 137). But such an assertion does not reflect mission realities on the ground. Besides the fact that non-Christians can replicate the philanthropic efforts of Christians, a rarely acknowledged truth on the part of holistic practitioners is that compassion ministries are "a bane as well as a blessing" (Hesselgrave 1999, 281). This is true in at least three ways: first, they lead to "unethical conversions" as people convert "to Christianity in order to receive charity or material advancements" (Somaratna 2012, 15); second, they produce "rice converts" as a result of the activities of "[r]ice missionaries" Bonk 2006, 77); and third, because "our natural inclination [is] to avoid the stigma and rejection associated with Jesus," it is easy "to find comfort in the notion that our deeds matter more than our words; indeed, that our deeds can *substitute* for our words" (Litfin 2012, 21). Hence, to assign the same intrinsic value to word and deed is both problematic and counterproductive.

In addition, what happens in situations where overtures to assist people are countered with the following?

> I do not want your help . . . despite all the nobility and charitableness of spirit in which you offer that help, for I have my own spiritual resources to draw upon and want to become saved according to my own fashion? There is, from the standpoint of secondary motives and purpose that have been falsely converted into primary ones, no valid answer to this argument. (Kraemer, 1963, 293)

Furthermore, the high aspirations of holism make "the church *alone* responsible for the disintegration of society [and thereby links] the church with a cause that cannot succeed in the present age"

(Hesselgrave 1990, 4). In reality, the church "never can *promise* the solution of economic, social, and political problems . . . for the simple reason that the church cannot pretend to govern the economic and political factors that determine the outward course of the world at large" (Kraemer 1963, 430). This truth should be a source of encouragement to those in mission because in the history of the church "the gospel has been spread abroad without [holistic ministries], and we need to be reminded that they are not indispensable. If we forget it we make social progress our gospel and become more concerned about social progress than spiritual regeneration" (Allen 1960, 99).

Last, there is a *financial* priority. The evidence shows that efforts to improve the socio-economic conditions of people have taken away from evangelistic ministries both in time and treasure. For instance, Frew Tamrat, principal of the Evangelical Theological College in Ethiopia, reports:

> Those ministers who have a clear calling to be evangelists prefer to involve in social work than preaching the gospel to the lost. If you are a social worker involved in development work, you will be paid more than the evangelist who labors in taking the gospel to unreached people groups. As a result, this has created among believers in Africa and especially in Ethiopia the idea that the work of preaching the gospel is the lowest job of the church. Even though the churches involvement in humanitarian work has brought significant improvements among several communities, its over emphasis has deprived the church from making the preaching of the gospel its priority. (Personal communication July 27, 2014)

One church in the same country was even shocked "by the fact that there were more [foreign] financial resources [made] available for relief and development work than for evangelism" (Thomsen 1999, 261). Such incidents are lamentable in and of themselves, but as Kevin

DeYoung and Greg Gilbert note, they fall short on another level altogether: "You can make a good case that the church has a responsibility to see that everyone in their local church community is cared for, but you cannot make a very good case that the church must be the social custodian for everyone in their society" (2011, 176). In fact, the "New Testament . . . never commands the church's diaconal work to assist people outside the church. What the New Testament authorizes . . . is that the church's diaconal ministry should be directed toward needy Christians" (VanDrunen 2010, 158). Therefore, in light of its limited funds, the "church should tend toward doing those activities and spending its resources on those projects that *more directly*, rather than *less directly*, further its central mission" of world evangelization (DeYoung and Gilbert 2011, 235).

CONCLUSION

After all that has been said, it is entirely possible that some may still find it difficult to decide which view to affirm. The following questions are meant to be of assistance in this regard:

1. Are the eternal needs of human beings more important than temporal ones?
2. Is what Jesus did for humanity on the cross infinitely more significant than anything the church can do for others?
3. Does the gospel involve what Jesus has done for others, not what the church can do for them?
4. Is the greatest injustice in the world today not social, economic, political, or environmental in nature, but the unequal distribution of the word of God whereby the lost may be reconciled with their Creator?
5. Is it acceptable to move on to unevangelized areas to introduce the gospel rather than remain behind to address the perennial humanitarian problems Christians face?
6. Is it appropriate to spend the majority of the church's resources in mission on evangelistic rather than social ministries?

If a person is able to answer most of these questions in the affirmative, then that person leans toward prioritism. Such a person will unapologetically defend and act upon the view that although the good news of salvation through Jesus Christ may not be the only blessing the church in mission has to offer the world, it is beyond measure the greatest blessing.[6]

REFERENCES

Allen, Roland. 1960. *The Ministry of the Spirit*. London: World Dominion Press.

———. 1962. *The Spontaneous Expansion of the Church: And the Causes Which Hinder It*. Grand Rapids, MI: Eerdmans.

Augustine of Hippo. 1950. *The City of God*. Translated by Marcus Dods. New York: Random House.

Beyerhaus, Peter. 1971. *Missions: Which Way? Humanization or Redemption*. Grand Rapids, MI: Zondervan.

Bird, Michael F. 2013. *Evangelical Theology: A Biblical and Systematic Introduction*. Grand Rapids, MI: Zondervan.

Bliss, Lowell. 2013. *Environmental Missions*. Pasadena, CA: William Carey Library.

Boer, Harry. 1961. *Pentecost and Missions*. Grand Rapids, MI: Eerdmans.

Bonk, Jonathan J. 2006. *Missions and Money: Affluence as a Missionary Problem*. Maryknoll, NY: Orbis.

Bosch, David. 1991. *Transforming Mission: Paradigm Shifts in Theology of Mission*. Maryknoll, NY: Orbis.

———. 1993. "Reflections on Biblical Models of Mission." In *Toward the 21st Century in Christian Mission*, edited by James M. Phillips and Robert T. Coote, 175–192. Grand Rapids, MI: Eerdmans.

---

6. This article was taken from one twice as long. The complete treatment of this subject by the author has been published in two parts in the *Great Commission Research Journal* 7, no. 2 and v. 8, no. 1.

Braaten, Carl E. 1985. *The Apostolic Imperative: Nature and Aim of the Church's Mission and Ministry*. Minneapolis, MN: Augsburg.

Burris, Stephen E., and Kendi Howells Douglas. 2012. "Introduction." In *River of God: An Introduction to World Mission*, edited by Doug Priest and Stephen Burris, 1–13. Eugene, OR: Wipf & Stock.

Carson, D. A. 2013. "The Hole in the Gospel." *Themelios* 38, no. 3: 353–356.

Chester, Theodore W. Jr. 2013. *Good News to the Poor: World Evangelical Economics*. Wheaton, IL: Crossway.

Crouch, Andy. 2013. *Playing God: Redeeming the Gift of Power*. Downers Grove, IL: Intervarsity Press.

DeYoung, Kevin, and Greg Gilbert. 2011. *What is the Mission of the Church? Making Sense of Social Justice, Shalom, and the Great Commission*. Wheaton, IL: Crossway.

Douglas, Robert. 2012. "Islam: How Christians are Learning to Create a Bridge Over Tumultuous Waters." In *River of God: An Introduction to World Mission*, edited by Doug Priest and Stephen Burris, 188–200. Eugene, OR: Wipf & Stock.

Eldred, Ken. 2005. *God Is At Work: Transforming People and Nations through Business*. Ventura, CA: Regal.

Engle, James F., and William A. Dyrness 2000. *Changing the Mind of Missions: Where have we Gone Wrong?* Downers Grove, IL: Intervarsity Press.

Ferdinando, K. 2007. "Gospel." In *Dictionary of Mission Theology: Evangelical Foundations*, edited by John Corrie, 137–141. Downers Grove, IL: Intervarsity Press.

Flemming, Dean. 2013. *Recovering the Full Mission of God: A Biblical Perspective on Being, Doing and Telling*. Downers Grove, IL: Intervarsity Press.

Glasser, Arthur F., and Tracey K. Jones, Jr. 1974. "What is 'Mission' Today? Two views." *Mission Trends No. 1: Crucial Issues in Mission Today*, edited by Gerald F. Anderson and Thomas F. Stransky, 6–11, Grand Rapids, MI: Eerdmans.

Glasser, Arthur F. 2003. *Announcing the Kingdom: The Story of God's Mission in the Bible*. Grand Rapids, MI: Baker.

Gordon, Wayne L. 2010. *Real Hope in Chicago: The Incredible Story of How the Gospel is Transforming a Chicago Neighborhood*. Grand Rapids, MI: Zondervan.

Greer, Peter, and Chris Horst. 2014. *Mission Drift: The Unspoken Crisis Facing Leaders, Charities, and Churches*. Minneapolis, MN: Bethany House.

Groothuis, Douglas. 2011. *Christian Apologetics: A Comprehensive Case for Biblical Faith*. Downers Grove, IL: Intervarsity Press.

Hesselgrave, David J. 1990. "Holes in 'Holistic Mission.'" *Trinity World Forum* 15, no. 3: 1–5.

———. 1999. "Redefining Holism." *Evangelical Missions Quarterly* 35, no. 3: 278–284.

———. 2001. "Evangelical Mission in 2001 and Beyond—Who Will Set the Agenda?" *Trinity World Forum* 26, no. 2: 1–3.

———. 2005. *Paradigms in Conflict: 10 Key Questions in Christian Missions Today*. Grand Rapids, MI: Kregel.

———. 2008. "The Eclipse of the Eternal in Contemporary Missiology." *Journal of Evangelism and Missions* 7 (Spring): 53–66.

Horton, Michael. 2009a. "Christ at the Center." *Christianity Today* 53, no. 11: 47–49.

———. 2009b. *The Gospel Driven Life: Being Good News People in a Bad News World*. Grand Rapids, MI: Baker.

Johnson, C. Neal. 2009. *Business as Mission: A Comprehensive Guide to Theory and Practice*. Downers Grove, IL: Intervarsity Press.

Johnson, Todd M., Gina A. Zurlo, Albert W. Hickman, and Peter F. Crossing. 2015. "Status of Global Christianity, 2015, in the Context of 1900–2050." *International Bulletin of Missionary Research* 39, no. 1: 29.

Kirk, J. Andrew. 2006. *Mission Under Scrutiny: Confronting Contemporary Challenges*. Minneapolis, MN: Fortress.

Kraemer, Hendrik. 1963. *The Christian Message in a Non-Christian World*. Grand Rapids, MI: Kregel.

Ladd, George Eldon. 1974. *The Presence of the Future*. Grand Rapids, MI: Eerdmans.

Larkin, William Jr. 1998. "Mission in Luke." In *Mission in the New Testament: An Evangelical Approach*, edited by William J Larkin Jr. and Joel F. Williams, 152–169. Maryknoll, NY: Orbis.

Liftin, Duane. 2012. *Word Versus Deed: Resettling the Scales to a Biblical Balance*. Wheaton, IL: Crossway.

Lausanne Theology Working Group. 2010. *Reflections of the Lausanne Theological Working Group*. Available from: http://www.lausanne .org/en/documents/all/twg/1177-twg-three-wholes.html.

Marshall, I. Howard. 2004. *New Testament Theology: Many Witnesses, One Gospel*. Downers Grove, IL: Intervarsity Press.

McGavran, Donald. 1980. *Understanding Church Growth*. Grand Rapids, MI: Eerdmans.

McKnight, Scot. 2011. *The King Jesus Gospel: The Original Good News Revisited*. Grand Rapids, MI: Zondervan.

———. 2014. *Kingdom Conspiracy: Returning to the Radical Mission of the Local Church*. Grand Rapids, MI: Brazos.

McQuilkin, Robertson. 2006. "Lost Missions: Whatever Happened to the Idea Of Rescuing People from Hell?" *Christianity Today* 50, no. 7: 40–42.

Micah Network. 2001. *Micah Network Declaration on Integral Mission*. Available from: http://www.micahnetwork.org/sites/default/files /doc/page/mn_integral_mission_declaration_en.pdf.

Moffett, Samuel. 2009. "Evangelism: the Leading Partner." In *Perspectives on the World Christian Movement*, 4th ed, edited by Ralph D. Winter and Steven C. Hawthorne, 598–600. Pasadena, CA: William Carey Library.

Moore, R. York 2012. *Making All Things New: God's Dream for Global Justice*. Downers Grove, IL: Intervarsity Press.

Moreau, A. Scott. 2012. *Contextualization in World Missions: Mapping and Assessing Evangelical Models*. Grand Rapids, MI: Kregel.

Myers, Bryant. 2002. *Walking With the Poor: Principles and Practices of Transformational Development*. Maryknoll, NY: Orbis.

Neill, Stephen. 1959. *Creative Tension*. London: Edinburgh House Press.

Nettles, Thomas. 1990. "A Response to Hesselgrave." *Trinity World Forum* 15, no. 3: 6–7.

Newbigin, Lesslie. 1989. *The Gospel in a Pluralist Society*. Grand Rapids, MI: Eerdmans.

Olsen, Ted. 2013. "Spotlight: the Way We Give Now." *Christianity Today* 57, no. 3: 11.

Padilla, C. René. 2005. "Holistic Mission." Accessed March 30, 2015.   http://www.lausanne.org/wp-content/uploads/2007/06/LOP33_IG4.pdf.

———. "Holistic mission." In *Dictionary of Mission Theology: Evangelical Foundations*, edited by John Corrie and Juan F. Martinez, 157–162. Downers Grove, IL: Intervarsity Press.

Peace, R. 2007. "Evangelism." In *Dictionary of Mission Theology: Evangelical Foundations*, edited by John Corrie and Juan F. Martinez, 115–118. Downers Grove, IL: Intervarsity Press.

Piper, John, and Justin Taylor. 2004. *A God-Entranced Vision of All Things: The Legacy of Jonathan Edwards*. Wheaton, IL: Crossway.

Piper, John. 2010. *Let the Nations Be Glad! The Supremacy of God in Missions*. Grand Rapids, MI: Baker.

Ramachandra, Vinroth. 2006. "Integral Mission: Exploring a Concept." In *Integral Mission: The Way Forward: Essays in Honour of Dr. Saphir P. Athyal*, edited by C. V. Mathew, 44–59. Kerala: Christava Sahitya Samithi.

Schnabel, Eckhard J. 2012. *Exegetical Commentary on the New Testament: Acts*. Grand Rapids, MI: Zondervan.

Sider, Ronald J. 1975. "Evangelism, Salvation and Social Justice." *International Review of Mission* 64, no. 255: 251–265.

Sider, Ronald, and James Parker III. 1985. "How Broad is Salvation in the Scripture?" In *Word and Deed: Evangelism and Social Responsibility*, edited by Bruce Nicholls, 85–107. Grand Rapids, MI: Eerdmans.

Smuts, Jan Christiaan. 1926. *Holism and Evolution.* New York: MacMillan.

Somaratna, G. P. V. 2012. "Buddhist Perceptions of the Christian use of Funds in Sri Lanka." In *Complexities of Money and Missions in Asia,* edited by Paul DeNeui, 1–22. Pasadena, CA: William Carey Library.

Stearns, Richard. 2009. *The Hole in Our Gospel: What Does God Expect of Us?* Nashville, TN: Thomas Nelson.

Stott, John R. W. 1970. "The Battle for World Evangelization." *Christianity Today* (January): 34–35.

Swanson, Eric and Sam Williams. 2010. *To Transform a City Whole Gospel, Whole City.* Grand Rapids, MI: Zondervan.

"Symposium." 2012. *Evangelical Missions Quarterly* 48, no. 3 (July): 264–271.

Tennent, Timothy C. 2010. *Invitation to World Missions: A Trinitarian Missiology for the Twenty-first Century.* Grand Rapids, MI: Kregel.

Thomsen, Mark. 1999. "In the Spirit of Jesus: a Vision Paper on Christian Service and Mission." In *Mission at the Dawn of the 21st Century,* edited by David M. Paton, 255–267. Minneapolis, MN: Kirk House Publishers.

Van Engen, Charles. 1991. *God's Missionary People: Rethinking the Purpose of the Local Church.* Grand Rapids, MI: Baker.

Van Drunen, David. 2010. *Living in God's Two Kingdoms: A Biblical Vision for Christianity and Culture.* Wheaton, IL: Crossway.

Witherington, Ben III. 2009. *Imminent Domain: The Story of the Kingdom of God and Its Celebration.* Grand Rapids, MI: Eerdmans.

Woodberry, Robert D. 2012. "The Missionary Roots of Liberal Democracy." *American Political Science Review* 106, no. 2: 244–274.

Woolnough, Brian. 2010. "Good News for the Poor—Setting the Scene." In *Holistic Mission: God's Plan for God's People,* edited by Brian Woolnough and Wonsuk Ma, 3–14. Eugene, OR: Wipf & Stock.

Wright, Christopher J. H. 2006. *The Mission of God: Unlocking the Bible's Grand Narrative.* Downers Grove, IL: Intervarsity Press.

———. 2010. *The Mission of God's People: A Biblical Theology of the Church's Mission.* Grand Rapids, MI: Zondervan.

Yannoulatos, Anastasios. 2010. *Mission in Christ's Way: An Orthodox Understanding of Mission.* Brookline, MA: Holy Cross Orthodox Press.

Yates, Timothy. 1994. *Christian Mission in the Twentieth Century.* New York: Cambridge University Press.

CHAPTER 3
CARL F. H. HENRY'S REGENERATIONAL MODEL OF EVANGELISM AND SOCIAL CONCERN AND THE PROMISE OF AN EVANGELICAL CONSENSUS

Jerry M. Ireland

The question of how evangelism and social concern relate to one another in the mission of the church has long occupied theologians, pastors, and missiologists. As Carl F. H. Henry once observed, "Perhaps no problem has distressed the modern churches more than determining the legitimacy of claims made upon Christian loyalties by champions of personal evangelism on the one hand and by those who call the church to social involvement on the other. These tensions now vex the church as never before in recent history" (Henry 1972, 3). The evangelical divide over this issue, though not entirely recent, became especially sharpened by the divisions that emerged from the fundamentalist-modernist controversy that peaked in the early decades of the twentieth century. Fundamentalism responded to the human-centered social agenda of liberal theology by mostly withdrawing from cultural engagement and social action. Rather than developing a more biblically balanced response to social issues, fundamentalism instead tended to truncate the gospel's temporal relevance in favor of an exclusive focus on eternal matters (Henry 2003, 6; Marsden 1987, 4).

From within fundamentalism though, there emerged in the latter half of the twentieth century, a theologian whom some have considered an evangelical prophet, calling the church back to a more balanced perspective (Neuhaus 1989, 30). His name was Carl Henry. In 1947, at the age of thirty-five, he published his clarion call for reform, *The Uneasy Conscience of Modern Fundamentalism*. In doing so, he established himself as a key thinker in the emerging neo-evangelical movement.

Henry devoted much of his academic life to the pursuit of evangelical unity. This is one of the things Russell Moore has shown in his book *The Kingdom of Christ: The New Evangelical Perspective* (2004). Henry's advocacy, along with that of others, for an evangelical consensus on the Kingdom of God as inaugurated eschatology emerged in part from Henry's concern for a united evangelicalism. But in 2009, six years after Henry died, a panel discussion at the Evangelical Theological Society (ETS), consisting of Moore, Richard Mouw, Craig Mitchell, and Peter Heltzel, all reflecting on the life and legacy of Carl F. H. Henry, agreed that Henry probably died a disappointed man. The primary reason for Henry's disappointment, according to the panel, was the reality of a still divided evangelicalism (cf. Thornbury 2013, 203).

It is worth pointing out, before I go further, that I have my theological differences with Carl Henry. He was a Reformed Baptist and I am an Arminian Pentecostal. That said, I am deeply convinced that Henry ought to be heard again by a new generation of thinkers and practitioners searching for solid biblical footing. In particular, I am persuaded that Carl Henry's regenerational model of evangelism and social concern—the focus of this essay—holds forth great promise for an evangelical consensus on an important issue that continues to divide the body of Christ.

THE RELEVANCE OF CARL HENRY

Why should we care what Carl Henry says about this issue? The simple answer is that no person in recent history has devoted more of their scholarly reputation or been at the center of more evangelical conferences, quests, or committees promoting a biblical view of both evangelism and social concern than Henry. Not only because of his extremely important book, *The Uneasy Conscience,* but also because, in addition to that volume, he wrote or edited over forty other books, plus hundreds of scholarly articles published in academic journals and in *Christianity Today* (CT). Henry not only helped found CT, but Fuller Seminary as well, and played important roles in the 1966 World Congress on Evangelism in Berlin, Key '73, Ronald Sider's *The Chicago Declaration* (also in 1973), and the first Lausanne Congress on World Evangelization in 1974. Undergirding every one of these was an effort to, in part, promote a very specific form of evangelicalism that exhibited biblical fidelity and embodied a passion for precisely the sort of social action and cultural engagement that had been missing in fundamentalism. This absence of temporal and social relevance was, in fact, what Henry considered to be fundamentalism's fatal flaw (Ireland 2015, 45–59; Cerillo and Dempster 1991, 369).

THE REVOLT AGAINST PRIORITISM

Prior to Lausanne I (1974), prioritism, or the declaration that evangelism is the church's primary task, remained the dominant view among evangelicals, even in the midst of neo-evangelical reforms. Yet, ambiguities arising from the first Lausanne Congress led to further consultations aimed at bringing some degree of clarity. In particular, holism advocates from the Global South challenged prioritism, claiming that this idea was rooted in western individualism and thereby a cultural corruption of the good news (Kirk 1983, 31; Stott 1996, 24; cf. Tizon 2008, 40–43). In recent years, this has led to an increased tendency away from a priority position in general and toward seeing evangelism and social concern as equally important in the church's mission. This perspective is evident in references that define these two mandates as "two wings of the same gospel bird" or "two sides of the same coin" (Miles 1986, preface).

People on both sides of this debate fear that the opposing perspective would lead to an imbalance. Priorists fear that holism diminishes evangelistic efforts (Little 2005). Holists, on the other hand, suspect that prioritism diminishes the church's ability to speak to issues of present human suffering and causes the church to be seen as uncaring. Some also argue that where social concern is not present, true disciples have not been made (cf. Sider 2011, 61; Kirk 1983, 92). As it relates to evangelical differences on this issue, Scripture plays the key role and both sides make their case based on various biblical texts (cf. Hesselgrave 2005, 118–138; Kirk 1983; Little 2013). But given the differences between the two perspectives, both positions cannot be right.

As the debate drags on, it becomes increasingly apparent that an evangelical solution capable of overcoming this divide must exhibit a passion for both evangelism and social concern, and be grounded in solid biblical principles. As I will briefly demonstrate, Henry achieves this and more because he develops the theological foundations for both, in greater depth than most. Most importantly, he does this specifically by a thorough defense of the doctrine of revelation. This emphasis on the doctrine of revelation is, furthermore, missing in almost every other attempt to resolve this issue. For example, John Stott, in his exposition of the Lausanne Covenant says that evangelism and social concern "are necessary expressions of our doctrines of God and man" (1996, 25). But as is almost always the case, there is no explicit mention of the doctrine of revelation; and yet for Henry, it is this doctrine above all others that proves *the* fundamental issue.

PRIORITISM AND INTEGRATION

There are many lessons to be learned from a study of Henry's thoughts on evangelism and social concern. Perhaps one of most important relates to a common assumption regarding the issue of priorities. In the evangelism-social concern debate, holism proponents have often argued that integration—the idea that evangelism and social concern are theologically and practically intertwined—can only be sustained within a holistic model. Or, put another way, holists claim that integration and prioritism are mutually exclusive. For example, David Bosch says:

> The moment one regards mission as consisting of two separate components, one has, in principle, conceded that each has a life of its own. One is then by implication saying that it is possible to have evangelism

without a social dimension and Christian social involvement without an evangelistic dimension. What
is more, if one suggests that one component is primary and the other secondary, one implies that one is
essential, the other optional. (1991, 405)

When I first began studying Henry (and in fact, one of the reasons I started studying Henry in the first place), I believed that I could
show that either he was inconsistent, or that his theological foundations did not support his conclusions. The reason I thought this was
because I had bought into this very popular claim made by David
Bosch and others, declaring that integration and prioritism are mutually exclusive.

One thing that becomes very clear in a study of Henry's thoughts
on evangelism and social concern is that he not only seems to speak
the language of both camps, but also challenges some of the basic assumptions of each side. For example, in *The Uneasy Conscience*, Henry
says, "the evangelical task primarily is the preaching of the gospel in
the interest of individual regeneration" (2003, 88). This is pretty standard fare for a priority argument. Yet, in one of his other works, Henry
says things that sound very much like the statements made by those
on the holism side. In *A Plea for Evangelical Demonstration*, he writes,
"the church must in life and word be the global echo of the Risen
Christ's invitation to turn from judgment to joy. This address to the
world is not only in audible words, but also in compassionate demonstration of gospel truth" (Henry 1971, 88). These two statements show
that Henry's position emphasizes the priority of evangelism and the
necessity of social concern. We are then forced to ask, on what theological grounds does Henry defend his position, and how does it relate
to the claim made by Bosch? We will return to these questions shortly. For now, though, it should be evident that articulating Henry's
priority argument requires some very careful nuancing.

The particular eloquence of Henry's position is this: one need not
deny the important biblical commands regarding social justice in order
to arrive at prioritism, and the way one does this is by understanding

the full weight of the doctrine of revelation within Christian theology. When this is done, it becomes clear that there is a direct correlation between the doctrine of revelation and the priority of proclamation. However, such a prioritist position by no means renders what the Bible says about social justice as irrelevant or unimportant. In fact, the opposite is true. A high view of the doctrine of revelation, especially concerning Scripture, also gives rise to a robust social concern because the moral imperatives for God's people are divinely revealed (Henry 1986, 15).

REVELATION AND REGENERATION: THE FOUNDATIONS OF HENRY'S APPROACH

For Henry, the whole issue of the evangelism and social concern debate is first and foremost a theological problem. In addition, theology itself is always driven by one's epistemology. Epistemological assumptions determine theological conclusions. Because of this, Henry believes the only way to remain true to the nature and content of revelation is for revelation to provide the basis for epistemology and thereby become the determining factor in theological formulation. Henry, therefore, articulates a revelational epistemology that builds on Augustine's *logos* doctrine wherein the eternally incarnate Word mediates truthful knowledge from God to man (Henry 1999, vol. 3, 168; Nash 1982, 59–68). As such, the *logos* doctrine underscores the personal nature of God's revelation. God does not simply infuse creation with information, but intends to use that information to reach humanity. Furthermore, Henry makes use, again following Augustine, of the *imago Dei* to establish that human creatures are endowed with a divinely ordained capacity to reason rightly. Not even the noetic effects of sin have rendered this capacity incompetent (Henry 1988, 121). Therefore, humanity is everywhere confronted with God's revelation in both nature and Scripture. At the heart of Henry's approach is the idea that God's own gracious self-revelation constitutes the central feature of the Judeo-Christian heritage, and that there exists a fundamental connection between the doctrine of revelation and church's proclamational task. Specifically, the doctrine of revelation necessitates prioritism and renders social concern as necessary. This is because Christianity is fundamentally a redemptive religion, and revelation is given particularly on that account.

HENRY AND HIS CRITICS

A number of Henry's critics have claimed that his propositional approach to theological method fosters a divide between right beliefs and right practice. In fact, this has become a standing critique of conservative evangelicalism in general, but it is particularly directed toward those who believe that theology can best proceed when the teachings of Scripture are formulated as true or false propositions. This criticism comes especially from proponents of a post-conservative theological method. Specifically, post-conservatives accuse Henry and others of holding to an epistemology that fosters an unbiblical rationalism emphasizing "information over transformation" (Olson 2007, chapter five).

The critique that post-conservatives make here is really directed at Henry's epistemology, which drives his approach to propositions and to Scripture as a whole. These critics, such as Roger Olson and Kevin Vanhoozer, uncritically lump Henry together with Hodge and Warfield and claim that Henry's passion for propositions is (1) based on Cartesian foundationalism, and (2) is a product of Scottish common sense realism, both of which are methodologically problematic (Vanhoozer 2005, 5; Olson 2007, chapter two). This then raises the important question of whether Henry's priority position, itself, is the product of an overly rationalistic epistemology.

Henry's chief concern was the doctrine of revelation and he believed this to be the most endangered doctrine in the twentieth century. In addition, he felt that the doctrine of the Bible was the control doctrine for every other doctrine. Upon closer inspection, one notices that Henry is not a foundationalist in the Cartesian sense, nor is his method at all based on Scottish common sense realism (like

Hodge's and Warfield's had been). He does not reduce all the genres of Scripture to propositions as he is accused of doing. Henry's method is Augustinian, not Cartesian (Henry 1990, 40). As such, Henry's foundational belief is not reason itself, but revelation and the necessity of revelation for all human knowledge. Human capacity for true knowledge of God and the world is possible only because God wills it and provides for it: "The Christian knows . . . that it is only by divine grace that he believingly participates in the epistemic and ontic realities affirmed by the Biblical heritage" (Henry 1990, 51).

That Henry has grounded his theology in an Augustinian foundation of faith seeking understanding is evident in his affirmation of both the priority of faith and of a correspondent theory of truth that depends on the reality of divine revelation (Henry 1990, 40; Brand 1999, 15; Trueman 2000, 52). This approach stands miles apart from Cartesian foundationalism and should, therefore, be a source of tremendous embarrassment to Henry's post-conservative critics because they are so far off base. No one who has taken the time to read Henry's *God, Revelation, and Authority*, Vol. 1 (1976) and Vol. 2 (1976), along with his *Toward a Recovery of Christian Belief* (1990), would ever come to these conclusions, for Henry directly refutes these very accusations. No wonder Gregory Thornbury asks, "Are these people reading the same Carl F. H. Henry that I am?" (2013, 59).

The fundamental difference between Henry and his critics lies in the tendency to equate *rationalism* with *rationality*. Rationalism can be defined as the elevation of supposed innate rational capacities built on a belief in the mind's unaided ability to reason rightly. Henry, however, does not believe that for a minute. Instead, he proposes a view of rationality (not rationalism) that allows reason to function within the provisions of God. Specifically, human reason is a product of the *imago Dei* and the mediating *logos*, both means by which God provides for the flow of knowledge from himself to humanity. On this view, human beings cannot know anything apart from God's provision. Since the people of God are called upon over and over again to reason rightly regarding true and false doctrine, the content of Christian theology must therefore lend itself to systematic and propositional forms. This, however, does not mean that ethical demands do not follow, nor as Olson wrongly assumes, that Henry is more concerned with information over transformation.

Henry's Augustinian model of revelation grounds knowledge in God's own nature and purposes and rests on two fundamental axioms. God himself constitutes the ontological axiom, and divine revelation constitutes the epistemological axiom. Henry argues, "On these basic axioms depend all the core beliefs of biblical theism, including divine creation, sin and the fall, the promise and provision of redemption, the incarnation of God in Jesus of Nazareth, the regenerate church as a new society, and a comprehensive eschatology" (1990, 49).

The core feature, therefore, of the doctrine of revelation is that God makes knowledge possible and does so, foremost, that He would be known among the nations. But God desires not to be known remotely, but personally and redemptively. This fundamental necessity of revelation and its grounding in God's regenerational purposes for lost humanity requires not only spiritual but also moral obedience (Henry 1999, vol. 1, 232). Humanity's responsibility and culpability in both areas find grounding in eternal truths published in God's gracious self-revelation. This constitutes the essential link between revelation and Henry's regeneration model. The transcendent and verbal nature of this revelation therefore casts its net over the whole of human existence, calling all to acknowledge the Lordship of Christ (Henry 1990, 54).

HENRY'S ARGUMENT FOR THE PRIORITY OF EVANGELISM

Henry frequently championed the priority of evangelism. Furthermore, he understands evangelism as primarily a verbal-proclamational task. For example, he says, "The *unmistakable priority* of God's people, the church in the world, is to proclaim God's revealed Word" (Henry 1999, vol. 2, 22; emphasis added). As such, evangelism constitutes the church's only unique role in the world. If the church fails to heed this mandate it becomes an affront to God (Henry 1999, vol 2, 22). This characterized the apostolic church and should characterize the modern one as well:

> To recall men to their created dignity, to rescue them from sin's hell and death, to renew them in salvation's grace and power, to awaken their sense of eternal destiny, and to renew them in the image of God, the church gave herself in glad obedience to the Great Commission of her Risen Head, and regarding fulfillment of this evangelistic mandate as her number one task in the world. (Henry 1971, 64–65)

What especially distinguishes Henry's prioritist perspective is that it flows primarily from his understanding of the doctrine of revelation and its essentially redemptive thrust. "The human species," he says, "is on the receiving end of a divine initiative" (Henry 1999, vol. 2, 30; cf. Thornbury 2013, 64). In other words, God's own gracious self-revelation has been given so that God may be personally known. God's revelation then is supremely evangelistic; "Like some piercing air-raid siren it sends us scurrying from life's preoccupations and warns us that no escape remains if we neglect the only sure sanctuary" (Henry 1999, vol. 2, 17).

Henry's understanding of the doctrine of revelation forms the central basis for his prioritizing evangelism and his emphasis on redemption. God's redemptive purposes lie at the very heart of God's special revelation in Scripture and in Christ. This can be seen in that Scripture defines revelation using the Hebrew word *galah* and the Greek verb *apokaluptō*–both of which center on the idea of an unveiling of something hidden (Henry 1999, vol. 2, 21). What is unveiled is God's own nature and purpose. The only manner in which this unveiling takes place is through the reality of Scripture, the *imago Dei*, and mediating *logos* (from John 1). Not only has God spoken a redemptive message, but through the *imago Dei* and the mediating *logos*, He sets humanity in a position to comprehend that revelation. Therefore,

sinful persons stand inescapably accountable to God, thereby height-
ening the urgency of the church's evangelistic efforts, for one never
knows when the offer of God's gracious self-revelation will come to
an abrupt end (Henry 1999, vol. 2, 301–334). The crucial idea here is
that Christianity exists as revealed religion and God acts in the world
to accomplish His redemptive purposes. Therefore, Henry finds cause
for concern among liberal and secular tendencies to downplay this
motif and warns against confusing evangelism and social concern—or
of reducing evangelism to merely attacking social or political evils. To
do so is to commit the ultimate act of lovelessness, for it neglects humanity's greatest need, namely personal redemption and supernatural
regeneration (Henry 1967, 36; cf. Henry 2003, 39; Henry 1964, 307).

Henry's critique of liberal and secular fallacies regarding the be-
nevolence of God might also be applied to some holism perspectives,
such as that of Scott J. Jones, who tend to equivocate evangelism and
social concern and define them in such a way that it becomes difficult
to know where one begins and the other ends (Jones 2003, 16, 60–61).
According to Henry, since Christianity exists particularly as a verbal-
ly-revealed religion, proclamation uniquely defines the very essence of
Christianity in a way nothing else does (Henry 1999, vol. 3, 13–63).
Because of this, it is slightly off base, then, to say that evangelism
and social concern are "two wings of the same bird" or "two sides of
the same coin." Scripture never equates these two things in such an
overtly parallel manner, even though Scripture upholds the necessity
and importance of both.

As it relates to the issue of priority, one can easily trace through
both the Old Testament and New Testament an emphasis on God's
otherwise hidden nature and purposes that are made known only because God has graciously revealed them. This emphasis is brought
into focus by looking at God's divinely revealed names, which from
YHWH to Jesus emphasize God's redemptive intents and progres-
sively self-revelatory acts. The names of God especially underscore
God's redemptive presence and initiative (Henry 1999, vol. 2,
151–240). Furthermore, God's nature and purposes are verbally

revealed through the prophets and apostles. This verbal revelation and its unique role in bringing forth true and accurate knowledge of God forms the basis of the church's evangelistic and redemptive mandate. Apart from this, God would remain obscured as general revelation only lends itself to condemnation and guilt, not to salvation (Henry 1999, vol. 2, 283–290). Therefore, "The content of church proclamation," Henry says, is:

> Not just about anything and everything. The church's message to the world is not about the energy crisis, pollution, white or black power, détente, the Israeli-Arab conflict, ad infinitum. It is the very specific Word of God . . . nor is the Christian minister anything and everything—a fundraiser, marriage counselor, pulpit orator, public relations specialist . . . He is primarily the proclaimer of God's revealed Word. (Henry 1999, vol. 2, 22)

If we were to stop here, we might all readily agree that Henry was a prioritist in the purest sense. But Henry does not stop here, and it is very important that we consider what he has to say about social concern as well. As we do, we discover that Henry is something of an anomaly among prioritists. This is evident in that Henry calls the church to actively address social evils in ways that go beyond its evangelistic task, even though evangelism and revival remain the primary well-spring of social change (Henry 1980, 26).

HENRY'S ARGUMENT FOR THE NECESSITY OF SOCIAL CONCERN

Henry held that all moral obligations were rooted in God's own nature and that, therefore, religious devotion and moral obedience could never be divorced from one another. In fact, they are never separated from one another in Scripture. God not only rescues sinners from hell and judgment, but creates a new society, the church, that sets before the world the qualities of the Kingdom of God. Thus, Christian social concern is not about the creation of a new society, but about providing evidence that one has come already, at least in part, through the person and work of Christ (Henry 1979, 98). As Henry explains, "The ascended Lord wants to extend his victory over sin and evil through us, the new society, and enjoins us to be light and salt to the world. We are to have an illuminating and a preserving role, one that includes the ministry of compassion, the benevolent ministry of the church throughout history" (Henry 1979, 99). Within this regenerational approach, Christian compassion is neither a means to an end nor an add-on to biblical faith. It is fundamental to it and cannot be viewed as optional or as merely a means to evangelism. Henry explicitly warns against this by declaring, "The church dare not be interested in social injustices merely as an occasion for evangelism. She has a standing responsibility to the province of social justice" (Henry 1980, 121). In this, Henry presents a direct challenge to Bosch's claim that integration and prioritism are mutually exclusive. More precisely, he defines his approach to social concern as a "regenerational model," which he says achieves "transformation through supernatural impulse in individual lives whereby the social scene is renewed through divine spiritual motivation" (Henry 1980, 16–17).

Henry believes that there are four common approaches to the issue of Christian social concern: revolution, reform, revaluation, and regeneration. Revolution can be defined as an approach that advocates all means necessary, even violence, to achieve its goals. Reform similarly relies on the power of government to compel social action from its citizens. Similarly, revaluation seeks to compel moral obligations by emphasizing the superiority of human creatures to the animal and material world. But only a regenerational model rests its success on spiritual power and on the gospel. As with evangelism, then, there exists a direct link between the doctrine of revelation and social concern. As Henry explains, "The new birth restores man to fellowship with God, and lifts him not only to the vision of truth and goodness but also qualifies him with a new nature and moral power to place his energies in the service of righteousness" (Henry 1980, 25).

We might be compelled to ask precisely how this differs from the fundamentalist paradigm that Henry challenged. The answer is that fundamentalism, for the most part, stopped short of encouraging an active social agenda based on the reality of reborn citizens within a society. In other words, fundamentalism rightly focused people on the centrality of the cross and the priority of evangelism, but failed to motivate them to fully appreciate the fullness of their spiritual rebirth. Henry called upon the church to recapture the moral power available through the risen Christ in a way reflective of the apostolic age:

> Christ founded neither a party of revolutionaries, or a movement of reformers, nor a remnant of reevaluators. He "called out a people." The twice-born fellowship of his redeemed church, in vital company with its Lord, alone mirrored the realities of the new social order. This new order was no mere distant dream, waiting for the proletariat to triumph, or the evolutionary process to reach its pinnacle, or truth to win its circuitous way through the world. In a promissory way the new order had come already in Jesus Christ and in the regenerate fellowship of the church. The Lord ascended; he reigned over all. Hence the apostolic church would not yield to other rulers or to other social visions. It could not obey some earthly leader, covet some power other than the gospel, or reverence some man-made commission. The Christian church knew Jesus Christ. He furnished the spiritual resources for its moral confrontation with the world. (Henry 1980, 28)

Henry argues that where social concern is absent, the power of evangelism is diminished. It is important to understand what Henry means here and what he does not mean. He does not mean that social concern is necessary in order for the gospel to be credible. The gospel is credible all on its own. Nor does he say, as some have, that social concern is the greatest way in which the gospel is demonstrated. The greatest demonstration of the gospel was in the person and work of Jesus and in the gospel's saving power. That said, Henry calls on the church to not just tell the world, but to also show the world what "life made whole truly is" (Henry 1984, 21). Therefore, Henry issues a strong warning about the dangers of ignoring social concern saying, "The temptation to stress evangelism only as 'the Christian answer' and to withdraw from social confrontation is dangerous and one that Protestant orthodoxy had best avoid" (1971, 43). For Henry, this is perhaps the most important lesson to be learned from fundamentalist withdrawal. As Moore has noted, this withdrawal "isolated fundamentalism from the society it sought to evangelize" with disastrous consequences (2004, 84).

One of the very important issues that Henry raises in developing his theology of social concern is that of the Kingdom of God. Henry helpfully points out that the biblical concept of the Kingdom of God—which is a vital biblical theme—has sadly become a point of contention. He specifically laments fundamentalism's apprehensions about the Kingdom, noting that this apprehension is, first of all, reactionary and theology should never be reactionary. In other words, evangelicals should never develop theological positions solely in response to the excess of others. The excess he refers to is of course the excess of the social gospel and theological liberalism which tended to interpret the Kingdom of God solely as participation in social good. This led many within fundamentalism to overly spiritualize the Kingdom in response. The problem with such a reactionary approach is that it is simply unbiblical since Scripture says a great deal about socio-ethical requirements for God's people and links those requirements to the reign of God. This is evident in numerous Old Testament passages that link God's own reign to His demand for justice and righteousness and also in New Testament passages in which Jesus' followers are called to "prayerful yearning and active working for the extension of God's Kingdom" (Luke 1:17; Matt 6:10; Henry 1999, vol. 6, 431–434). Henry argues forcefully that the church is called to show forth the qualities of the Kingdom, and that there is an evangelistic component to this as well as a social component. The evangelistic component flows from the fact that when the church lives according to the ethical demands of the Kingdom of God, then in doing so it proleptically sets the world before the judgment seat of Christ by declaring the standards by which God will judge the world (Henry 2003, 37–88). Again, the regenerational emphasis emerges as the central feature.

George Marsden helpfully sums up exactly why Henry succeeds in advocating a Kingdom ethic for the people of God while so many others on both sides of the debate have struggled to find the right balance. Marsden writes:

> Henry worked out more clearly than did most of his evangelical colleagues the puzzling question of how social and political efforts could be Kingdom work while the Kingdom could never be equated with social, political, or national programs. His solution was essentially a version of Augustine's two cities conception, which sees a distinction between the city of God and the city, or civilization, of earth. Kingdom principles can influence the earthly city, but can never be fully realized there in this age. (1987, 81)

TOWARD A REGENERATIONAL MODEL

In closely examining Henry's perspective, it becomes evident that he has related these two tasks of the church in a manner similar to that of C. H. Dodd, who distinguished *didache* from *kerygma*. Dodd pointed out that *kerygma* represents the church's unique message of salvation, namely the gospel, whereas *didache* refers to the church's teachings and Scripture's ethical demands. Similarly, Henry has said that *kerygma* especially relates to what it means to fulfill the Great

Commission. But that is not all. The church sent into the world to share the good news of Christ is also called to live as citizens of two worlds and witness to the world of the abundant life Christ offers (Henry 1971, 62; Dodd 1964, 8–38; cited in Stott 2008, 67–68). Both *kerygma* and *didache* are essential, but they are not essential in the same way. *Kerygma* (proclamation) is essential because it is the only means given in Scripture by which God's will and offer of salvation are known. *Didache,* the process of discipleship that includes moral formation and ethical demands, is crucial to spiritual growth. But without proclamation there can be no disciples. Therefore, holism advocates like Orlando Costas who wish to label any differentiation between the gospel and its effects as dichotomizing, must come to terms with the problematic reality that such a distinction is found in Scripture itself (cf. Costas 1992, 38). It is, therefore, important that we distinguish the gospel from the demands of the gospel and avoid equivocating the two if we are to be faithful to Scripture. When this is done, then we can advocate for both the priority of evangelism and for a robust Christian social concern.

The claim, such as that made by Bosch, that prioritism and integration are mutually exclusive is simply a false claim. As mentioned, I had previously believed this claim to be true and have said so in print. But Henry presents a potent challenge to this notion because he was clearly a prioritist, but also evidenced a clear passion for social concern. He saw them both as necessary and, thus, he helps us to see how a prioritist position can indeed hold these together. Certainly, we can point to advocates of a prioritist position who lacked interest in social action. But this does not mean that there is, therefore, a *necessary* correlation. Plus, we can readily conceive of examples from everyday life that demonstrate the weakness of Bosch's claim. For example, I might say that I am going to go to the bank to make a deposit and then to the post office to mail some bills. I furthermore declare that the bank is my top priority because if I do not deposit my paycheck, then the bills cannot be paid. Clearly, one has here a case of priority in which both things remain necessary. I still must deposit my check and I still must pay my bills. Yet one of these takes priority because the second thing depends on the first thing having taken place. It is the same with evangelism and social concern. The gospel must first be preached before converts can be discipled and, indeed, the content of Christian discipleship remains mired in obscurity apart from the proclamational foundations of the apostles and prophets, which is divine revelation. Thus, the logical priority of evangelism does not render compassion as optional. It simply affirms the ultimate place of Scripture and the unequivocal role given to proclamation in the life of the church.

MACRO PRIORITY, NOT MICRO PRIORITY

Henry's priority position refers to a macro priority not a micro priority, though he never uses these precise terms. This notion has since been echoed by a number of scholars who have recently written on the subject (Litfin 2012, conclusion; Flemming 2013, 264–269; Wright 2006, 317–318). Henry argued that Scripture deals almost exclusively in macro priority, focusing especially on guiding principles rather than specific programs (1980, 129). In advocating this idea, Henry criticized both the Jesus movement of the 1960s and 1970s along with the group of socially-active Christians associated with Ron Sider's *Chicago Declaration* because of their individualism and anti-institutionalism. In other words, these seemed more concerned with promoting specific social programs than with fostering local churches that functioned as salt and light in the community. Henry was concerned that though both groups importantly tackled social issues, they did so generally from a stance of antipathy toward the church. This very problem also lay at the center of almost all imbalances regarding Christian social concern, including those of theological liberalism and fundamentalism. In all of these, there was a tendency to ignore the New Testament understanding of church as a visible institution. The church formed by Christ was to display certain characteristics in the world as the body of Christ, and these were to define its very nature (macro priority). As Henry explains:

> From one biblical perspective the Jesus movement, the Chicago Declaration of young evangelicals, independent fundamentalist churches and even the so-called evangelical establishment, no less than the ecumenical movement which promoted structural church unity, all suffer a basic lack, namely, public identity as a "people," a conspicuously unified body of regenerate believers. Evangelical Christians in their fragmented condition no less than ecumenical Christians in their structural affiliation seem to lack the realization that Christ's church is to be a "new community." (1999, vol. 1, 133)

For Henry, a focus on broad scriptural principles is necessary to maintain the institutional church's primary focus on making disciples. Where biblical principles have not been kept central, the result has been confusion over the church's role in society and the neglect of personal social ethics, which is fundamentally a discipleship issue (Henry 1980, 121–125). Regarding the move from principles to practice, Henry argues that the Christian believer must evaluate each situation with concrete biblical teaching. He writes, "To avoid being dismissed as indifferent to the culture in which it exists . . . the Christian movement will need to evaluate the live contemporary options, and to indicate whether they conform with sound biblical principles" (Henry 1980, 126; cf. Litfin 2012, conclusion).

In other words, though such a priority must govern the church's self-understanding (macro priority), proclamation will not always take priority in everyday life (micro priority). There will be times when it is necessary to feed the hungry or rescue victims of trafficking before sharing with them the good news. The priority of evangelism, though, simply means that ultimately we want every person to know Jesus, the Word made flesh, and accept his offer of salvation. Therefore, all that the church does should either begin with or find its way back to that central feature. Since God's will and offer of salvation are verbally given, and because there is no other name under heaven by which men can be saved (Acts 4:12), there must be, as Christopher Wright says, an "ultimacy" to the evangelistic task that is uniquely definitive for the mission of the church (Wright 2006, 319). This is, I think, precisely what Henry meant when he talked about the priority of proclamation.

Henry's instructive theology of evangelism and social concern highlights the need to recover a manner of talking about the church's missionary mandate in a way that emphasizes macro priorities. Contemporary discussions have largely become bogged down, though, and the terms prioritism and holism appear to have too much baggage to be of much use owing to various misconceptions. For example, when prioritists hear the word holism, many inherently attribute to it the neglect of evangelism. Conversely, when holists hear the word prioritism, this implies Bosch's paradigm and the relegation of social concern to optional status. These concepts, false as they are, have become ingrained in the evangelical conscience. Yet we gain nothing by continuing to talk about prioritism and holism if we cannot even agree what those terms mean. Perhaps then, it is time to adopt better terminology that captures the ultimate nature of evangelism as a macro priority, along with the necessary nature of social concern. I think Henry's terminology—a regenerational model—has great promise in this regard. The need for individual regeneration is the driving force behind evangelism and is the central focus of the doctrine of revelation. Similarly, from the regenerate life flows a Kingdom ethic in which the church models for the world life made whole. In this life, Christ's followers become salt and light (Matt 5:13–16), a city on a hill that cannot be hidden, (Matt 5:14) radiant with practical expressions of love and compassion in a world of increasing darkness and moral ambiguity.

REFERENCES

Brand, Chad Owen. 1999. "Is Carl Henry a Modernist? Rationalism and Foundationalism in Post-War Evangelical Theology." *Trinity Journal*, 20, no. 1: 3–21.

Bosch, David. 1991. *Transforming Mission*. Maryknoll, NY: Orbis.

Cerillo, Jr. Augustus, and Murray W. Dempster. 1991. "Carl F. H. Henry's Early Apologetic for an Evangelical Social Ethic, 1942–1956." *Journal of the Evangelical Theological Society* 34, no. 3: 365–379.

Costas, Orlando. 1992. *Christ Outside the Gate: Mission Beyond Christendom*. Maryknoll, NY: Orbis.

Dodd, C. H. 1964. *Apostolic Preaching and Its Development*. New York: Hodder & Stoughton.

Flemming, Dean E. 2013. *Recovering the Full Mission of God: A Biblical Perspective on Being, Doing, and Telling*. Downers Grove, IL: IVP Academic.

France, R. T. 1989. *Matthew: Evangelist and Teacher*. Grand Rapids, MI: Zondervan.

Henry, Carl F. H. 1967. *Evangelicals at the Brink of Crisis*. Waco, TX: Word Books.

———. 1971. *Plea For Evangelical Demonstration*. Grand Rapids, MI: Baker Book House.

———. 1972. "The Tension Between Evangelism and Christian Concern for Social Justice." *Fides et Historia* 4:3–10.

———. 1979. "Evangelicals and the Social Scene: God's Plan for Salvation and Justice," In *The Ministry of Development*, edited by Robert Lincoln Hancock, 96–103. Pasadena, CA: William Carey Library.

———. 1980. *Aspects of Christian Social Ethics*. Grand Rapids, MI: Eerdmans.

———. 1984. *The Christian Mindset in a Secular Society: Promoting Evangelical Renewal & National Righteousness*. Portland, OR: Multnomah Press.

———. 1986. *Christian Countermoves in a Decadent Culture*. Portland, OR: Multnomah Press.

———. 1988. *Twilight of a Great Civilization*. Westchester, IL: Crossway.

———. 1990. *Toward a Recovery of Christian Belief: The Rutherford Lectures*. Wheaton, IL: Crossway Books.

———. 1999. *God, Revelation, and Authority*, 6 vols. Wheaton, IL: Crossway.

———. 1947, 2003. *The Uneasy Conscience of Modern Fundamentalism*. Grand Rapids, MI: Eerdmans.

Hesselgrave, David J. 2005. *Paradigms in Conflict: 10 Key Questions in Christian Missions Today*. Grand Rapids, MI: Kregel Publications.

Ireland, Jerry. 2015. *Evangelism and Social Concern in the Theology of Carl F. H. Henry*. Eugene, OR: Pickwick.

Jones, Scott. J. 2003. *The Evangelistic Love of God and Neighbor*. Nashville, TN: Abingdon.

Keener, Craig. 1997. *Matthew*. Downers Grove, IL: IVP Academic.

Kirk, J. Andrew. 1983. *The Good News of the Coming Kingdom*. Downers Grove, IL: Intervarsity Press.

Litfin, Duane. 2012. *Word vs. Deed: Resetting the Scales to a Biblical Balance*. Wheaton, IL: Crossway.

Little, Christopher. 2005. "What Makes Mission Christian?" *Mission Studies* 22, no. 2: 207–226.

———. 2013. *Polemic Missiology in the 21st Century*. Amazon Digital Services.

Marsden, George. 1987. *Reforming Fundamentalism: Fuller Seminary and the New Evangelicalism*. Grand Rapids, MI: Eerdmans.

Miles, Delos. 1986. *Evangelism and Social Involvement*. Nashville, TN: Broadman Press.

Moore, Russell D. 2004. *The Kingdom of Christ*. Wheaton, IL: Crossway.

Nash, Ronald H. 1982. *The Word of God and the Mind of Man*. Phillipsburg, NJ: P&R.

Neuhaus, Richard John. 1989. "A Prophetic Jeremiad." *Christianity Today*. April.

Olson, Roger. 2007. *Reformed and Always Reforming: A Postconservative Approach to Theological Method*. Grand Rapids, MI: Baker Academic.

Sider, Ronald. 1993. *Good News and Good Works*. Grand Rapids, MI: Baker.

Stott, John. ed. 1996. *Making Christ Known: Historic Mission Documents from the Lausanne Movement, 1974–1989*. Grand Rapids, MI: Eerdmans.

———. 2008. *Christian Mission in the Modern World*. Downers Grove, IL: Intervarsity Press.

Thornbury, Gregory Alan. 2013. *Recovering Classic Evangelicalism: Applying the Wisdom and Vision of Carl F. H. Henry*. Wheaton, IL: Crossway.

Tizon, Al. 2008. *Transformation After Lausanne*. Eugene, OR: Wipf & Stock.

Trueman, Carl. 2000. "Admiring the Sistine Chapel: Reflections on Carl F. H. Henry's God, Revelation, and Authority." *Themelios* 25, no. 2: 48–58.

Vanhoozer, Kevin. 2005. *The Drama of Doctrine*. Louisville, KY: Westminster John Knox.

Wright, Christopher. 2006. *The Mission of God: Unlocking the Bible's Grand Narrative*. Downers Grove: IVP Academic.

CHAPTER 4

RECONSIDERING THE FORMATIVE ROLE OF ETHICS WITHIN MISSIOLOGICAL PRACTICE

Greg Mathias

Among ethicists there has been a renaissance of sorts regarding the importance of the connection between character and action. G. E. M. Anscombe's 1958 essay "Modern Moral Philosophy" marks the beginning of this renaissance. This essay reintroduced the classical Aristotelian notion of virtue theory to the modern ethical discussion. Essentially, it called for a return to Aristotle in shaping both individuals and their actions. Subsequently, this article paved the way for Alasdair MacIntyre's (2007) seminal work *After Virtue*. MacIntyre's work built on Anscombe while providing mainstream ethical acceptance of virtue theory.

According to Anscombe, contemporary moral philosophy suffers from an identity crisis due to Christianity with its ethic of law and the subsequent loss of a collective Christian conscience in the West (Anscombe 1958, 4). Anscombe argues that Christianity bequeathed categories of moral obligation and duty to moral philosophy categories, yet these categories are nonsensical without the divine lawgiver, God. One cannot lose the moorings of an ethical system while retaining the robust meaning of its categories. Otherwise, as Anscombe perceptively observes, there is the "survival of a concept outside the framework of thought that made it a really intelligible one" (1958, 5). MacIntyre builds upon these observations and argues that contemporary ethics is in a "state of grave moral disorder" and lacks any basis for rational moral agreement (2007, 2). He recommends an ethics of virtue as the way out of the wilderness in which contemporary ethics finds itself. Daniel Harrington and James Keenan write, "MacIntyre re-personalized ethics and proposed we start discussing not only what we are now doing, but more importantly, who we are now becoming"

(2002, 24). This question of becoming is a question of virtue, and it is a question that Christians need to be asking of themselves.

To emphasize this point, consider Peter Kreeft's argument that ethics without virtue is a dangerous thing. Kreeft explains that the highest purpose of ethics "is to make people good" (1992, 30). Further, unless one has a "road map of the virtues and vices," all that is understood is an ethic of doing at the expense of being (Kreeft 1992, 31–32). According to Kreeft, without virtue, ethics are rendered as mere illusion since it gives unsatisfactory answers to life's most important questions and betrays a less than Christian worldview. As Kreeft writes, "Our ethics are always rooted in our metaphysics, and modern ethics is rooted in modern metaphysics, the modern worldview, which is the superstition that all that is objectively real is nature which in turn we have reduced to matter" (1992, 32). The modern metaphysic, unable to support a Christian view of the world, then, betrays an unsatisfactory ethical system.

If Kreeft is correct in his contention that modern ethical theory is rooted in materialistic assumptions about metaphysics, then Anscombe and MacIntyre's point seems to hold. While the language of ethics may remain from an earlier time—with different metaphysical assumptions about the ultimate nature of the universe in play—in a post-Enlightenment environment, the foundations of the ethical system undergirding the language are no different now. The pursuit of the right and good is no longer based on a worldview that incorporates a Divine Being who creates the world with a set teleology. Deontic instructions, which adhere to the created nature of the universe and also shape the person toward *eudaimonia* or flourishing, no longer act as a guide for image bearers in behavior. In short, action commands are disconnected from the rightly ordered formation of character. This modern metaphysic which Kreeft introduces leaves no place for the Divine, including the role of the Holy Spirit, within the realm of virtue and character formation. Rather, the claims to proper behavior and the language of right and good are measured by what would best bring efficiency and convenience. Measurements of success shift from standards that cohere with an inherent human nature to utility maximization and pragmatic efficiency based on cost-benefit analysis.

This paper argues for a reconsideration of the formative role of ethics within missiological practice. This argument assumes that the shift in metaphysical grounding of ethical theory and the subsequent shift in emphasis on what determines "success" in ethics, has also affected the realm of missiological practice and motivations. While an increase in theological grounding of missions is on the rise as a whole, there is a general lack of thought in the realm of moral theology and missiology. In 2010, the Evangelical Missiological Society published its annual monograph based upon the current year's focus for research, writing, and conversation. The theme of the year, and subsequent published work, was *Serving Jesus with Integrity: Ethics and Accountability in Mission* (Baker and Hayward 2010). While the theme of ethics and missions is a vital one, it is interesting to note that not one of the sixteen chapters contained contributions from an ethicist. The current emphasis is to be on mission with God in every area of life; but in the rush to be "on mission," task completion supersedes moral richness when it comes to the Great Commission.

Further, David Bosch demonstrates this tragic missiological shift in his *magnum opus*, *Transforming Mission*. According to Bosch, the Enlightenment paradigm eliminated the certainty of ontological grounding and, therefore, the teleological dimension from the universe (2011, 363). Sans the teleological dimension, humans ultimately attempt to ground meaning, morality, and the rational determination of them in other things. Once human rationality is untethered from a settled ontology and clear *telos*, what results is a change in valuation. Progress measured largely in terms of numerical growth and utilitarian evaluation becomes the new hallmark virtue.[1]

---

1. Warren I. Susman (2003, 273–285) notes in his book the shift from a "Culture of Character" to a "Culture of Personality" within American Society in the twentieth century. This present paper is not concerned as much with the typology of a Culture of Personality, but notes that the move away from character or virtue is addressed on a societal level by Susman, a cultural historian. In line

The church has not been immune from the influence of this Enlightenment rationally-based understanding and use of progress and power. The shift in ontological and teleological uncertainty allowed a new metric of thinking about success to infiltrate the church. Instead of an emphasis on virtue and character formation, progress and power became the measure of success. Numbers were the new display of progress as opposed to transformed lives. Missiologist Samuel Escobar (2001) terms this type of numbers-based missiology, "managerial missiology." Escobar writes, "There are some aspects of missionary work that cannot be reduced to statistics . . . Managerial missiology has diminished those aspects of missionary work which cannot be measured or reduced to figures. In the same way, it has given predominance to that which can be reduced to a statistical chart" (2001, 110). Although numbers are not unimportant, as a display of progress, this focus represents a clear move away from the biblical ethic of love of God and neighbor as motivation for the missions endeavor. In light of this Enlightenment framework, people and even the gospel message were then employed as instruments of transformation toward progress and power (Bosch 2011, 270–279, 343). In labeling the modern missionary enterprise "a child of the Enlightenment," Bosch summarizes the tragic influence

---

with this study, the contention is that this shift takes place on a missiological level as well as an American cultural level, in part due to Enlightenment impact. Without the teleological dimension, humans are, in a sense, finite and material beings only and so are not concerned with the answer to the question, For whom? The primary focus then shifts to function in society and perception by others. This being the case, developing virtue is conflated with things such as accomplishment, progress, and expediency. Susman notes, "The older vision [character] no longer suited personal or social needs; the newer vision seemed particularly suited for the problems of the self in a changed social order, the developing consumer mass society . . . The new stress on the enjoyment of life implied that true pleasure could be attained by making oneself pleasing to others" (2003, 280–281).

of the Enlightenment upon the missional endeavor (2011, 280).[2] Within this dominant cultural milieu of ideas, biblically grounded principles of missiological practice slowly but surely gave way to ideals of efficiency, and character-based ethical practice gave way to utilitarian methods and measures of success.[3]

Philosopher Bruce Little (2012) recognizes a similar shift in evangelical life, which leads him to correctly observe, "Most evangelicals would deny commitment to pragmatism as a means of determining truth or morals, but when it comes to achieving a good goal it is an entirely different matter. In pragmatism, the first question asked is 'does it work' instead of 'is it right?'" With the foundational ideals now altered, Bosch is correct when he says, "An inadequate foundation for mission and ambiguous missionary motives and aims are bound to lead to an unsatisfactory missionary practice" (2011, 5). If this statement is true and Bosch and Little are correct, then this foundational shift signals a tragic turn of events for the field of missiology. Almost unwittingly, pragmatism now drives missiology and the foundational place of virtue has eroded, leaving the missions endeavor anemic.

MISSIONS AND THE DEVALUING OF ETHICS

It is now appropriate to explore two examples illustrating a devaluing of the role of ethics within missiology: the Church Growth Movement and the reliance upon marketing strategies.

---

2. The entire quote is "It was inevitable that the Enlightenment would profoundly influence mission thinking and practice, the more so since the entire modern missionary enterprise is, to a very real extent, a child of the Enlightenment." For a further discussion of the Enlightenment impact on missiological practice, see Bosch (2011, 324–325, 342–347).

3. This shift toward utilitarian methods and measures of success was a catalyst for the Iguassu Missiological Consultation in October 1999.

The Church Growth Movement

Donald McGavran is known as the father of the Church Growth Movement. His writings and methodologies originated from his experience as a missionary. He began with a simple but genuine question: "How do peoples become Christians?"[4] He goes on to give fuller expression to this question in writing:

> The question is how, in a manner true to the Bible, can a Christward movement be established in some class, caste, tribe or other segment of society which will, over a period of years, so bring groups of its related families to Christian faith that the whole people is Christianized in a few decades? It is of the utmost importance that the church should understand how peoples, and not merely individuals, become Christian. (McGavran 1981, 7)

From this initial question, McGavran proposed the idea of a Homogenous Unit Principle (HUP) where entire tribes or castes come to Christ as opposed to individuals. In other words, the goal in missions expanded from individual salvation to People Movements. The idea of the HUP produced a seismic shift in missiological thinking.

It is from within his concepts of a HUP and People Movements that McGavran proposes two stages of Christianization—discipling and perfecting (1981, 13–16). It is precisely at this juncture of conversion and discipleship where a de-emphasis upon ethics begins to emerge within missiological practice.[5] In writing about the roles of discipling versus perfecting, McGavran argues for somewhat of a

---

4. In McGavran's groundbreaking work, *The Bridges of God* (1981) this question of how peoples are saved is the main thrust of his first chapter, "The Crucial Question in Christian Missions." The understanding of how peoples, not individuals, come to faith drives McGavran's theology and missiology.

5. The purpose of highlighting these elements is not to argue for or against the HUP or People Movements, it is only to demonstrate the shift away from ethical consideration.

delineation between a converted life and an ethical life, while un-abashedly criticizing those who would disagree:

> Originally, it is said, to be a Christian meant some-thing ethical. A Christian was a spiritual person, seeking the things which are above, forgiving enemies, renouncing the works of the flesh, and man-ifesting the fruits of the Spirit. After Constantine, and particularly after these rough tribal conversions, Christians were little better than baptized heathen, and the Christian faith had more affinity with the worship of Thor than with that of the Prince of Peace. How much better it would have been, runs the armchair argument, for the church to have been dis-criminating, to have maintained an ethical standard and required those accepting baptism to conform to the law of love, or to have baptized only those indi-viduals who gave proof of spiritual rebirth. Needless to say, those who so argue either are speaking igno-rantly out of the ease of modern western civilization or are thinking in terms of that extreme individual-ism which marks the Christian churches of the West after the industrial revolution. (1981, 40)

To be clear, McGavran is not advocating for a total dismissal of ethical transformation. He states, "Discipling is the essential first stage. Much else must, however, follow" (McGavran 1981, 14). Mc-Gavran clarifies elsewhere that "biblical barriers must not be removed" (1970, 229). The barriers he is alluding to are the cross, repentance, and confession of Christ through baptism and joining the church (McGavran 2008, 229–230). He is addressing a misplaced emphasis of requiring people to cross undue linguistic, class, or race barriers prior to becoming Christians. For McGavran, these unwarranted bar-riers are unscriptural, and they halt church growth.

While the thrust of McGavran's sentiment is toward highlighting the continual need for evangelism, his proposal of a two-stage process of discipleship and perfecting is without scriptural warrant. In John 14:15 (ESV), Jesus declares, "If you love me, you will keep my commandments." Far from making discipleship at odds with conversion, Jesus addresses both the inner and outward orientation of the believer within this brief exhortation. Jesus equates love and obedience because, as Dallas Willard writes, "His gospel is a gospel for life and Christian discipleship" (2007, 273). Lesslie Newbigin highlights this misstep of McGavran when he writes, "There cannot be a separation between conversion and obedience. To be converted in any sense that is true to the Bible is something that involves the whole person. It is a total change of direction, which includes both the inner reorientation of the heart and mind and the outward reorientation of conduct in all areas of life" (Newbigin 1995, 135). The two-stage model proposed by McGavran is disjointed and needlessly bifurcates conversion and ethical or moral transformation. Paul Hiebert highlights the intimate connection between these two elements when he writes of the importance of the evaluative dimension of transformation.[6] Evaluative transformation includes "the moral dimensions of cultures and their worldviews. Christians are called not only to know the truth and experience beauty and joy but also to be holy people" (Hiebert 2008, 313). Hiebert's understanding of conversion and sanctification is an ongoing process from the moment of conversion.

Thus, the concern is not with McGavran and his desire to remove barriers to the gospel, but the consequences of his two-stage model of discipling and perfecting upon missiological practice. Unfortunately, McGavran's proposal of a sequential two-stage Christianizing process of peoples paves the way for an emphasis on numerical growth and the subsequent missiological model which Samuel Escobar terms "managerial missiology" (Escobar 2001, 109–112). As discussed earlier in

---

6. For a full discussion of the biblical view of transformation including the cognitive, affective, and evaluative dimensions, see (Hiebert 2008, 310–316).

this paper, managerial missiology is built upon the new metrics for success uncovered by David Bosch.

Modern Marketing and Missions

David Sills cautions contemporary missionaries against over-reliance upon modern marketing techniques. He writes, "One of the most important things missionaries should do is keep their Bibles open. When we set them aside to consider the latest marketing and management strategies, we can very easily slip into the pit of pragmatism and 'whatever works' mentalities" (Sills 2011, 188). In other words, when the methodology and techniques of the missional endeavor are emphasized at the expense of the Scripture, it allows marketing principles and task-orientation to characterize the missions enterprise over and above the work of God.

Sills goes on to discuss the impact of modern marketing philosophy on missiological strategy. He writes, "Initially, missionaries were working with the figure of twenty percent evangelical as sufficient to consider a group reached; this was based on a sociological axiom that if twenty percent of a population accepts a new idea, the adopters can perpetuate and propagate it within that group without outside help" (Sills 2010, 108). However, according to Sills, this twenty percent adjudication seemed too high to some, so more discussion led to the now prevailing less than two percent evangelical as the criterion for tagging a people group as "unreached" (Sills 2010, 189). The less than two percent rule drives a vast majority of missionary method and strategy, particularly when determining missionary assignments and relocation. Again, Sills writes:

> Unfortunately, the arbitrary two percent figure is employed in exactly this way in the deployment and reassignment of missionaries, and the significance of the definition and determination has drifted into missiological lore as an accepted fact on par with the laws of physics. Often, it is just as missionaries have learned culture, language, survived culture shock,

developed relationships with nationals, and become effective in evangelizing, preaching, teaching, and discipling that they are reassigned to another people group because their current one is drifting toward the two percent mark. (2010, 189–190)

While this paper recognizes the need for missional strategy, too often contemporary missiology takes a "pragmatic approach to the task, which de-emphasizes theological problems, takes for granted the existence of adequate content, and consequently majors in method" (Escobar 2001, 110). Thus, methodological pragmatism saturates missionary strategy and reduces the missionary endeavor "to a linear task that is translated into logical steps to be followed in a process of management by objectives, in the same way in which the evangelistic task is reduced to a process that can be carried on following marketing principles" (Escobar 2001, 109). This pragmatism of methodology is birthed more from the elevation of human reasoning and modern marketing than from biblical emphasis.

Within managerial missiology the focus moves too heavily toward human endeavor as opposed to a work of God. Eckhard Schnabel holds up Paul as the antithesis of this kind of missiology. Commenting on the potential reasons for the success of Paul's ministry in the New Testament, he comes to this conclusion: "Paul does not rely on a 'method' understood in terms of 'a defined, and regular plan' for the success of his missionary preaching but, rather, on the power of God" (Schnabel 2008, 371).

Although this paper contends that the Great Commission is more than a task, Sills' evaluation of modern marketing's impact on the missional endeavor is pertinent: "The task of reaching the unreached is necessary and biblical, but it is simply the first step in our obedience to Christ's Great Commission among the peoples where we serve. Jesus did not send us to 'Go therefore and get decisions from all men' but rather to 'make disciples of all nations'" (2011, 190). The question is not one of biblical motivation, but of unhealthy emphases within the missional endeavor.

The point here is that much contemporary missiology is lacking a proper ethical perspective. This reality leads to a utility ethic that often relies upon pragmatic methodologies. In turn, the *missio Dei* is cast as a mere task for completion, which is accomplished via the correct methods and strategies. Subsequently, human beings are then measurable numbers as opposed to men and women created in the image of God. The shift away from proper ethical consideration is damaging to both the *missio Dei* and the *imago Dei,* therefore exposing the need for an ethics-centered missiology.

With all of this in mind, missiologists must pursue what Anscombe has identified as a renaissance of virtue ethics to once again ground and guide the missiological conversation. Such a recapitulation of virtue ethics must be decisively grounded in a robust moral theology including a settled ontology and a clear teleology, which in turn leads to a re-emphasis on virtue and character formation. Kreeft reminds us, however, that the modern metaphysic does not allow for the Divine in this realm of virtue and character formation. So while Anscombe is right to call for a true return to virtue, perhaps the better way to do so in relation to missions is not to call upon Aristotle but upon Aquinas' notion of virtue ethics since he has a place in his metaphysic for the important role of the Holy Spirit who infuses virtue into the life of the Christ follower. For this reason, there must be greater attention given to the formative role of ethics within missiological practice.

This idea provokes an interesting point of evaluation for the field of missiology and the missional endeavor. Is the missiological task one that is driven primarily by one's cognitive beliefs about God, sin, the state of a fallen world, and the recognition of a possible eternity in hell? Or should one's love of God and love of neighbor be the primary driving force behind the missiological task?

Certainly one would be wise to avoid an either/or conceptualization of the missions endeavor; but interestingly enough, when one considers the driving motivations articulated in the preeminent missiological writings, there is a surprising lack of engagement of the moral motivations for modern evangelism and missions. That is, moral motivations for the missional endeavor tend to focus more on cognitive information and skill training of the missionary. They often exhibit a striking neglect of discussions related to the moral formation of the missionary who is called to engage the mission as a lover of God and a lover of neighbor.

A MISSIOLOGY OF VIRTUE

Building from the preceding observations, it is evident that missiology must recover an ethical emphasis in order to rightly engage the whole person in the missional endeavor. This paper will now suggest three foundational elements toward the shaping of a missiology of virtue in which there is a consideration of the formative role of ethics.

Emphasizing Pneumatology

In his classic work, *God's Empowering Presence,* Gordon D. Fee notes, "The health of the contemporary church necessitates that its theology of the Spirit and its experience of the Spirit correspond more closely" (1994, 2). A closer connection between a theology and experience of the Spirit is applicable not only in the church, but also within missiological practice. The ongoing role of the Spirit needs to be emphasized within the life of the believer as he participates in the *missio Dei.*

Sanctification

The Holy Spirit creates an ethical trajectory in believers (Gal 5:16–25) in order that they might be a demonstration of God's glory (Matt 5:13–16, 48), while reveling in new life now and for eternity (John 10:10; 1 Cor 13:12–13; Rev 21). These processes describe the continuing work of sanctification as the Spirit renews believers into the image of Christ (Col 3:10). John Frame correctly observes that believers are called "to a godly life based upon the Spirit's activity" (2013, 1105). The Spirit's ongoing activity in a believer's life is integral to the sanctification process and the subsequent cultivation of virtue.

Two New Testament examples serve to demonstrate this important connection between sanctification and a cultivation of virtue. In 2 Peter 1:3, Peter writes that God's divine power "has granted to us all things that pertain to life and godliness, through the knowledge of him who called us to his own glory and excellence [virtue]." Building from this foundation, in verse 5, Peter exhorts believers to "make every effort to supplement faith with virtue." While all things pertaining to life and godliness have been granted from God, believers are still expected to pursue a life of virtue. The implied expectation, then, is that there would be an ongoing process of growth and sanctification because there is an already/not yet sanctifying dynamic in the Christian life. Summarizing this dynamic, Kenneth Matthews writes, "Concomitant with the believer's participation in the divine 'glory' is the believer's 'new life,' made in the 'image of its Creator'" (1996, 164). Put another way, the cultivation of virtue is an expected part of the Christian life as believers pursue becoming that which they have already been declared to be in Jesus (2 Cor 5:17).

Turning now to Galatians 5:16–25, Carl Henry refers to this passage as one of the "best known of Paul's passages on the Christian virtues" (1957, 491). In similar fashion to 1 Peter 1, a familiar pattern emerges. In this passage, Paul twice exhorts believers to "walk by the Spirit" (Gal 5:16, 25). While this exhortation calls on the believer to exhibit fruit or virtue, Paul reminds his readers in verse 25 that this exhortation is grounded in the ongoing work of the Spirit. Gordon Fee is again helpful here. He explains, "The Spirit is the empowering for life that is both over against the flesh and in conformity to the character of God" (Fee 1994, 422). There is a symbiotic relationship between walking in the Spirit and exhibiting the fruit of the Spirit, or virtue.

Speaking of the fruit of Spirit in Galatians 5:22–23, Martin Luther writes, "They who have them [fruit of the Spirit] give glory to God, and allure others to embrace the doctrine of faith in Christ" (1979, 349). In other words, the virtuous life is a gospel-attractive life, a missional life. In this light, the cultivation of virtue is a necessity in the life of the believer in all his roles, especially that of a missionary. Put another way, the ongoing work of the Spirit orients the believer to the *summum bonum* of the Christian life, which is to bring glory to God by loving Him and reflecting Him to all those around by exhibiting an ever increasing virtuous life.

Character Formation

As already implied, the Christian life is an exercise in sanctification, or becoming what one has already been declared to be. The primary goal of sanctification is conformity to the image of Christ. The transformation of one's character from ungodly to godly is a continual process. N. T. Wright (2012, 3–4) argues that transformation of character is the primary purpose of the Christian life post-conversion. Wright then proceeds to intimately connect the formation of character with the cultivation of virtue. He writes, "After you believe, you need to develop Christian character by practicing the specifically Christian 'virtues'" (Wright 2012, 25). Since virtue relates directly to character formation, and each of these constitute a primary part of the Christian life, then virtue should be emphasized in all arenas of ministry including missions. Cultivation of virtue is a fundamental goal of the Christian life and is, therefore, a necessary part of healthy missionary practice. Christian missions is consequently tied directly to Christian ethics.

A transformed life, a life of godly character and Christian virtue, was an assumed part of the gospel message for early believers. Steven McKinion points out that in the early church, "Christians attempted to convert their neighbors and others through evangelism, or the personal proclamation of the teachings of Christ. They did this not simply by sharing the message of Jesus but also by living a life that demonstrated their own conversion" (McKinion 2001, 115). Second-century Christians understood that without a changed life, the gospel message is meaningless. Michael Green echoes this sentiment when he notes from Clement, "For when unbelievers hear from our mouth the oracles of God, they wonder at their beauty and greatness.

Then, discovering that our deeds are not worthy of the words we utter; they turn from their wonder to blasphemy, saying it is all a myth and delusion" (Green 2004, 72). Historically then, character and a virtuous life is understood as an essential part of the missionary enterprise. Separation of word and deed is not an option in the life of a believer.

When mission is understood primarily as a task to complete, then the fulfillment of this goal pushes even the most careful missiologist or missionary toward defining success in light of "does it work?" as opposed to "is it right?" This cannot be the foundational question for a missionary strategy ("MR #26: The Missional Helix: Example of Church Planting" 2011). When ethics is subsumed under strategy then the barometer of success is bent toward efficiency and pragmatism. Often, strategic missionary initiatives are undertaken with little to no consideration of the impact a particular strategy will have upon the cultivation of virtue within the missionary agent and upon the missionary enterprise.

Addressing the Motivation for Mission

A robust pneumatology also transforms motivation for mission into a whole-life response. Michael Reeves describes this truth well when he writes, "Because the Christian life is one of being brought to share the delight the Father, Son, and Spirit have for each other, *desires matter*" (2012, 99). Obedience-based motivation alone belies a truncated view of life and mission in the Spirit.

In Acts 1:8, Luke records that when the Holy Spirit comes, the disciples will "receive power" and "will be witnesses" for Christ. Often this passage is emphasized in relation to enablement for the task of missions, but this emphasis does not capture the full meaning. Reeves again explains, "The Spirit of the Father and the Son would never be interested in merely empowering us to 'do good.' His desire is to bring us to such a hearty enjoyment of God through Christ that we delight to know him, that we delight in all his ways, and that therefore we want to do as he wants and we hate the thought of ever grieving him" (2012, 101–102). The presence of the Spirit does not merely give the disciples the ability to take part in the task of mission, but He transforms their affections and desires into action motivated by an overflow of love for God.

Roland Allen further captures the intimate connection between life in the Spirit and motivation for mission in Acts 1:8. He explains that the disciples whom Luke is describing are not men "who, being what they were, strove to obey the last order of a beloved Master, but of men who, receiving a Spirit, were driven by that Spirit to act in accordance with the nature of that Spirit" (Allen 2006, 5). Life in the Spirit transforms motivation for mission from a merely outward orientation (obedience/task) to an accompanying inner orientation of the heart (virtue/formation).

In the same way that life in the Spirit involves the whole person, so too should missional motivation. Appealing to mission in this way only serves to affirm Paul's exhortation in Ephesians 6:6, to do the will of God "from the heart." As Dennis Hollinger summarizes:

> Thus, ethics in the Bible is not blind obedience to laws, principles, or virtues but rather a response to the living, all-powerful God of the universe, who is himself the foundation of those moral guidelines. The content of our moral responses are certainly known and shaped by the biblical norms in their various forms, but ultimately they are reflections of God's character, purposes, and actions in the world. (2002, 64–65)

The inter-connection between response and reflection appeals to motivation for both the moral and missional life.

Re-envisioning the Great Commission as a Formative Endeavor

As proposed in this paper, the Great Commission needs to be re-envisioned not merely as a task for completion, but as a formative endeavor in the life of the believer. James K. A. Smith's (2009) work, *Desiring the Kingdom*, proposes a similar project, although in a different field.

Smith provokes his readers to consider re-visioning Christian education as a formative rather than just an informative project (2009, 18). He bases this invitation for a recapitulation of education on the idea that humans are creatures of desires or loves and are not primarily cognitive creatures. Basing his investigation heavily on Augustinian themes, he writes:

> This Augustinian model of human persons resists the rationalism and quasi-rationalism of the earlier models by shifting the center of gravity of human identity, as it were, down from the heady regions of mind closer to the central regions of our bodies, in particular, our *kardia*—our gut or heart. The point is to emphasize that the way we inhabit the world is not primarily as thinkers, or even believers, but as more affective, embodied creatures who make our way in the world more by feeling our way around it. (Smith 2009, 47)

Smith's discussion has significant parallels for the field of missiology. His argument would challenge the missiologist to re-envision the Great Commission imperative to "go" to all nations as a loving command grounded in the very nature of God and reflected in humans as image bearers, thereby being guided and shaped by proper theological and practical instruction.

Seen in this new light, obedience to Matthew 28:18–20 could then be primarily understood as a crucial expression of God's image bearers to not only obey the command given in the Great Commission, but to do so in love and in the hope of pleasing the One who has given the command. Further, this loving act of obedience develops Christlikeness and character virtues that are proper expressions of image bearers. In other words, obedience to follow the Great Commission would be understood primarily as a command to love God and love neighbor. In turn, introducing sinners to the One worthy of all love and affection can be seen as the highest possible act of neighbor love.

Stated another way, this important connection between the moral nature of God and the commands of God should play a defining role in the contemporary *missio Dei* discussion. In the Great Commission, a command is certainly given but, because God is a loving and good moral lawgiver, it is by its very nature a loving, good, moral command. Thus, it should come as no surprise that the commands given by God are meant to orient the ones created in His image to experience the love of God as well as reciprocate that love to Him as a demonstration of their love.

Remarkably, the highest expression of human flourishing, involves a loving encounter with the God of the universe. Note that Jesus renders the two greatest commandments as commandments of love in the form of an ethical obligation: "And he said to him, 'You shall love the Lord your God with all your heart and with all your soul and with all your mind. This is the great and first commandment. And a second is like it: You shall love your neighbor as yourself'" (Matt 22:37–39). In the Gospel of John, Jesus also makes the explicit connection between moral obligation and the proper expression of love for God. In John 14:15, Jesus states: "If you love me, you will keep my commandments." Later in verse 21 of the same chapter, Jesus makes even clearer the symbiotic connection between love and obedience: "Whoever has my commandments and keeps them, he it is who loves me. And he who loves me will be loved by my Father, and I will love him and manifest myself to him." Thus, our acts of moral obedience are designed by God to be loving acts of worship before a holy and loving God.

At this juncture, the Great Commission of Matthew 28:18–20 is inextricably linked to the Great Commandment in Matthew 22:35–40. With this understanding in mind, one can begin to appreciate the important connection between the *missio Dei* and the flourishing of the *imago Dei*. By anchoring missiology in moral theology, the importance of considering a human *summum bonum* becomes paramount. Gordon Lewis and Bruce Demarest are helpful on this point:

Because God first loved us, we respond by loving God with more of our heart, soul, strength, and mind. The chief end of forgiven and regenerated people is not only to glorify God but also to enjoy him forever. People were created not only to serve God but also for loving communion with him. We are here not only to be of influence in the world but also to love, worship, contemplate, and meditate upon God. (1996, 245)

The *imago Dei* must be rightly engaged in and through the *missio Dei*, or the entire missional endeavor becomes anemic. The danger of this grand divine commission to love God and introduce others to God runs the risk of becoming a mere duty-based task understood primarily through cognitive evaluation of strategies to save the highest numbers of souls possible.

On the other hand, when the full participation in the life and love of God is understood as the highest human good or *summum bonum,* "ethical evaluation involves more than just the acts that are committed . . . events that qualify for moral evaluation always involve conduct, character, and goals" (Jones 2013, 15). Missions becomes an act of love-motivated obedience toward God and neighbor flowing from a character shaped by love of God, with the goal of bringing all peoples into a loving relationship with their Creator. While still recognizing the importance of obedience, the missiological task must be grounded in moral theology. Then the primary question of the *missio Dei* shifts from a mere action-based inquiry about what deeds must be done to accomplish the task, to "Just what kind of person is this habit or practice trying to produce, and to what end is such a practice aimed?" (Smith 2009, 83)

Ultimately, the missionary is challenged to consider the Great Commission in terms of the Greatest Commandment: "Am I acting out of love for God and love for neighbor?" (Jones 2013, 113). Questions of this nature connect the *imago Dei* with the *missio Dei* because they engage the motive and intent of the acting agent and not just the behavior. In this way, an emphasis on the formative nature of the

Great Commission becomes central, because it connects the importance of sanctification and character formation with the mission of
God for the redemption of the world.

CONCLUSION

The conclusions and subsequent proposal of this paper should not
be understood as a wholesale rejection of obedience-based missional motivation, nor should they be construed as a uniform criticism
of contemporary missiological practices. The emphases in this paper
serve to highlight the need for ethics and missions to be more intimately connected, particularly through the realm of virtue. This
connection allows for the Great Commission to move from the realm
of mere task completion to the realm of worship.

Jesus renders the two greatest commandments as commandments
of love in the form of an ethical obligation: "And he said to him, 'You
shall love the Lord your God with all your heart and with all your
soul and with all your mind. This is the great and first commandment.
And a second is like it: You shall love your neighbor as yourself'"
(Matt 22:37–39, ESV). Our acts of obedience are therefore designed
by God to be loving acts of worship before a holy and loving God. In
this light, the Great Commission intersects with our obligations as
well as our loves and desires. In other words, seeing the Great Commission as a worshipful response, transforms the focus from strategies
and means in accomplishing a task into a focus on being the kind of
people from whom the Great Commission naturally flows.

REFERENCES

Allen, Roland. 2006. "Pentecost and the World: The Revelation of the Holy Spirit in the 'Acts of the Apostles.'" In *The Ministry of the Spirit: Selected Writings of Roland Allen*, edited by David M. Paton. Grand Rapids, MI: Eerdmans, 2006.

Anscombe, G. E. M. 1958. "Modern Moral Philosophy." *Philosophy* 33, no. 124: 1–19.

Baker, Dwight P., and Douglas Hayward, eds. 2010. *Serving Jesus with Integrity: Ethics and Accountability in Mission*. Pasadena, CA: William Carey Library.

Bosch, David J. 2011. *Transforming Mission: Paradigm Shifts in Theology of Mission*. 20th Anniversary Edition. Maryknoll, NY: Orbis.

Escobar, Samuel. 2001. "Evangelical Missiology: Peering into the Future at the Turn of the Century." In *Global Missiology for the 21st Century: The Iguassu Dialogue*, edited by William D. Taylor, 101–122. Grand Rapids, MI: Baker Academic.

Fee, Gordon D. 1994. *God's Empowering Presence: The Holy Spirit in the Letters of Paul*. Peabody, MA: Hendrickson.

Frame, John M. 2013. *Systematic Theology: An Introduction to Christian Belief*. Phillipsburg, NJ: P&R Publishing.

Green, Michael. 2004. *Thirty Years That Changed the World: The Book Acts for Today*. Grand Rapids, MI: Eerdmans.

Harrington, Daniel, S. J., and Keenan, James F. 2005. *Jesus and Virtue Ethics: Building Bridges between New Testament Studies and Moral Theology*. Lanham, MD: Sheed & Ward.

Henry, Carl F. H. 1957. *Christian Personal Ethics*. Grand Rapids, MI: Eerdmans.

Hiebert, Paul G. 2008. *Transforming Worldviews: An Anthropological Understanding of How People Change*. Grand Rapids, MI: Baker Academic.

Hollinger, Dennis P. 2002. *Choosing the Good: Christian Ethics in a Complex World*. Grand Rapids, MI: Baker Academic.

Jones, David W. 2013. *An Introduction to Biblical Ethics*. Nashville, TN: B&H Academic.

Kreeft, Peter. 1992. *Back to Virtue: Traditional Moral Wisdom for Modern Moral Confusion*. San Francisco, CA: Ignatius.

Lewis, Gordon R., and Demarest, Bruce A. 1996. *Integrative Theology*. Grand Rapids, MI: Zondervan.

Little, Bruce. 2012. "Pilgrim and Progress: Enlightenment Assumptions and American Christianity," Southeastern Baptist Theological Seminary Faculty Lecture.

Luther, Martin. 1979. *Commentary of Galatians*, translated by Erasmus Middleton. Grand Rapids, MI: Kregel.

MacIntyre, Alasdair. 2007. *After Virtue: A Study in Moral Theory*. Notre Dame, IN: University of Notre Dame.

Matthews, Kenneth A. 1996. *Genesis 1–11:26*. New American Commentary. Nashville, TN.: B&H Academic.

McGavran, Donald A. 1981. *The Bridges of God: A Study in the Strategy of Missions*. New York: Friendship Press.

———. 1990. *Understanding Church Growth*. 3rd ed. Grand Rapids, MI: Eerdmans.

McKinion, Steven A. ed. 2001. *Life and Practice in the Early Church: A Documentary Reader*. New York: NYU Press.

"MR #26: The Missional Helix: Example of Church Planting : The Missiology Homepage." Accessed December 5, 2015. http://www.missiology.org/?p=157.

Newbigin, Lesslie. 1995. *The Open Secret: An Introduction to the Theology of Mission*. Grand Rapids, MI: Eerdmans.

Reeves, Michael. 2012. *Delighting in the Trinity: An Introduction to the Christian Faith*. Downers Grove, IL: IVP Academic.

Schnabel, Eckhard J. 2008. *Paul the Missionary: Realities, Strategies and Methods*. Downers Grove, IL: IVP Academic.

Sills, David M. 2011. "Mission and Discipleship." In *Theology and Practice of Mission: God, the Church, and the Nations*, edited by Bruce Ashford, 186–199. Nashville, TN: B&H Academic.

Sills, David M. 2010. *Reaching and Teaching: A Call to Great Commission Obedience.* Chicago, IL: Moody.

Smith, James K. A. 2009. *Desiring the Kingdom: Worship, Worldview, and Cultural Formation.* Grand Rapids, MI: Baker Academic.

Susman, Warren I. 2003. *Culture as History: The Transformation of American Society in the Twentieth Century.* Washington D.C.: Smithsonian Institution.

Taylor, William D. ed. 2001. *Global Missiology for the 21st Century: The Iguassu Dialogue.* Grand Rapids, MI: Baker Academic.

Willard, Dallas. 1998. *The Divine Conspiracy: Rediscovering Our Hidden Life in God.* New York, NY: HarperCollins.

Wright, N. T. 2012. *After You Believe: Why Christian Character Matters.* New York, NY: HarperCollins.

PART TWO   The People of Mission

CHAPTER 5

POWER PLAY IN THE KOREAN AMERICAN CHURCH

Eunice Hong

The remarkable growth of the Korean American church is well known and well documented (Chang 1998, 17). However, division has accompanied this growth, with numerous splits into separate first- and second-generation congregations (Han 2009; Kim 1999; Chang 1998). While God can and does transform church splits into church growth, these splits "are definitely painful experiences for all those involved" (Park 1997, 20).

This paper reports the findings of a study on factors contributing to church splits in multi-generational Korean American churches. Specifically, it gives voice to second-generation pastors who felt compelled to break away from their Korean American churches. Data was collected through semi-structured interviews with seventeen second-generation pastors from various denominations in the greater Los Angeles region. Data was analyzed using grounded theory procedures described by Kathy Charmaz (2006).

THE EMERGENCE OF ENGLISH MINISTRIES

The Korean church in the 1970s focused all its efforts on first generation Koreans. As a result, the first generation Korean church had "no extra energy to pay attention to their second generation children," and almost all Sunday school programs were conducted in Korean (Park 1997). It was not until the 1980s that the first generation became aware of the need to conduct Sunday school in English for their children who could not speak the Korean language. However, due to the lack of qualified English-speaking teachers, anyone that could speak English was appointed as a Sunday school teacher (Park 1997).

Paul Kim (1980) stated that though there were leaders in the Korean American church, their backgrounds were that of first-generation immigrants; hence, the programs they presented to the congregation did not meet the needs of the second-generation students (56). Instead of benefiting the church, "such leadership was not effective because it created conflict between the first-generation leader and the second-generation youth" (Kim 1980, 56). As those Sunday school children grew older, the Korean church then further realized the need for a separate English service for college students and young adults; hence, there emerged what is now known as English Ministry (EM).

The Korean American church today, however, continues to prioritize the needs of the first-generation congregation because first-generation individuals founded it. As a result, English Ministries and second-generation pastors share the feelings of frustration having to conform to the patterns, worldview, and administration of first generation immigrants.

POWER PLAY

In analyzing data, it is clear that the struggle for power in the Korean American church is prominent. Fred Prinzing says, "When in a conflict situation the question to ask is not, 'Who is right and who is wrong?' but 'Who is in charge?'" In other words, the question to ask in a conflict situation is, 'Who has the power and authority?'" (1986, 86). Prinzing goes on to say that:

> The basic tension is not one between right and wrong, but between power and authority . . . Authority is the right a person or group has to govern, control, or command. Power, on the other hand, refers to the ability to act or do. Another way of stating the difference is that authority comes through the positions designated in the constitution and organizational

structure of the church. Power is the ability to make decisions outside of this structure. In all churches there is the formal system (authority) and the informal system (power) that effect the decision making process. (1986, 86–87)

Young Lee Hertig stated that the role of power in the assimilation of immigrants is significant "because many immigrants face a sense of powerlessness from social dislocation" (1991, 12). He suggested that powerless people often turn to violence as a response to oppression and injustice and notes:

As in the case of Korean American immigrants, violent clashes in the family and church are direct results of powerlessness . . . When power is not mutually given there is more possibility of coercive power by the power holder. Consequently empowerment is scarce. Korean churches and families struggle mainly with the coercive power that is shortsighted, costly domination of the one against the other. Korean family and church structures demonstrate coercive power due to the weak social power in the immigrant context. (Hertig 1991, 17)

The struggle for power, or power play, is a main contributing factor for second-generation Korean American pastors leaving the Korean American immigrant church. As one participant pastor shared, "The real struggle is feeling this need to try to create leverage, or trying to create political power or ministry power, to be able to get what I want, but the reason why that tension exists is because there is one authority base where you try to contend." Another pastor shared, "The issue of power dynamics . . . this is the reason why first- and second-[generation] ministry partnerships don't work out. Because at the end of the day, a first-generation pastor has to look at a second-generation pastor with equal regard, and that is a barrier that has not been broken yet."

Many second-generation pastors are frustrated because they feel as if they are part of a political game in which they do not even know the rules. Some participants even suggested that the political game was specifically divided due to language:

> We [second-generation Korean Americans] have to go under the Korean-speaking deacons and elders, that is political power struggle. Of course, they won't say it that way, but that's what it is. So we don't see our future in that. Why? Because the leaders are all Korean-speaking leaders, and I don't speak Korean.

Though there also may be other factors that contribute to power struggle, the data pointed to three main components of the phenomenon. These interrelated components are: control, cultural ambiguity, and ownership. One participant reflected, "The balance between ownership and control is a difficult balance. How do you have ownership, and at what point do you have ownership where you don't have to control, and how do you make sure you have a healthy ownership and not an over-controlling one?" Another pastor's statement plainly demonstrates the interplay and equal importance of these categories: "Looking back, it was more of a power struggle. [The senior pastor] was unwilling to let go and let me take it over. He was insecure in that sense in my eyes." Implied in this previous statement, the second-generation pastor revealed that because the first-generation senior pastor experienced cultural ambiguity, he was unwilling to let go of the ministry (control) so that the second-generation pastor could take over (ownership). The participant's mention of the first-generation pastor's cultural ambiguity, or "insecurity," inferred the threat the senior pastor faces as a minority living as an immigrant in the United States. The following sections will examine more closely the power struggle found in Korean American churches as it is displayed by control, cultural ambiguity, and the right to exercise ownership.

Control

Power struggle may be used synonymously with the term "control." The Korean American church has experienced great difficulty because there is a continual struggle for control. One pastor recalled, "It really comes down to control. Who wants control and who has control . . . in the end, one group will dominate the other."

Most of the participants shared a similar opinion of being restrained in the immigrant church. One person admitted his frustration of always having to adjust to the needs of the first- generation congregation, "There wasn't much direction. The nature of the church was, 'Okay, we're doing this for the [Korean adult congregation]. What do they want to see happening?'" Another member shared a similar thought: "I was part of the church for nine years. I had credibility, but they did not have me to support the growth of the second-generation. They had me there to grow the first-generation via the second-generation program."

Many felt they wanted to spread their wings and fly but were restricted and pinned down—"I just felt stuck and constrained . . . It's rare to find a church, Korean church, where the first-generation allows the second-generation to experiment and allow them to be who they are."

Contributors were upset at being told what to do by the first-generation community. These second-generation pastors felt that they were not only old enough but also in positions of authority to make decisions and take responsibility. Pastor Andrew said he left his previous church because he felt there was a set of ideologies imposed on not only his ministry but also on himself:

> I wasn't against the first generation, but I was against those who wanted to impose an "ism" upon the new generation. I would do the same thing [leave] if someone wanted to impose something on my kids, some "ism." If some schoolteacher wanted to impose that, I would tell my kids to respect your teachers,

> but at the same time, I trust my kids to show what is
> natural and God-given.

Though people may not consider a church plant as an issue of control, interviews revealed that many first-generation pastors consider second-generation pastors leaving the immigrant Korean church as rebellion. As a result, "Mutual accusation and a bitter split follow. The split causes acute pain and bitterness in the hearts of the first-generation pastors" (Han 2009, 21).

It is interesting to note that fourteen of the seventeen participants shared similar stories of clashing with either the senior pastor and/or the elders before deciding to leave the first generation Korean church. What caused such tension for power among the KM (Korean Ministry) and EM leadership? The category that emerged from the participants' responses was "cultural ambiguity," the second component to define power struggle.

Cultural Ambiguity

Before clarifying the second component in the dynamics of power struggle, it is important to reiterate that all interviews were with second-generation Korean American pastors. As a result, only second-generation pastors' perceptions of first-generation Korean pastors are portrayed and may not accurately reflect true feelings of first-generation immigrant pastors.

Contributors suggested that first-generation pastors may feel threatened by second-generation Korean American pastors. Due to cultural factors (such as performance-orientation and shame), however, first-generation pastors may never reveal such stances. These feelings may be further understood as an expression of cultural ambiguity resulting from immigrants' unfamiliarity with a new culture.

After Pastor Billy was forced to resign from his fifteen-year post, he shared the following story:

> I worked with the senior pastor for fifteen years; he
> retired, and a new senior pastor came in. He was, I

think, one year older than me, and I knew that in terms of the transition, I wanted it to be smooth. So I went to him first and I told him, "I'm going to be fully supportive of you. I'll follow you, I'll submit to you, no problem." I wanted to just let him know just so that he would not think otherwise. And he kind of pulled an interesting trick on me, which I to this day, am baffled by. He asked me a question about the Greek language. He asked me to define a word for him, to explain it to him, so I did. And we talked about it for about a deep twenty minutes, and then he said, "Oh, thank you." And he just walked out. I didn't think anything of that until I talked to Koreanized pastors later on, and found out that I got played, a back door, side played. Do you know what word he asked me to explain to him? He asked me to explain to him the Greek word for "authority." And so I did, and then he asked me, "What does authority look like?" and I explained it to him, and I thought he was just asking me a propositional question. But all of my older Korean friends said, "No, he wasn't asking you. He was telling you something in a kind of roundabout way." So I thought, "Hmm, that sure is strange" because I went to him and said, "You know, I'm going to submit to you, I'll be totally fine" . . . I think he was a bit fearful about how much influence I had because at the time, the ministry was growing was so large that it was becoming 50/50, 50 percent KM, 50 percent EM. So maybe he was fearful of my influence.

Pastor Peter shared that he too had a similar experience in a parachurch setting. With his growing popularity in the church, the senior pastor felt threatened and ended up pushing him out of the ministry altogether.

I was vice-president of the organization and a lot of people who knew me tried to push me to become the president. They were actually trying to push out [the current president], which didn't help me at all, that was not my intention. And somehow, those things all played a role, so he pushed me out.

After his para-church experience, Pastor Peter joined a first-generation immigrant church where he encountered another similar situation.

So I moved in, and it was a very nice facility; everything was fine. And then difficulty began two years later. [The senior pastor] asked me if I can preach at the Morning Prayer on Thursday, he said, "This will help our congregation get to know you better." So I thought, "Well as far as the preaching is concerned, as a preacher, I love to go and preach when there is an open door." So I spoke on a Thursday, and when I went there were about twenty to thirty people at the 5:30 morning service. But the next week eighty people showed up. And then, he called me to the office, and said, "Your preaching is filled with bitterness and resentment, and it comes from a wounded soul." And he was kind of judging me and attacking my motivation. He attacked me in a way that nobody ever did before. So he pushed me out of that place, and so I stopped preaching . . . Looking back I think he was threatened; here is this bilingual guy who comes in, his preaching is powerful, he triples the number, and so he pushed me out.

During another interview another person said something very interesting:

The biggest problem the KM will face is not if the second generation will do poorly; the issue is whether it will ever do well. Not only does that mean that there will be a fight for resources but also for space, and it's also an issue of pride. KM pastors want to grow, but they don't want the EM pastor to be a true leader and visionary because what that means is that their leadership and vision might take them away from their vision and their leadership and that's problematic, to have two leaders under one roof.

Why are first-generation pastors fearful? Why do they feel threatened by second-generation Korean American pastors? Participants suggested that having two powerful, influential leaders under one roof means that one will grow in popularity while the other does not.

When participants were asked if the same phenomenon of feeling threatened was true of pastors in Korea, interviewees replied that pastors in Korea were more secure and free to take risks. Participants also shared that, ironically, pastors in Korea tended to have a more global mindset than did immigrant Korean pastors. This difference is best understood in terms of cultural ambiguity; pastors in Korea do not suffer from this because they are anchored in their home environment.

> [First-generation pastors] are so alienated, and there is inferiority in terms of not being able to speak the language. Then here comes the young buck who speaks the language. So there is a language element and there is a sense of marginality, that they are not part of the mainstream culture so that the whole estimate enclave, there is not much social upward mobility for them. Whereas in Korea, there is no language barrier, I mean, there is a classism that divides them, but you don't have this lack of access and cultural differences. So I think that's always playing in the back of their heads that is "I don't belong to the

majority class." Then people who are inferior tend to be very, very controlling; that's how they deal with it. So you become a control freak even as a pastor. And "my way is the high way." So in that kind of setting there is no way you can negotiate anything. Dialogue is impossible. It's not even a language thing; it becomes a personality disorder.

Another person specified, "The immigrant church is so small. I would have to say, 90 percent of the immigrant church pastors are smaller than the pastors in Korea, in terms of world perspective." In fact:

> [Immigrant Korean pastors] have a smaller world perspective than a lot of the Korean pastors that I've met in Korea because they're living in a bubble of [the] immigrant community . . . where the Korean pastors have already embraced everything already. What happens is that because the USA has influence, the immigrant church is all in their own pockets trying to protect themselves from the outside influence. So the guys in Korea are the ones who end up with a global perspective; here, it's just a local perspective.

Participants suggested that cultural ambiguity among first generation immigrant pastors is the result of KM pastors living as strangers in a foreign land. Living as marginalized individuals, first-generation pastors have controlled the church and have not given others, including second-generation pastors, the ability and/or right to have ownership of the church.

Ownership

Another factor contributing to power struggle is lack of ownership. Sukhwan Oh states, "the lack of ownership is the key issue" as to why second-generation pastors have left the first-generation immigrant church (1998, 7). In other words, many second-generation pastors left the first-generation church because they did not feel like the immigrant church was their church. Han agrees, noting further that:

> The lack of ownership is a significant reason for the weakness of the second-generation Korean American church. The authoritarian decision making model greatly discourages the second-generation pastors. Most second-generation pastors do not feel that they can stay in the first generation Korean church for a lifetime because they are not given ownership of the ministry; they are not invited into the decision making process of the church. (2009, 39)

Various interviews suggested that second-generation pastors have not had the opportunity to step up into positions of leadership and influence because they were restricted in making decisions concerning their ministries. While serving in a KM, one young pastor asked himself, "When I turn 50, will that church be mine?" He answered, "No. Why? Because I didn't see a future there. It's not my church. It belongs to the KM." Pastor Caleb agreed that the Korean American church does not belong to English speakers but Korean speakers.

> When English speakers grow up they don't hold the same position as the deacon or elder; they are outside the decision making body. They could be in their 30s and 40s, they can be professionals with lots of people working under them, but just because of the virtue of speaking English, they are lumped with the junior high students. That mentality hasn't changed, and because of that, people as they grow, in their faith, in their profession, in their family life, and all that, they have a need of their own.

Not only did second-generation Korean American pastors feel that they could not take ownership of the church, but many also felt betrayed because the first-generation church did not hire second-generation pastors full time. In the Korean American church, most education department pastors are hired part-time, and because EM is structurally part of the education department, most churches do not hire full time EM pastors.

Although Pastor Christian served at a Korean American church for many years, he left because the church was not able to support him financially. "Part of the reason [why I left] is because they don't believe in hiring full time staff, and I have two boys and my wife, and we can't survive if that was my single job."

Having mentored second-generation pastors, Pastor Bob said:

> You know what the dilemma is? Second-generation pastors all come to me saying, "Pastor, I want to do second-generation ministry. I need a full-time job, but they will not hire me as full time." Why? Because they don't want to invest. Money talks.

The irony is that though pastors are not hired as full-time staff at the church, they are expected to work over full-time hours. A well-known saying among second generation Korean American pastors when describing work in the immigrant church is, "Full-time hours, part-time pay." One interviewee recounted:

> When I was in seminary I had to stop studying because you know how the Korean church is so pressuring. They pay you part time and entrust you with 200 people. My first paycheck was $700, and I was in charge of the entire children's department. I just couldn't afford to go to school. I was too busy with church and had no time. I asked them to send me an associate pastor because the ministry was getting too big, but they wouldn't even do that.

Another pastor faced something similar:

> Since I was finishing at seminary I was looking to be hired as a full-time pastor. My wife had just decided

to quit her job at UCLA so that we could focus on the ministry. But then the elder board tells me, "No. You can become the associate pastor, but we don't have the funds to hire you full time." But that's absolutely not true. They do have the funds. They just didn't think that they needed a full-time pastor at EM. And that was my first experience where I felt sort of betrayed . . . I had given my life here; I grew up here, I was the high school pastor, then the college pastor, and even still they decided not to give that to me. And at that point I decided to find another job.

Second-generation Korean American pastors have left the immigrant church because of the absence of ownership. Second-generation pastors are given many tasks to complete, but due to the lack of support, financially and politically, they do not feel as though the Korean American church belongs to them. Instead, the Korean American church has become a place for second-generation pastors to work temporarily until they finish school and have enough experience to begin a church of their own.

TENSION AND CONFLICT

One veteran youth pastor described the relationship between first- and second-generation Korean Americans by saying, "The second generation belongs to the first generation because they were born of the parents who are the first generation, but it's very much like oil and water. There are just so many conflicts of issues." Second-generation Korean American pastors revealed their frustrations and shared situations that led to their exodus from the first generation immigrant church. Differences and relational dynamics reveal the tensions experienced due to the intergenerational power struggle. The majority of the study's participants explained their departure in terms of differences; careful analysis of the interview transcripts revealed these differences to be the direct result of, or the playing out of, power struggle tensions. During the interview, Pastor Bob said:

> When you ask young people why they are leaving the church, they will say, "Oh, because we're different. It's cultural. It's linguistics." They don't have the mental capacity to interpret what they are feeling or why they are feeling that way. That's what I've found out. This took me a long time to figure out . . . So the reason they're leaving is not because of cultural differences. Differences are just what is on the surface.

Pastor Bob revealed during his interview that most individuals blame differences (of culture, linguistics, visions, values, etc.) as the reason for leaving the immigrant church. The fact is, however, that differences are merely the result of something that is much deeper—power struggle. So, though people think that they are leaving because of differences, it is actually power struggle that drives the second-generation pastors out of the first-generation church.

Like all organizations, the church has its share of tension and conflict. According to Shawchuck, conflict arises when "the actions of one party threaten the values, goals, or behaviors of another party" (1983, 35). Of course, intra-church tension and conflict are not unique to the immigrant church. From the first century forward the church has had its share of difficulties and separation.

> The prevailing interpretation of Acts 6:1–8:4 holds that the Hellenists and Hebrews were separate, ideologically based parties within the earliest Jerusalem church . . . That the early church, almost from its inception, was divided into two distinct ideological groups corresponding to the terms Hellenists and Hebrews is not a new idea. (Hill 1992, 3)

Donald Palmer stated that conflict is inevitable, and it is because of humankind's disobedience that conflict began. Even Jesus experienced conflict and God sometimes permits conflict within His will (Palmer 1990, 5).

Conflict itself is not bad. As a matter of fact, there can be positive results of conflict. Palmer proposed that conflict is the evidence of life and vitality; it can lead to renewed motivation and permits the venting of frustrations. Even more, conflict can lead to personal growth and maturity (1990, 16). Palmer even identified that avoiding conflict can be dangerous for resentment may build up, emotions may be displaced, and discontentment, gossip, and backbiting may grow when conflict is avoided (1990, 18).

> The problem is not with having some conflict. Too little conflict in an organization may very well mean that its leaders and members are apathetic and need to be awakened and challenged. On the other hand a progressive organization that is changing to meet new demands and opportunities will experience conflicts. (Palmer, 1990, 19)

Though conflict itself is not sinful, the way individuals react to conflict may be sinful.

> Some conflicts in the church result in sinful behavior, such as the inquisitions and the resulting assassinations; or a conflict in your own church which results in malicious backbiting and character assassination. On the other hand, some conflicts in the church result in a clearer understanding of the will of God and in more effective ministries. (Shawchuck 1983, 9)

As a pastor who both observed and experienced relational dynamics between first- and second-generation pastors, Pastor James stated:

> The reason why there is conflict and disappointment among first and second generation is because we think we're very similar and we get very frustrated when we don't think alike, speak alike, and do things

alike. The first generation presumes that the second generation should be like the first, and vice versa. First generations think, "Why don't you look like and think like every other pastor at our church?" And then second generations wonder, "Why don't you look like and talk like the professors at my seminary?" And you know, we say, "You're wrong." But when you see things differently, different is not wrong. Different is just different. If you call it wrong, then you're creating separation and not unity.

CONCLUSION: A SUGGESTION FOR RECONCILIATION

Intergenerational church splits do not just happen. In analyzing data, it was clear that the struggle for power in the Korean American church is prominent. The interplay of control, cultural ambiguity, and ownership among leaders in the Korean American church have brought hurtful separation and need for reconciliation. As Pastor Billy said:

> If there is a problem found in the church, it's a both-and problem. I'm not trying to blame one or the other. Whether it be 80 percent one and 20 percent the other, there is still a combination of conflict. So we need to start owning up to our stuff and not play the blame shifting game.

Some second-generation individuals may feel as though first-generation pastors treated them unjustly. Nevertheless, as Pastor Billy stated, "it's a both-and problem." Looking at the situation from hindsight, many realized that there was a lot of blame shifting when the second- generation church decided to leave the immigrant church. Upon reflection one pastor said, "I realized what was going on in my heart was arrogance. There was a lot of pride on both sides, and there is enough blame to go around for everyone."

When Pastor Mike was leaving the immigrant church he remembered:

> The EM felt like we were being kicked out—that was their perception. The KM elders probably felt like, "You abandoned us." So there are different perspectives based on what happened. We felt like we got kicked out, they felt like we abandoned them, and it's like everyone was shifting blame.

Many veteran EM pastors shared their wisdom and explained carefully that it is not always the first generation pastors who are at fault. One pastor said:

> The second-generation pastors need to understand what the KM pastors are thinking. And I don't mean to poo poo on second-generation pastors, but a lot of second-generation pastors are lazy. They are less accountable in many ways, and I find them to be more selfish and less sacrificial.

Another EM pastor who left the first generation church to begin his own church plant said:

> The second generation, why did they leave? They can't just say, "We're victims. The first generations are tyrants." That's what the younger generation would like to think, but it's not like that. I know some young people who will stick by until the end, and I know others who are just rebels, and for whatever reason, they just bad mouth everything and they think if they find a refuge and think it's going to work out, but then what happens? Something may happen that is not favorable to them and they rebound again and again until they eventually forfeit the ministry. Instead of owning their part in this, everything is the blame game. Before long you demonize everybody,

and what happens to you? You're not even interested in God anymore.

What the second generations don't realize is that we have our own set of blinders, our own presuppositions that prevent us from seeing the whole picture. So who's really more righteous? I don't think the second generation is necessarily more righteous, and I can say that because I'm an elder to them. We realize that the youngins don't see everything so crystal clear in the way they think they have. So we have to own up to our blind spots, and if we don't, we'll continue to blame each other; we'll never grow beyond that.

Though society says that one must exert his/her power upon others to gain respect, leadership as it is found in the Bible is not one that dominates, but one that is humble and serves others. Part of God's ingenuity is that the gospel does not impose a cultural uniformity but rather fosters reconciliation (Gibbs 2000, 123).

Second-generation pastors have become discouraged as they struggle with first- generation Korean pastors for power and control. Applicable to both first-generation and the second-generation pastors, however, is the need for leaders to first be great servants.

The greatest leadership principles, Brian Dodd argued, are not found in motivational strategies or secular leadership books but within the pages of Scripture. The struggle does not lie in "which is a better, egalitarian or hierarchical method of leadership?" A new generation of Spirit-empowered leaders is needed; people who, like the Apostle Paul, are willing to yield to the Spirit's direction and guidance (Dodd 2003, 16).

To begin a dialogue of reconciliation, I would like to suggest that the discussion among Christian leaders should not be whether the church should follow a hierarchical model or an egalitarian model of leadership, but rather how the church might follow Jesus' model of servant leadership. Jesus' ministry radically affected underlying notions of what servant leadership really was. Jesus' model of servant leadership was not associated with national leadership or authority based on age and status as it had been in the Old Testament days. Instead, Jesus' servant leadership necessitated a new power base and new values. Jesus' leadership was concerned with spiritual leadership. The leadership that we are called to follow is an upside hierarchical model in that those in leadership be made lower so that he/she might serve others.

As followers of Christ, we must look within cultural and generational differences and find areas for reconciliation through servant leadership; we are called to humble ourselves and serve others as Christ humbled himself to serve others. As found in Matthew chapter twenty, to be a leader is to be a servant first. Servant leaders in both generations can foster understanding and mutual appreciation despite cultural and generational differences. I pray this study will aid both first- and second-generation Korean pastors in their genuine pursuit of the expansion of His church and in advancing His Kingdom.

REFERENCES

Chang, Jay. 1998. "Overcoming Conflicts in the Korean Immigrant Churches in the United States: In Pursuit of Reconciliation and Renewal," Ph.D. diss., School of Theology at Claremont.

Charmaz, Kathy. 2006. *Constructing Grounded Theory: A Practical Guide through Qualitative Analysis.* London: Sage.

Dodd, Brian. 2003. *Empowered Church Leadership: Ministry in the Spirit According to Paul.* Downers Grove, IL: Intervarsity Press.

Gibbs, Eddie. 2000. *I Believe in Church Growth.* Pasadena, CA: Fuller Seminary Press.

Greenleaf, Robert K. 1977. *Servant Leadership: A Journey into the Nature of Legitimate Power and Greatness.* Mahwah, NJ: Paulist Press.

Han, Tauhun. 2009. "A Strategy to Promote Reconciliation between First- and Second- Generation Korean-American Pastors," Ph.D. diss., Fuller Theological Seminary.

Hertig, Young Lee. 1991. "The Role of Power in the Korean Immigrant Family and Church," Ph.D. diss., Fuller Theological Seminary.

Hill, Craig C. 1992. *Hellenists and Hebrews: Reappraising Division within the Earliest Church*. Minneapolis, MN: Fortress Press.

Hoge, Dean R. 1976. *Division in the Protestant House: The Basic Reasons behind Intra-Church Conflicts*. Philadelphia, PA: The Westminster Press.

Kim, Jason Hyungkyun. 1999. "The Effects of Assimilation within the Korean Immigrant Church: Intergenerational Conflicts between the First and the Second Generation Korean Christians in Two Chicago Suburban Churches," Ph.D. diss., Trinity International University.

Kim, Paul Shu. 1980. "A Study of Ministry to Second Generation Korean Immigrants in the Church," D.Min. diss., Drew University.

Oh, Sukhwan. 1998. "A Strategy for Planting Cell Based Churches for the Emerging Asian Americans: A Case Study Based on Oikos Community Church," D.Min. diss., Fuller Theological Seminary.

Palmer, Donald C. 1990. *Managing Conflict Creatively: A Guide for Missionaries and Christian Workers*. Pasadena, CA: William Carey Library.

Park, Sung Kyu. 1997. "An Analysis of English Ministries in the Korean Church in Southern California," Ph.D. diss., Fuller Theological Seminary.

Prinzing, Fred W. 1986. *Handling Church Tensions Creatively: Adjusting Twelve Tensions to Avoid Conflict*. Arlington Heights, IL: Harvest.

Shawchuck, Norman. 1983. *How to Manage Conflict in the Church*. Vol. 1. Schaumburg, IL: Spiritual Growth Resources.

CHAPTER 6

SUBMISSION OR COOPERATION?
Two Competing Approaches to Conflict Management in Mission Organizations
David R. Dunaetz

Conflict between missionaries, often within the same organization, is one of the most difficult and common phenomena that missionaries must face (Hale 1995; Carter 1999; Hay et al. 2007). Experiencing opposition from a team member in a difficult ministry context may be extremely painful. Rather than receiving support from one of the few people who should understand the missionary, he or she may feel condemned, misunderstood, or the target of misplaced hostility. Such conflicts often slow down the work to which both parties feel called (Dunaetz 2010a) and, even worse, may dishonor God who calls Christians to love one another as a sign of their discipleship (John 13:35) and who condemns fighting among Christians as a form of hatred toward him (Jas 4:1–10). It is a significant source of missionary attrition (Global Mapping International 2009) and may have long lasting negative consequences on a missionary's emotional health, physical health, and career (Tanner et al. 2012a; Tanner et al. 2012b; Romanov et al. 1996).

Because the consequences of conflict can be devastating, most Christians desire to resolve conflict in order to limit the damage it causes. Two competing paradigms can be observed in Christian contexts. The first paradigm, which focuses on the subordinate's need to obey authority, can be identified as the Submission Paradigm. This approach argues that the best way to resolve conflict is to submit to God-ordained authorities. The second paradigm, which focuses on finding a solution that responds to both parties' concerns, can be identified as the Cooperation Paradigm. This approach argues that the best solution to a conflict is found by negotiating a solution that responds to the God-honoring interests of both parties. This study will examine the reasons for and against each approach and will argue that the cooperation model is the superior paradigm for dealing with missionary conflict.

PARADIGMS OF CONFLICT MANAGEMENT

We will begin by summarizing these two paradigms of conflict management. Undoubtedly, the actual approaches to conflict used by missionaries are much more diverse, but we will limit the discussion to two global approaches that could be considered opposite poles of a spectrum.

The Submission Paradigm

On Being a Missionary by Thomas Hale (1995) can serve as a source for a description of the Submission Paradigm to conflict management.[1] Hale argues that the effective functioning of a team requires "that the team members submit to their leader, regardless of his qualities" (1995, 219) and that the purpose of authority is to "mediate God's will in the Christian community" so "if one has a problem submitting to authority, his problem is basically with God" (1995, 231). This means that, when a missionary finds himself or herself in a conflict, it is God's will for him or her to submit to whomever has authority. Hale continues, "All Christians are commanded to submit to authority over them, up to the point where that authority forces them to violate Scripture" (1995, 231). Hale argues that missionaries must continue to submit even when "mission authorities may themselves unknowingly violate Scripture in the exercise of their duties, but that is a different matter; that does not give a worker license to disobey or rebel against

---

1. Although this book is chosen to represent the point of view that I argue against, Thomas Hale (1995) has much to say that is beneficial to missionary candidates preparing to leave for the field and for young missionaries. The critiques in this paper are only of his view on authority and conflict, not of him or his ministry that the Lord has richly blessed.

their authority" (1995, 231). In unfortunate situations, depending on the motives that would cause an authority to unknowingly sin, this could mean a missionary should continue to submit when faced with belittling, condescending insults, outbursts of anger, or other types of abuse, including physical or sexual abuse.

A key assumption of the Submission Paradigm is that people who hold power know the will of God for people who are under their authority, even when the authority makes a decision that a subordinate considers unwise or abusive. "Submitting to such decisions," Hale says, "is the only sure way we have of ultimately knowing what God's will is . . . We need to start out with the attitude of accepting our leaders' decisions as from God. . . . We need, first of all, to tell God that we will submit to anything the leadership says, and then trust him with the outcome" (1995, 233).

Hale admonishes the missionary to not be afraid of submitting to authority: "Remember, your leaders are kindly disposed to those under them . . . Submit to your leader's decision and let God cover the consequences. That is the only scriptural option you have" (1995, 233). The key verse for this position is Hebrews 13:17, "Have confidence in your leaders and submit to their authority" (NIV). For Hale, if a person is not willing to submit, he or she is not fit to be a missionary: "We must state clearly: willingness to submit to authority is indispensable to a successful missionary career. The person who is not prepared to submit willingly to the decisions of his leaders should not come to the mission field" (1995, 233).

The origin of much of this type of authoritarianism (Adorno 1950; Gabennesch 1972) in modern evangelicalism can be traced back to Bill Gothard's *Institute of Basic Youth Conflicts* seminar (Gothard 1975b), which was very influential in the 1970s. Gothard continued to be a leader within evangelicalism until he resigned in 2014 from his organization when faced with accusations of sexually abusing numerous young female employees (Bailey 2014; Recovering Grace 2015). Gothard argued that the purposes for authority were to help a person grow in wisdom and character, to be protected from temptation, and to receive direction in life (1975a, 1). Disobeying authority results in permanent damage by limiting our potential to be used by God (Gothard 1975a, 9). Thus, to resist the chain of authority in Christian organizations is to resist God, even if the authority's behavior, wisdom, or motives are questionable. Gothard's *Advanced Seminar* argued that obeying authority is the means by which a person discovers God's will and that "as long as you are under God-given authority, nothing can happen to you that God does not design for your ultimate good" (Gothard 1986, 297). This has far reaching consequences. For example, Gothard taught that people who are sexually abused by people in authority should question if they were the source of temptation, repent if they were, and not see themselves as victims, but as having the opportunity to "become mighty in spirit," forgiving the offenders and letting God take care of them (Gothard n.d.). If inappropriate behavior in Christian leaders needs to be addressed, "we must come as a learner and as their servant. We must appeal to them on the basis of what is best for them, not what is offending us" (Gothard 1976, 22).

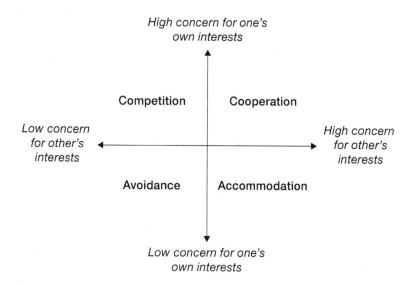

Figure 1. The Dual Concern Model of Conflict Resolution
(Pruitt & Kim 2004; Dunaetz 2011a; Wilmot & Hocker 2001).

Thus, in the submission approach to conflict management in mission organizations, the person lower in hierarchical power is responsible to obey the person with greater power. There is little room for discussion and the threat of being removed from ministry is real.

The Cooperation Paradigm

In contrast to the Submission Paradigm, the Cooperation Paradigm of conflict management views conflict as an opportunity to find solutions to problems that respond to the interests and desires of both parties. "Do not merely look out for your own personal interests, but also for the interests of others" (Phil 2:4, NASB). The idea of submission is not absent from this approach, but rather than a superior requiring the submission of a subordinate, the two are to "be subject to one another in the fear of Christ" (Eph 5:21, NASB). Rather than demanding or expecting obedience, rather than lording it over a subordinate, "If anyone wants to be first, he shall be last of all and servant of all" (Mark 9:35, NASB; cf. Matt 20:25–27, 1 Pet 5:2–3).

In the social sciences, the Cooperation Paradigm is described in the dual interest model of conflict resolution (Rubin et al. 1994; Pruitt and Carnevale 1993; Rahim 2001). This model assumes that conflict occurs when two parties have interests (concerns or desires) that at least one party perceives as being incompatible. For example, within a church planting team, one missionary may want the young church to start a new evangelistic activity and another might want to work on discipling and consolidating the initial group of believers which has started to meet together. The first missionary might believe that the group will lose its momentum without a new emphasis on evangelism, while the second missionary might believe that burnout is inevitable if he and the young believers feel they need to be involved in another program. Thus, the first missionary may see the other missionary's concern for stability as incompatible with his own desire for growth. This perceived incompatibility of goals or interests sets the stage for a conflict between the two missionaries.

Furthermore, each missionary may have a low or high concern for his own interests and a low or high concern for the interests of the other missionary. The combination of levels of concern will predict to a great degree the conflict resolution strategy that each party will choose (de Dreu et al. 2000; Rahim 2001). These strategies are illustrated in Figure 1. If one person is more concerned about the other's goals (e.g., he or she is more concerned about the relationship) than his or her own goals, he or she will adopt a strategy of *accommodation* in response to the conflict. In the opposite situation, when a person is primarily concerned about his or her own goals rather than those of the other person, he or she will adopt a strategy of *competition* to try to achieve them, which will typically occur if he or she has more power than the other party; this strategy is characterized by the use of threat or force. If a person is not especially concerned about either party's goals, he or she will tend to adopt a strategy of *avoidance* to limit the likelihood that the conflict damages the existing status quo. Finally, if a person is concerned about both his or her own goals and those of the other party, the person will try to adopt a strategy of *cooperation* which might include dialogue, negotiation, or persuasion; this strategy is likely to be successful if the two parties are willing to generate a large number of possible solutions to the conflict in order to find that which would be optimal.

In our example of the two missionaries, if neither missionary is very concerned about preventing burnout nor losing momentum, they are both likely to avoid discussing the topic; the cost of an emotionally draining and relationship damaging conflict will be too high. If the missionary who is concerned about losing momentum is more concerned about his relationship with the other missionary, this first missionary may *accommodate* the missionary who is concerned about burnout and let him have his way. If the missionary is more concerned about losing momentum than damaging his relationship with the other missionary, he may willingly enter into combat with the other missionary to determine whose strategy will be adopted. However, if the missionary is concerned not just about his own interests (continuing the momentum), but is also concerned about the interests of the other missionary (preventing burnout), a situation which typically occurs when the two parties are trying to act in loving ways, he will try to *cooperate* with the other missionary to find a solution that will allow both parties to achieve their goals. Such a solution might include one missionary focusing on discipling a group of young believers and the other missionary continuing to organize evangelistic activities without applying pressure on the believers in the other missionary's discipleship group to participate.

If one missionary chooses a competition strategy and the other an accommodation strategy, there will be no conflict; the interests of the missionary choosing competition will prevail. However, if both missionaries choose to compete, the missionary with more power will win and his interests will prevail. In the Submission Paradigm of conflict management, these two ways of resolving conflict are considered normal. The missionary lower in hierarchy is expected to voluntarily submit to the superior missionary. If he chooses to not do so, he can expect the other missionary to use his power to prevail. However, in the Cooperation Paradigm of conflict management, both missionaries are to avoid competing and seeking to have only their concerns addressed, but are to cooperate and find a solution that responds to both of their concerns. When a power differential exists between the missionaries, the more powerful missionary is expected to not use his power to force his will upon the other missionary; he is expected to empower the other missionary so that they can work together to find an optimal solution, viewing the conflict as a problem to be solved as brothers and sisters in Christ rather than a case of spiritual rebellion.

An optimal solution to a problem is typically found through the brainstorming of many possible solutions accompanied by discussion and negotiation concerning the best to choose (Greenberg 2005; Kuhn and Poole 2000; Whyte 2000). If done in a spirit of mutual submission, each party will be able to provide servant leadership to the conflict resolution process in order to ensure that the other's concerns will be addressed (Greenleaf 1977).

CRITIQUES OF THE TWO PARADIGMS

The Submission Paradigm focuses on the necessity of missionaries to obey those who are higher in the organizational hierarchy; conflicts are resolved by submitting to the person in authority. The Cooperation Paradigm focuses on the needs and concerns of both people who are in conflict, regardless of their hierarchical status; conflict is resolved by both people working together to find a solution that responds to each person's interests and concerns. Both paradigms claim to be biblical and have been used by sincere Christians who wish to serve the Lord. We will examine the scriptural basis for each, as well as empirical evidence concerning what we may expect as outcomes from each approach.

Critique of the Submission Paradigm

The strongest biblical argument for the Submission Paradigm is in Hebrews 13:7, "Obey your leaders and submit to them, for they keep watch over your souls as those who will give an account" (NASB). It should be noted that the text does not indicate that this is how God's will is revealed to someone in a subordinate position. It does, however, indicate that leaders will be held accountable for the use of their power. In the context, the author of Hebrews has made it clear that a priority for both leaders and followers in the church is "to live in peace with all" (Heb 12:14, NASB). In the broader context of the New Testament, Jesus warned against using one's power to "lord it over" those in subordinate positions but rather to use one's power to serve and set an example (Matt 20:25–28, I Pet 5:2–3). Submission is certainly a result of being led by the Spirit, a means of revering Christ, but Christians are called to mutual submission, not one Christian forcing his or her will upon another (Eph 5:21).

In light of both the specific context of Hebrews 13:7 and the general context of the New Testament, the author of Hebrews would undoubtedly expect differences of opinion in the church or perceptions of interference to be dealt with constructively, with mutual respect being shown, in order that those in conflict may find a jointly acceptable, even beneficial, solution that enables them to live in peace with one another. Forcing the weaker person to submit to the more powerful person's authority, or expecting the weaker person to not have a voice in a decision that concerns him or her, is more like a sin for which the power holder would be held accountable than a strategy for godly leadership.

Understanding the Effects of Power

One of the underlying assumptions of the Submission Paradigm is that the power holders will use their power in a godly and Spirit-led way, depending on the Lord to provide the necessary checks and balances. Although some Christian leaders may use power this way, it is, unfortunately, not always the case. The experiences of the young women who worked for Bill Gothard or the pastoral staff working at Mars Hill Church serve as contemporary warnings that even the most trusted, respected, and influential Christian leaders may abuse their power in very destructive ways (Recovering Grace 2015; Tertin 2015). But how often does power lead to abuse? To what degree is Lord Acton's dictum true that "Power tends to corrupt, and absolute power corrupts absolutely" (Dalberg-Acton 1907)?

Christians are not alone in wanting answers to these questions. A number of research psychologists have sought to understand the effects of power (i.e., the ability to influence others). It is important, first, to note that there are various types of power. A schema created by French and Raven (1960) describing five bases of power is still relevant for today. *Reward Power* is the ability to provide a material or non-material reward. In a mission organization, this might be a favorable ministry location or public recognition for one's work. *Coercive power* is its opposite; it is the ability to provide a material or non-material punishment, which acts as a threat. Examples in mission organizations would include the ability to refuse a reimbursement request or the power to demand that a missionary resign. *Legitimate power* comes from culturally agreed upon lines of authority.

When one joins an organization, one agrees to respect the decision-making processes that are in place. *Referent power* comes from a person liking, admiring, or appreciating the power holder. Helpfulness, celebrity, beauty, warmth, and caring are all associated with referent power. *Expert power* comes from competence and expertise in some valued domain. A missionary may have expert power due to his or her knowledge of the local culture, church planting strategies, or the Bible.

In organizations, including missionary organizations, these five power bases may be classified into two groups, *position power* and *personal power* (Northouse 2013). Position power comes from one's position or office that is assigned by those higher in an organization's hierarchy. Position power includes both reward and coercive power, as well as legitimate power. It is independent of the person and can be transferred to another member of the organization if the organizational hierarchy chooses to do so. In the Submission Paradigm, position power determines who is supposed to submit and who has the right to demand submission. In contrast, personal power comes from personal characteristics of an individual which cannot easily be separated from him or her or transmitted to others by an administrative decision. Personal power includes referent power and expert power.

Personal power typically does not cause as many problems of abuse as position power does in organizations. Certainly a person might be attractive and charming and use his or her referent power in a hurtful way. Similarly, expert power may be used to actively pursue evil. However, in Christian contexts, referent power is most commonly associated with love for others (John 15:9–17, 1 Cor 13:1–13) and expert power is associated with wisdom and knowledge (Prov 1:8–4:27, cf. Exod 31:3–4). In contrast, position power (the focus of the Submission Paradigm) is easily abused. A series of experiments by the social psychologist David Kipnis of Temple University has shown how readily positional power is abused (Kipnis 1976; Kipnis 1972; Kipnis 1984).

Kipnis (1972) found that having position power, especially coercive power, changes the power holder's view of self and of others with less power. Self is evaluated as being more important and more deserving, while others are evaluated as being less important and less worthy of respect. In a typical experiment, volunteers were primed to think of themselves as being powerful by arbitrarily being designated as managers (versus employees) in an experiment (legitimate power). Sometimes this power was increased by giving them coercive power, such as the ability to reduce the employee's wages or to fire the employees, or by giving them reward power, such as the ability to give raises or bonuses to employees.

There are several reasons that people who are assigned position power may have an elevated sense of self-worth. The power holders may feel the need to justify their power over other people (Kipnis 1976). Since they have the power to punish or reward others, this must mean that their opinions and beliefs are superior to those of their subordinates. A missionary who is put in power over other missionaries will be tempted to justify such a power differential by concluding that he is more worthy of this position than those over whom he has power.

A second reason that power holders have a high view of themselves (relative to their subordinates) is because they fairly continuously receive compliments and flattery from those around them (Kipnis and Vanderveer 1971; Kipnis 1972). Because flattery is a relatively effective way to gain the goodwill of power holders (Westphal and Stern 2007; Gordon 1996), it occurs quite frequently in organizational settings, including mission organizations. When power holders continuously hear how good they are and how wonderful their work is, they are more likely to start believing in their superiority than if they did not hear the flattery. In addition, subordinates who do not verbally acknowledge the power holder's superiority are likely to be evaluated negatively because the power holder may feel that these subordinates are incapable of seeing that which is so clear to others. Similarly, power holders start believing that they are especially worthy of controlling resources because of their superiority. They may see themselves as having more rights because of their superior abilities. This may enable them to justify immoral behavior. They may view their well being as so much more important to the organization than the well-being of others that fits of anger, various forms of theft, and taking sexual liberties with their subordinates may be justified in their minds.

A consequence of this elevated view of self and devaluing of others, especially in power holders with the ability to punish subordinates, is less willingness to cooperate and compromise in order to resolve conflicts (Deutsch and Krauss 1960; Kipnis 1976; Kipnis 1984). Power makes people more aggressive and less concerned about the relational consequences of this aggressivity. Power holders with the ability to punish subordinates tend to avoid developing much of a relationship with those whom they can punish (Fiedler 1967; Magee and Smith 2013). For example, Kipnis (1972) found that 79 percent of people randomly assigned a high status position without the ability to punish a subordinate expressed an interest in meeting the person and having a coffee together. However, only 35 percent of the power holders who had the ability to punish were interested in meeting the person socially. Leaders with the power to punish may avoid socializing with subordinates because they believe that they would lose some of their power if they started friendships which would cause them to be less willing to use coercion on them. Alternately, they may avoid socialization because they know they would feel bad about punishing someone who had become their friend. They may fear losing status if they were to fraternize with a person potentially worthy of punishment. Thus forcing, coercion, or demanding obedience becomes the normal way of resolving conflicts, rather than cooperation.

Thus the abuse of power in Christian organizations with leaders using the Submission Paradigm should not be surprising. Such an approach to conflict resolution sets the stage for lording it over the less powerful, abusing them, keeping them at an emotional distance, and devaluing them and their work. When conflicts occur with a missionary leader using the Submission Paradigm, the junior missionary is left feeling unworthy and unheard. This approach provides discouragement rather than encouragement, contributing to ineffective missionary teams (Dunaetz 2010a), a sense of being unjustly treated (Dunaetz 2010c), and even missionary attrition (Hay et al. 2007; Global Mapping International 2009).

Critique of the Cooperation Paradigm

Although the Cooperation Paradigm of conflict resolution looks very attractive from a biblical point of view with its emphasis on responding to both parties' interests (Phil 2:4), servant leadership (Matt 20:26), optimal solutions (Prov 15:22), and healthy relationships (Heb 12:14), there are several costs and dangers involved. Managing conflict with the Cooperation Paradigm is time consuming and mentally demanding. In extreme cases, it can also distract from the mission of the organization.

Whereas the Submission Paradigm can result in quick decisions requiring little reflection or communication, the Cooperation Paradigm by nature requires much time and effort. It seeks to find solutions to problems other than the solutions that might be immediately available to the missionary with hierarchical authority. One of the fundamental requirements to finding optimal solutions to a problem in organizations is creating a set of possible solutions from which to choose (Greenberg 2005; Whyte 2000). Creating such a set of alternatives may require much mental effort and time.

This might be especially difficult for Christian leaders who do not feel the need to evaluate strategies for their effectiveness or want to compare the merits of one alternative over another. Individuals differ in their *need for cognition,* a personality trait characterized by the "tendency to engage in and enjoy effortful cognitive activity" (Cacioppo et al. 1996, 197). Some people are motivated to think through problems, come up with alternatives, and evaluate the merits of each, while others feel less internal pressure to do so. People high in need for cognition might experience more success in cognitive activities and, thus, are willing to expend more effort in creating and evaluating activities. People low in the need for cognition may not receive much satisfaction for exerting the effort necessary for effective problem solving (Cacioppo et al. 1996; Dunaetz 2011b). Thus, mission leaders with a low need for cognition may find the Cooperation Paradigm exasperating and the Submission Paradigm especially attractive.

Another ability that influences the amount of effort needed to function within the Cooperation Paradigm is *perspective taking,* the ability to see the issues from the other person's cognitive and emotional point of view (Johnson 1975; Johnson et al. 2000). This ability enables a person to see the value in alternative solutions that the other person proposes while they discuss the issues. Typically it is expressed as paraphrasing what the other person has said to receive feedback indicating correct or incorrect comprehension of the others point of view, or as imagining the other person's emotional response to a proposal. This is typically a skill that is developed during childhood and adolescence (Sandy and Cochran 2000). Some people have greater perspective taking skills than others. Those in authority who find it difficult to take another person's perspective will view the Cooperation Paradigm as more difficult and less attractive.

Nevertheless, mission leaders with limited need for cognition or perspective taking skills may still find that the Cooperation Paradigm is worth the effort it requires because of its biblical justification. Mission executives may notice that field leaders may not be attracted to the Cooperation Paradigm and prefer requiring submission from those under their authority. If this is a possible scenario, mission executives need to make sure that a conflict management system is firmly in place in the mission organization (Costantino and Merchant 1996). Such conflict management systems typically provide mediation whenever one party requests it. In order for the system to be effective when there is a hierarchical power differential between the missionaries, it must be designed so that:

1. The more powerful party cannot deny a request for mediation.
2. The system must provide a mutually acceptable mediator who is perceived as trustworthy and neutral by both parties.

3. The system is not simply created to reduce liability in case of conflict; the use of the system must be promoted by all levels of authority within the organization.

Such a system may be implemented even in cases of long-distance separation of mission members when the determination exists to create constructive, cooperative solutions to missionary conflict (Dunaetz 2010b).

Another critique of the Cooperation Paradigm is that it could distract from the mission of the organization. Here is an extreme case to illustrate this point. Suppose the mission of an organization is evangelism and church planting but a junior missionary develops a passion for animal rights. In this case, a cooperative solution to a conflict which might occur concerning the placement of a junior missionary would be to assign him to a ministry of evangelism and church planting among animal rights activists. However, if the junior missionary is no longer interested in evangelism and church planting, such a placement would be ineffective and inappropriate. In fact, any cooperative solution might divert resources from the organization's mission. If the organization provides resources for the junior missionary to pursue his interests, a phenomena known as mission shift occurs. No longer is the organization's mission limited to evangelism and church planting, but it would also now include the defense of animal rights. In cases such as this, to prevent mission shift, mission leadership might rightfully conclude that cooperation is not appropriate; requesting the resignation of the junior missionary might be more appropriate. Similarly, agreement to the organization's doctrinal statement or other foundational documents might also be non-negotiable; cooperation which involves compromise with what the organization believes is God's will for it would not appropriate. However, these types of situations where cooperation presents a danger are most likely relatively rare. It is far more likely that self-serving biases of power holders would motivate them to believe their interests are God's will because they feel threatened by a subordinate (Ross 1977; Ross et al. 1977). The "tall poppy effect" occurs when high achievers, especially those without hierarchical power, are cut down, resulting in positive emotional re-actions in those who no longer fear being compared to them (Feather 1989). In Christian circles, a popular way of cutting down someone is to declare their interests outside the will of God. If the Submission Paradigm is being used, this would include any interest that the hier-archical superior opposes. Power holders who have doubts about their own competence or have low self-esteem are especially likely to be motivated to seek the downfall of high achievers and, thus, make the appropriate accusations (Feather 1991; Rucker & Petty 2003; Rucker & Pratkanis 2001). Once again, the best way to prevent such abuse is to have in place a mediator-based conflict management system which the mission organization's leaders encourage the less powerful mem-bers to use (Costantino & Merchant 1996; Dunaetz 2010b).

Understanding the Effects of Cooperation
The most obvious effect of cooperation in organizations is an increase in the quality of group decisions (Kuhn and Poole 2000). When faced with a problem, considering a greater number of possible responses enables a group to find better solutions than when it only considers one or two options. This effect not only occurs in small groups and teams, but also in organizations as a whole (Rahim 2001; Tjosvold 1991) when the organizational culture promotes healthy conflict res-olution cooperation. Additional research (Jehn 1997b; Greer & Jehn 2007; de Dreu and Weingart 2003) has found that for conflict to be most productive, the conflict should focus on the task at hand. When the conflict becomes personal, it quickly becomes emotional (Dunaetz 2014; Jehn 1997a). Negative emotions prevent constructive dialogue and reduce the ability to find the optimal solution. Therefore, cooperation is most likely to occur when both parties are committed to focusing on a single issue related to accomplishing the goals of the organization, and are willing to avoid criticizing each other personal-ly, whether it be one's behavior, background, or preferences.

CONCLUSION

We have looked at two approaches to conflict management in mission organizations, the Submission Paradigm and the Cooperation Paradigm. Some missionaries will prefer operating under the Submission Paradigm, but this paper has argued for the use of the Cooperation Paradigm because of its congruency with the Christian values of love, mutual understanding, servant leadership, and mutual submission to seek the well-being of others. The dangers of abusing the power associated with a strict hierarchy of authority in the Submission Paradigm are great, and have often resulted in abuses that have nothing to do with the gospel. Mission organizations which promote the Cooperation Paradigm will, thus, create an atmosphere that is safe for missionaries, enables the organization to better achieve its goals, and is in harmony with biblical values and principles.

REFERENCES

Adorno, Theodor W. 1950. *The Authoritarian Personality.* New York, NY: Harper.

Bailey, Sarah Pulliam., 2014. "Conservative Leader Bill Gothard Resigns Following Abuse Allegations," *Washington Post,* March 7.

Cacioppo, John T., Richard E. Petty, Jeffrey A. Feinstein, and W. Blair G. Jarvis. 1996. "Dispositional Differences in Cognitive Motivation: The Life and Times of Individuals Varying in Need for Cognition." *Psychological Bulletin* 119, no. 2: 197–253.

Carter, Joan. 1999. "Missionary Stressors and Implications for Care." *Journal of Psychology and Theology* 27: 171–180.

Costantino, Cathy A., and C. S. Merchant. 1996. *Designing Conflict Management Systems.* San Francisco, CA: Jossey-Bass.

Dalberg-Acton, John E. E., 1904. "Letter to Bishop Mandell Creighton, dated April 5, 1887." In *Life and Letters of Mandell Creighton,* Vol. 1, edited by Louise Creighton, 372. London, UK: Longmans, Green, and Co.

de Dreu, Carsten K. W., and Laurie R. Weingart. 2003. "Task Versus Relationship Conflict, Team Performance, and Team Member Satisfaction: A Meta-Analysis." *Journal of Applied Psychology* 88, no. 4: 741–749.

de Dreu, Carsten K. W., Laurie R. Weingart, and Seungwoo Kwon. 2000. "Influence of Social Motives on Integrative Negotiation: A Meta-Analytic Review and Test of Two Theories." *Journal of Personality and Social Psychology* 78, no. 5: 889–905.

Deutsch, Morton, and Robert M. Krauss. 1960. "The Effect of Threat Upon Interpersonal Bargaining." *The Journal of Abnormal and Social Psychology* 61, no. 2: 181–189.

Dunaetz, David R. 2010. "Good Teams, Bad teams: Under What Conditions Do Missionary Teams Function Effectively?" *Evangelical Missions Quarterly*, 46, no. 4 (October): 442–449.

———. 2010. "Long Distance Managerial Intervention in Overseas Conflicts: Helping Missionaries Reframe Conflict Along Multiple Dimensions." *Missiology* 38, no. 3 (July): 281–294.

———. 2010. "Organizational Justice: Perceptions of Being Treated Fairly." In *Serving Jesus with Integrity: Ethics and Accountability in Mission,* edited by Dwight Baker and Douglas Hayward, 192–221, Pasadena, CA: William Carey Library.

———. 2011. *Personality and Conflict Style: Effects on Membership Duration in Voluntary Associations.* Saarbrücken, Germany: Lambert Academic Press.

———. 2011. "Understanding the Effects of Diversity in Mission from a Social Science Perspective." In *Reflecting God's Glory Together: Diversity in Evangelical Mission,* edited by A.Scott Moreau and Beth Snodderly, 335–353. Pasadena, CA: William Carey Library.

———. 2014. "The Achievement of Conflict-related Goals Leads to Satisfaction with Conflict Outcomes." CGU Theses & Dissertations. Paper 89. Accesesed December 7, 2015. http://scholarship.claremont.edu/cgu_etd/89.

Feather, N. T. 1989. "Attitudes Towards the High Achiever: The Fall of the Tall Poppy." *Australian Journal of Psychology* 41: 239–267.

———. 1991. "Attitudes Towards the High Achiever: Effects of Perceiver's own Level of Competence." *Australian Journal of Psychology* 43: 121–124.

Fiedler, Fred E. 1967. *A Theory of Leadership Effectiveness*. New York, NY: McGraw Hill.

French, John R. P. and Bertram Raven. 1960. "The Bases of Social Power." In *Group Dynamics*, edited by D. Cartwright and Alvin Zander, 607–623. Evanston, IL: Row, Peterson, and Co.

Gabennesch, Howard. 1972. "Authoritarianism as Worldview." *American Journal of Sociology* 77, no. 5 (March): 857–875.

Global Mapping International. 2009. "The Engage! Study Executive Summary," Accessed December 7, 2015. http://www.gmi.org/files/9613/6096/6908/Engage_Executive_Summary.pdf.

Gordon, Randall A. 1996. "Impact of Ingratiation on Judgments and Evaluations: A Meta-Analytic Investigation." *Journal of Personality and Social Psychology* 71, no. 1 (July): 54–70.

Gothard, Bill. 1975. "Authority and Responsibility." In *Institute in Basic Youth Conflicts: Research in Principles of Life*, edited by Bill Gothard, 1–21. Oak Brook, IL: Institute in Basic Youth Conflicts.

———. 1975. *Institute in Basic Youth Conflicts: Research in Principles of Life*, Oak Brook, IL: Institute in Basic Youth Conflicts.

———. 1976. *Instructions for Our Most Important Battle*. Oak Brook, IL: Institute in Basic Youth Conflicts.

———. 1986. *Advanced Seminar Textbook*. Oak Brook, IL: Institute in Basic Life Principles.

———. n.d. *Counseling Sexual Abuse*. Oak Brook, IL: Advanced Training Institute of America.

Greenberg, Jerald. 2005. *Managing Behavior in Organizations*. Upper Saddle River, NJ: Prentice Hall.

Greenleaf, Robert K. 1977. *Servant Leadership: A Journey into the Nature of Legitimate Power and Greatness*. New York, NY: Paulist Press.

Greer, Lindred L., and Karen A. Jehn. 2007. "The pivotal role of negative affect in understanding the effects of process conflict on group performance." *Research On Managing Groups and Teams* 10: 23–45.

Hale, Thomas. 1995. *On Being a Missionary.* Pasadena, CA, William Carey Library.

Hay, Rob, et al. 2007. *Worth Keeping: Global Perspectives on Best Practice in Missionary Retention.* Pasadena, CA: William Carey Library.

Jehn, Karen A. 1997. "Affective and Cognitive Conflict in Work Groups: Increasing Performance Through Value-Based Intragroup Conflict." In *Using Conflict in Organizations,* edited by C. K. W. de Dreu and E. Van de Vliert, 87–100. Thousand Oaks, CA: Sage Publications.

———. 1997. "A Quantitative Analysis of Conflict Types and Dimensions in Organizational Groups." *Administrative Science Quarterly* 42: 530–557.

Johnson, David W. 1975. "Cooperativeness and Social Perspective Taking." *Journal of Personality and Social Psychology* 31, no. 2 (Feb): 241–244.

Johnson, David W., Roger T. Johnson, and Dean Tjosvold. 2000. "Constructive Controversy." In *The Handbook of Conflict Resolution,* edited by M. Deutsch and P.T. Coleman, 65–85. San Francisco, CA: Jossey-Bass.

Kipnis, David. 1972. "Does Power Corrupt?" *Journal of Personality and Social Psychology* 24, no. 1 (October): 33–41.

———. 1976. *The Powerholders,* Chicago, IL: University of Chicago Press.

———. 1984. "The Use of Power in Organizations and in Interpersonal Settings." *Applied Social Psychology Annual* 5: 179–210.

Kipnis, David, and R. Vanderveer. 1971. "Ingratiation and the Use of Power." *Journal of Personality and Social Psychology* 17, no. 3: 280–286.

Kuhn, Tim, and Marshall Scott Poole. 2000. "Do Conflict Management Styles Affect Group Decision Making?" *Human Communication Research* 26, no. 4 (October): 558–590.

Magee, Joe C., and Pamela K. Smith. 2013. "The Social Distance Theory of Power." *Personality and Social Psychology Review* 17, no. 2 (May): 158–186.

Northouse, Peter G. 2013. *Leadership: Theory and Practice.* Los Angeles, CA: Sage Publiations.

Pruitt, Dean G., and Peter J. Carnevale. 1993. *Negotiation in Social Conflict.* Pacific Grove, CA: Brooks Cole.

Pruitt, Dean G., and Sun Hee Kim. 2004. *Social Conflict: Escalation, Stalemate, and Settlement.* Boston, MA: McGraw Hill.

Rahim, M. Afzalur. 2001. *Managing Conflict in Organizations.* Westport, CT: Quorum Books.

Recovering Grace, "A Gothard Generation Shines Light on the Teachings of IBLP and ATI" Accessed December 7, 2015. http://recoveringgrace.org.

Romanov, Kalle, Kirsi Appelberg, Marja-Liisa Honkasalo, and Markku Koskenvuo. 1996. "Recent Interpersonal Conflict at Work and Psychiatric Morbidity: A Prospective Study of 15,530 Employees Aged 24–64." *Journal of Psychosomatic Research* 40: 169–176.

Ross, Lee. 1977. "The Intuitive Psychologist and His Shortcomings: Distortions in the Attribution Process." In *Cognitive Theories in Social Psychology: Papers from Advances in Experimental Social Psychology,* edited by L. Berkowitz, 173–220, New York, NY: Academic Press.

Ross, Lee, David Green, and Pamela House. 1977. "The False Consensus Effect: An Egocentric Bias in Social Perception and Attribution Processes." *Journal of Experimental Social Psychology* 13: 279–301.

Rubin, Jeffrey Z., Dean G. Pruitt, and D. G. Sun Hee Kim. 1994. *Social Conflict: Escalation, Stalemate, and Settlement.* New York, NY: McGraw-Hill.

Rucker, Derek D., and Richard E. Petty. 2003. "Effects of Accusations on the Accuser: The Moderating Role of Accuser Culpability." *Personality and Social Psychology Bulletin* 29, no. 10: 1259–1271.

Rucker, Derek D., and Anthony R. Pratkanis. 2001. "Projection as an Interpersonal Influence Tactic: The Effects of the Pot Calling the Kettle Black." *Personality and Social Psychology Bulletin* 27, no. 11 (November): 1494–1507.

Sandy, Sandy V., and Cochran, K.M. 2000. "The Development of Conflict Resolution Skills in Children." In *The Handbook of Conflict Resolution: Theory and Practice,* edited by Morton Deutsch and Peter T. Coleman, 316–342, San Francisco, CA: Jossey-Bass.

Tanner, Marcus N., Jeffrey N. Wherry, and Anisa M. Zvonkovic. 2012. "Clergy who Experience Trauma as a Result of Forced Termination." *Journal of Religion and Health* 52, no. 4 (December): 1–15.

Tanner, Marcus N., Anisa M. Zvonkovic, and Charlies Adams. 2012. "Forced Termination of American Clergy: Its Effects and Connection to Negative Well-being." *Review of Religious Research* 54, no. 1 (March): 1–17.

Tertin, Ben. 2015. "The Painful Lessons of Mars Hill: What Can We learn from the Collapse of Mark Driscoll's Church?" *Leadership Journal* 37, no.1: 18–22.

Tjosvold, Dean. 1991. *The Conflict-Positive Organization.* Reading, MA: Addison-Wesley.

Westphal, James D., and Ithai Stern. 2007. "Flattery Will Get You Everywhere (Especially if You are a Male Caucasian): How Ingratiation, Boardroom Behavior, and Demographic Minority Status Affect Additional Board Appointments at US Companies." *Academy of Management Journal* 50 no. 2 (April): 267–288.

Whyte, Glen. 2000. "Make Good Decisions by Effectively Managing the Decision-Making Process." In *The Blackwell Handbook of Principles of Organizational Behavior,* edited by Edwin A. Locke, 316–330, Oxford, UK: Blackwell Publishers.

Wilmot, William W., and Joyce L. Hocker. 2001. *Interpersonal Conflict.* Boston, MA: McGraw Hill.

CHAPTER 7

THE CONTROVERSIAL IMAGE OF THE US AMERICAN IN MISSIONS

Kenneth R. Nehrbass

INTRODUCTION

Even as the United States wields substantial cultural influence in this era of globalization, US Americans are controversial figures. US Americans who sojourn overseas are even more controversial. Expatriates from any country are often received with ambivalence, whether they are migrant workers, refugees, or successful business owners, but among controversial others, the US American missionary is especially provocative, as the United States of America represents "Gospel and gold, ointment and gun, oppressor and oppressed" (Conn 1984, 55). Opposing images of missionaries from the United States are portrayed in major motion pictures and best-selling novels, and they are coupled with the ubiquitous metaphor of the "Ugly American" (who is presumably NOT from Canada). Evening news broadcasts of flag-burnings and protesters holding signs that read (in Arabic) "Death to America" (Al Jazeera 2013) further reify the notion of anti-western and especially anti-American sentiment.

Such negativity is prevalent to different degrees across the globe—sometimes reflexively in the form of "western self-loathing." However, the United States continues to receive a fairly high international approval rating in polls. And in the midst of this ambivalence about the West and the United States in particular, the country which sends out the largest number of missionaries is still the United States (see Steffan 2013). In what ways do missionaries from the United States experience this phenomenon of anti-American sentiment? How do international stakeholders in Christian mission perceive US Americans and especially missionaries from the United States? Is the "ugly

American" any more of a reality than "the ugly Canadian" (or the ugly German, Russian or Pakistani, etc.?) Are images of the US missionaries in film and news broadcasts congruent with the experiences of missionaries abroad? And how do international perceptions of US Americans affect mission strategies?

Since an understanding of international opinions of US Americans in the twenty-first century can help shape how we design mission strategies for the future, this chapter examines the pervasiveness and lived reality of anti-American sentiment in the setting of missionary work. To accomplish this, I interviewed nineteen participants (US Americans and internationals) who have resided outside of the United States for at least two years to gain insight regarding the broad spectrum of international perceptions of US Americans. I then analyzed this data in order to develop a theory that explains the impact of anti-western sentiment on missionary work.

IMAGES OF THE UGLY AMERICAN

The controversy of American missionaries is manifested in major motion pictures and best-selling novels, where portrayals range anywhere from the selfless Bible translator Rachel Lane in John Grisham's *Testament* (1999), to the self-absorbed Nathan Price in Barbara Kingsolver's *Poisonwood Bible* (1998). An unspoken rubric seems to be employed in popular culture as the basis for rating missionaries. And while the rubric is not directly based on missiological metrics (e.g., whether the missionaries plant sustainable churches, or their ability to leverage cultural knowledge to effectively teach doctrine), the method of evaluation turns out to be surprisingly well aligned with Christian values. In film and fiction, missionaries are graded on their ability to embrace their host culture. They seem to be assessed by the degree to which they make significant contributions to the standard of living in their mission context. Put another way, Hollywood seems to evaluate missionaries based on how closely they resemble the incarnational ministry of Jesus, minus the teaching.

Missionaries are most positively depicted when their social action defends the rights of the powerless. British missionary Gladys Aylward, portrayed by Ingrid Bergman in *The Inn of the Sixth Happiness* (Robson 1958) fought to end foot-binding in China, and adopted nearly a hundred orphan children whom she led to safety during WWII. The Spanish Jesuit priests Gabriel and Mendoza fought to the death to defend the rights of the Guarani natives of Brazil in *The Mission* (Joffe 1986). And despite his checkered past and penchant for violence, the US American preacher Sam Childers is a semi-heroic character in *Machine Gun Preacher* (Forster 2011) as he defends an orphanage in Uganda against the Lord's Resistance Army. In fact, Hollywood's value of cultural identification works both ways in this film: Childer's failure to identify with his home country (the USA) makes him increasingly less effective back home.

Complex images of well-meaning but naïve missionaries also abound. In *The Other Side of Heaven* (Davis 2001), the neophyte Mormon missionary John Groberg has no success until he eventually dedicates himself to learning the local language and culture. We are likewise left feeling ambivalent about the fervent yet almost reckless US missionaries to Ecuador in *The End of the Spear* (Hanon 2005). On the one hand, their theological commitment to "all tribes and nations" compels them to engage the Woadani. On the other hand, their ignorance of Woadani history and culture leads to their death before they make any progress among them.

On the more critical side, Barbara Kingsolver's *Poisonwood Bible* (1998) portrays missionaries whose naïve mono-cultural attitudes are directly proportional to their fervor for evangelism. The patriarch of the missionary family, Nathan Price, is culturally clueless and eventually dies a failure. To be sure, we would also find levels of ambivalence toward Korean or Brazilian or Canadian missionaries (and so on) in popular culture; but the dominant image in film and news media has focused on the controversy of US Americans who serve in missions overseas.

Constantino Arias' famous photo titled "the Ugly American" conveys all the undesirable qualities people assign to US Americans who travel overseas. A hairy overweight older man, wearing shorts that are as bare as his sombrero is broad, smokes a cigar while saluting the camera with a quart of liquor in each hand. This was the "Ugly American" of Cuba in the 1950s when international tourism was a privilege only available to westerners. "Ugly Americans" can still be found, wearing cutoff shorts in Muslim countries that value modesty, or letting their kids run wild in Japan, despite the cultural value of orderliness there; or ordering Coca Cola in an Irish pub. It is not that they are physically ugly, but that their "ugly" behaviors draw attention to themselves from the second they step off the tour bus and start snapping pictures to the time they run back into the air conditioning of their safe hotel.

The moniker "Ugly American" was both challenged and popularized in a political novel by Lederer and Burdick (1958), which was later made into a film starring Marlon Brando (Englund 1963). Homer Atkins, the rugged protagonist, was physically ugly in contrast to the polished delegation of US government advisors who were sent to combat the communist agenda in a fictional country called Sarkhan (set in Southeast Asia). Atkins, though physically unattractive, was compassionate and helpful. Meanwhile, his compatriots were too self-absorbed and culturally isolated (cross-culturally illiterate, really) to connect with the people of Sarkhan. So in a twist of literary irony, the true "ugly Americans" turn out to be the polished workers of the US Foreign Service. The tragic end of this ugly behavior is that the US workers lack social influence; they are unable to persuade the Sarkhanese to adopt a Western free market system, and Sarkhan succumbs to communism. Lederer and Burdick wrote their novel to argue subtly that for US Americans to win the Cold War and spread democracy, they needed to understand and engage with Southeast Asians. In other words, to be world changers, cross-cultural workers need to be culturally literate.

Ethnophaulisms change over time, and nowadays the "ugly American" can refer to all US Americans—even those who do not travel—or to westerners in general. The evening news gives the impression that the rest of the world—at least many in Europe, Asia, Africa, the Middle East, and South America—have hostility toward US Americans. Who actually feels this way? And is the sentiment specifically anti-American, or is it anti-western in general? Or is it just plain old xenophobia, with a geopolitical spin?

INTERNATIONAL IMPRESSIONS OF US AMERICANS

We cannot say definitively how the "rest" feel about the United States, since hatred cannot be quantified for statistical comparison. But the BBC has tried to quantify each year how 29,000 adults throughout the world feel about twenty-seven prominent nations including the United States. It turns out that the world feels most positive about Germany, with a global approval rating of 59 percent. Canada is in second place with 51 percent. But the United States is a close number three, seen by 49 percent as positive, while 34 percent hold a negative impression.[1] The country with the lowest global approval rating was Iran, with a 15 percent approval rating. Russia, Israel, North Korea, and Pakistan also have ratings at 30 percent or below (BBC World Service 2010).

So, the "ugly American" is no more of a reality than "the ugly Canadian, German, Russian or Pakistani." In an era of globalization, with China losing jobs to Malaysia, with Lebanon receiving refugees from Syria, and with globetrotting tourists going everywhere, there will be anti-other sentiment, wherever the other comes from. For example, the *Seattle Times* recently reported that the "ugly American" has shifted to the "ugly Chinese" tourist in Thailand (Gray 2014). Anti-western sentiment is as real as anti-eastern, or anti-Asian, or anti-African—these are permutations of anti-other sentiment (which goes by a number of other labels, including xenophobia, ethnocentrism, etc.). The BBC survey does not teach us much about international sentiment of people from various nations, except that everyone seems to have feelings that

---

1. The remaining 17 percent abstained.

range from negative to ambivalent toward *all* the world's nations. If the BBC surveyed people from all 220 or so of the world's nations, we would find the same mixed reviews regarding each of them.

The global impression of the United States, however, may be worsening. Another study (Pew Research) showed that twenty-six countries had a less favorable view of the United States in 2007 than in 2002. Of forty-seven nations surveyed, the nations with the highest view of the United States are in Africa. In fact, three nations—Ivory Coast (88 percent favorable), Kenya and Ghana—had a higher view of the United States than US citizens did (80 percent of US residents had a favorable view of their own country). Other countries with considerably high opinions of the United States include Mali, Nigeria, Israel, and Ethiopia. The lowest opinions were found in Morocco, Palestine, Turkey, and Pakistan, all with approvals of 15 percent or less.

Katzenstein and Keohane (2006) theorize that anti-western sentiment has to do more with western wealth than political policies. The United States and western nations in general, possess an indefatigable economy and hegemony. Since many novices see the economy as a zero-sum game, conventional wisdom says that "if the USA is wealthy, then we will be poor." The "ugly American," in this case, is a self-absorbed businessman who gets rich off the poor. One participant in my study named John (a college professor who taught in Brazil from 1965 to 1989) described how he observed discourse against western hegemony in light of a Brazilian national agenda:

> I think the biggest thing was political. It was resentment of the power, of the dominance of the US . . . how much they resented that all the name brands for toothpaste, and home goods come from the USA. One Brazilian asked, "How come we export our long fibers for US toilet paper and our own children have to wipe with second rate toilet paper?"

Such reports of negative sentiments cause some cognitive dissonance for US Americans who have traveled extensively, since they have observed quite positive attitudes toward their homeland. Americans report that they were seen by their hosts as "exotic, or a demigod" (Iyer 1991 in Kelly 2008, 268); they were "treated extremely well" and shown "tremendous curiosity and kindness" (Kerr 1996 in Kelly 2008, 268). Kelly reports that as an English teacher in Japan, he was complimented, flattered, and made comfortable (2008, 269). I have personally noticed that many Pacific Islanders feel a similar sense of awe about the United States because of the aid that comes from the United States in the form of dollars, healthcare, and technical training. Note that in the BBC's report (BBC World Service 2010), 82 percent of Filipinos see US American influence as positive. The same is true for 85 percent of Kenyans and 64 percent of Central Americans. In many other developing nations, westerners, if not appreciated, are at least seen as an important source of income for the tourism industry. In that sense, they are respected and even pandered to. US American missionaries who have worked in East Africa, Turkey, Morocco, Kazakhstan, Brazil, India, Indonesia, and Thailand told me that they are often pleasantly surprised to find that they are not despised (not outwardly, anyway) as the news reports intimated they would be; rather, they are often received hospitably and go on to develop rewarding relationships in their host country. However, some missionaries told me that the more "ugly" US Americans behaved, (i.e., the less cross-culturally literate they are), the less successful their cross-cultural experience became.

When we actually study international perceptions of US Americans, a theory emerges: anti-western discourse, like all discourse, is communicated for a purpose. That purpose seems to have more to do with the speaker in his own context, than with US Americans or the United States.

ANTI-AMERICAN SENTIMENT AS A TOOL FOR IDENTITY MANAGEMENT

One feature of any communicative act is the management of identity (Goffman 1958), and it turns out that internationals are finding that they can use anti-American discourse as a useful tool for managing their own identities. For example, one participant from Nigeria explained that it is largely the educated elite who use anti-American discourse to separate themselves from the commoners: "They think that by speaking against America they can show how sophisticated they are—that they understand [global] issues better than others do." The "sophisticated" are able to articulate alternative, complicated explanations to counter the "commoner's" simplistic notion that America represents freedom and opportunity. Daniel, a Ugandan pastor described a similar breakdown of discourse in his country:

> Daniel: When they see an American, they say, "There is the answer to all my problems." There is a sponsor . . . Others say that Americans only come to Africa for their own interests.
>
> Ken: How do you reconcile the two very different attitudes about America?
>
> Daniel: It is usually the elite who have the view that America is imperialist.

However, there seems to be a contradiction: often, the international academics and elites who tout anti-western sentiment are the very ones that rely on the West for their own upward mobility and comfortable lifestyle. If such communicators of anti-western sentiment employed the rhetoric about the evils of capitalism and the West, their own consumerism and social mobility would be hypocritical. However, if we reframe anti-western discourse as identity management, rather than a firmly held ideology, the contradiction is resolved. Talking bad about life in the West is simply another tool available for elites to separate themselves from the lower classes in their nation. One West African participant in my study said that those who speak against Europe and the United States are the ones who "own condos in London and send their kids to the US for education . . . they cannot succeed without the West." Will, a missionary who worked in North Africa, said that immediately after witnessing a USA flag burning, protesters approached him to ask him to help them get visas to the United States.

A participant who worked in Brazil told me, "There was this strong resentment and anger toward the US, but also a desire to have the benefits of living in the US." Joseph, an Indian community development worker who has lived in several countries in the Arabian Peninsula, said, "I would hear people talk [negatively] about American values, but then if I asked, 'Would you like to move there?' They would answer, 'Oh, yes!'"

If what people say is different than what they actually feel, their communication must serve a purpose other than the construction of plausible propositional truths. I have argued here that anti-western discourse is often a tool for branding self-identity. And this sort of discourse is especially useful for managing one's religious identity. Participants from India, Turkey, Cameroon, Indonesia, Eastern Europe, and East Africa indicated that Christians in their home countries express a more favorable view of the United States than Hindus or Muslims in the same context do. Since the United States and Christianity are often seen as coterminous, pro-western discourse is a way for Christians in these nations to show their solidarity with missions and Christianity. Likewise, anti-western discourse is a way of expressing concerns about Christianity in general.

ANTI-AMERICAN DISCOURSE AS A TOOL FOR NATIONALISTIC MOVEMENTS

Anti-western sentiment is most visible to all of us through the news media. And, as with all communication, anti-western discourse is utilized for a specific purpose. Most commonly, political movements leverage stereotypes of unjust US American hegemony and greed in order to muster feelings of nationalism. One participant explained to me that in India, the anti-western discourse becomes particularly useful as any political party can demonize its opponents by labeling them "puppets of Europe and America." A missionary who spent extensive time in Brazil, Portugal, and Poland between 1979 and 1990 indicated that nationals' responses to US Americans were dependent on their own political orientation. Those who were sympathetic to communism had animosity toward US Americans, even accusing missionaries (in a national newspaper in Brazil) of sterilizing women to reduce the population for an eventual takeover. On the other hand, those who did not identify with communism were more accepting of US Americans. In these cases, the use of anti-western discourse is really a tool for the management of political identities.

Anti-western (especially anti-American) discourse in the media is focused on military force—employing strong words like invasion, aggression, meddling, and interfering. Before Korean rapper Psy became a beloved icon in the United States due to the one hit wonder "Gangnam Style" on YouTube, he severely denounced the United States in his song "Dear American." The translated lyrics read: "Kill . . . Yankees who have been torturing Iraqi captives . . . who ordered them to torture . . . Kill their daughters, mothers, daughters-in-law and fathers . . . Kill them all slow and painfully." At a pause in the song, Psy smashed a small replica of a US Tank on stage, to adoring fans (TMZ 2012). The "ugly American" as the overweight tourist or the wealthy capitalist has been replaced by a new ugly American: the meddling, violent soldier. Hussein (2012) argued, "Occam's Razor, the logical principle that the simplest explanation is most often the correct one suggests that the American militarism which once ravaged Korea and which has now been set upon the Muslim world is the cause of this growing antipathy."

But even in the midst of this political conflict, US missionaries in Muslim countries report that they enjoy strong social relationships with people in their host culture. A doctoral student who was living in Istanbul told me that after the attacks on the World Trade Center in 2001, he received several calls from his Turkish friends, offering their condolences. "We hope nobody in your family suffered," a Turkish friend told him.

The use of anti-western sentiment as a tool for burgeoning nationalism highlights the need for cross-cultural workers to understand the history of colonialism, and the psychology of nationalism. "In Nigeria, we say that we divorced Britain to marry America" one participant told me. He explained that the independence movement specifically involved anti-British strategies: A rejection of the parliamentary system, and switching driving to the right side of the road. These were outward symbols of an alliance with US American values rather than colonial ones. In this case, anti-British sentiment and pro-American sentiment were more about burgeoning Nigerian nationalism than underlying feelings about the United States or the United Kingdom.

Each nation state has its unique experience with colonialism, so the discourse and sentiment about certain western powers will be nuanced, and will in fact change over time. But several themes emerged from interviews with missionaries who work around the globe, as I will describe below.

PERCEPTIONS RELATED TO THE COLONIAL PAST

Sociologists refer to the tendency to project one behavior on all members of an ethnic group as essentialism (Holliday 2011). For instance, participants said they regularly heard nationals say that US Americans are rich. In this case, the nationals are essentializing US culture. This "flattened" view of the other's culture causes outsiders to attribute an individual's actions to his or her ethnic culture. To take an example from India, a missionary from the United States paid too much for a watch at an open air market, and a man in his host culture attributed the swindling to his American-ness: "He doesn't know how to bargain, because he is a rich American." Rather than seeing sojourners as individuals, the tendency to essentialize causes people in a host culture to filter expatriate's behaviors through their pre-conceived idea of US Americans.

Participants who work in nations which have been demoralized due to communism or colonialism especially evidenced this sort of essentialism: US Americans are rich, and they throw money around "because they are Americans." So the role of westerners is to be the benefactor. One participant who worked in a former territory of the

USSR said, when she arrived with just a suitcase her host expressed dismay, "The other American team brought a truckload full of pallets, piled up with goods—but is that all you brought?" Participants from East Africa said their compatriots also engage in this sort of essentialism about post-colonial benefactors. "When a westerner moves into a village, we say, 'You have a white man. Now you're rich.'"

Essentialist views are easily reinforced when expatriates live in homogenous enclaves. In many former colonies, westerners have created their own wealthy neighborhoods, thus, limiting their interaction with the dominant culture. The isolationism makes it difficult for members of the host culture to get to know westerners in particular, so host country nationals use the minimal observations of westerners to make ethnic attributions about westerners in general. Participants told me that these enclaves have created the (sometimes true) perception that whites/Europeans/Americans only live cross-culturally to advance their own interests. "They think Americans see cultural engagement as a hassle or necessary evil." One participant who worked in East Africa described an enclave of large European houses in Dar es Salaam:

> Often Tanzanians think that Europeans want to stick to themselves, "They don't care about us . . . They don't want to eat the food, don't want to learn Swahili" . . . Once a shop owner asked me, "You're white . . . why are you speaking Swahili? White people don't like Swahili."

This participant theorized that the sterile and posh western enclaves can make the hosts feel like idiots, dirty, or backwards. In another case, a Thai woman said, "We can tell the missionaries from the business owners, because only missionaries bother to learn our language." A visitor to Haiti told me that she observed an expatriate aid worker in Haiti blurt out, "These Haitians need to know that when Americans come all this way to help them, we need the air conditioning to be working." Such attitudes of aloofness and entitlement reinforced a global stereotype that US Americans are elites who like to stay in their comfortable enclaves.

While expatriates have set up more or less permanent enclaves throughout the world, the majority of westerners actually live overseas on a temporary basis. A recurring theme that emerged from my research was that missionaries may leave any time: if they get sick, or if their organization moves them, or if their kids go to school. The perception that the US American is transient has a number of effects on mission work. First of all, one Filipino pastor explained to me:

> We feel like since the US missionaries are temporary, we must be good hosts to them as our guests. So we don't tell them when we disagree. We want to make them happy. We don't open up to them about our problems, because they may soon be gone.

In other words, the ephemeral nature of an overseas mission assignment affects rapport building and creates an environment where the missionaries are unable to receive candid feedback. The temporariness also gives the impression that US missionaries work abroad for somewhat selfish motives. A professor who worked in Romania at the fall of communism said that host country nationals were ambivalent about the US aid that was coming in. "Americans only think of themselves. As soon as they find another way to spend their money, they'll stop giving to us."

Another common perception of westerners, especially due to colonialism, is that no matter the background, all westerners are experts. Expatriates typically have desirable skills like a superior grasp of English, or literacy in computers, or have attained higher education. Participants who worked in East Asia, East Africa, Indonesia, and Central Europe related that their hosts often defer to them with far more respect than makes them comfortable. Western sojourners are known to occupy positions of leadership, so they are sent to the front of the queue, seldom carry heavy objects, and when they make a point, nobody is willing to argue with them. A missionary who worked in Indonesia said,

"We live in a hierarchical society, with leaders and underlings. And we're perceived as leaders." Prior training in the legacy of colonialism, and in cultural value orientations, helped these missionaries to form a more accurate understanding of how they were being perceived in their host cultures, and how to fit within their expected social roles.

The extraordinary status that western expatriates are afforded also gives the impression that they are above the law. Missionaries and host country nationals alike mentioned that while nationals are held to one standard by local officials and the police, westerners have the clout to get out of trouble with the police. The effect is that nationals as well as local officials can resent expatriates for their special status.

A major criticism of US missionaries working from India all the way to East Asia is the use of their "special status" to operate above the law by persuading people to convert. John, from India explained, "Missionaries ostensibly come to start a business, or hand out supplies, but then ask for open conversions in large numbers." John suggested that missionaries who challenged this perception of US Americans as duplicitous, and who made their motives clear from the beginning were often better received. A participant who works in Thailand said it was the same dissonance between ostensible motives (business) and actual work (evangelism) that caused some local authorities to distrust missionaries in her area.

The colonial past has played its part in creating many of these perceptions of US Americans as benefactors, or temporary experts who live in enclaves and operate above the law. But the byproducts of industrialization and globalization also lead to ambivalent impressions of the West. This is especially seen in the values (or anti-values) coming from Hollywood.

ANTI-VALUE

Of course, Hollywood plays a part in global perceptions of the United States. Pearse (2004) records the intense ambivalence that people from many developing nations have regarding North America and Europe, based on what they see on the television. On the one hand, western values are enticing at a visceral level—illicit sexuality, immense wealth, and unfettered individualism. But at the same time, non-westerners instinctively know that these very values are antithetical to their own pre-industrial cultures, which often place high values on duty, the community, and modesty. It is precisely this ambivalence—this simultaneous enticement plus "anti-value" which engenders a recipe for the "rest to hate the west." While Pearse's erudite essay on anti-western sentiment is plausible, international and US participants in my study only considered the "anti-value" as one of many factors contributing to anti-western discourse. Instead, as I have argued here, anti-western discourse is more about identity management, nationalism, and essentialist ethnic attributions that were formed as a legacy of colonialism. Below, we will see how these perceptions of US Americans affected their cross-cultural strategies.

IMPACT OF ANTI-WESTERN SENTIMENT ON CROSS-CULTURAL STRATEGIES

By this point, we must conclude that global opinions of the west in general, and of the United States in particular, are multi-vocal and complicated, and these various opinions of "ugly Americans" or "beautiful Americans" require a multi-layered strategy for any sort of cross-cultural work. The responses missionaries are implementing are somewhat contradictory: at times accepting or leveraging the international perceptions, at times challenging them, but always mindful of them.

Self-loathing

Despite the generally positive reception that many of us actually receive when we travel overseas, a fear (or snobbery) of being portrayed as the "ugly American" has caused some sojourners to be ashamed of their nationality. In fact, participants in my research indicated that they experienced more anti-American sentiment from people who originate from western nations, with less negative sentiment from their hosts in Asia or Africa (usually Muslim or Buddhist). Our sharpest criticisms are of people that we are similar to—not of people halfway around the globe. An Indian participant said that he experienced more anti-western discourse from US Americans than he heard at home in India.

McLaren describes this self-loathing:

> [US Americans] think small, do nothing daring or prophetic or entrepreneurial, never offend the indigenous Christians . . . don't innovate, don't act American even if that's what [we] are. Meanwhile, North American popular music, film, and culture in general are—for better or worse—arguably the most universal cultural phenomena in the world. So ironically, just as the missionary movement begins to feel snobbish toward all things American, more people around the world have more in common with North Americans than ever before. (1988, 127)

Professors of intercultural studies observe a mild form of this self-loathing as their students begin to understand how European cultural values differ from the value orientations in other parts of the world. We observe students enthusiastically embrace the collectivism, relational-oriented, hospitable, and flexible cultural values that are characteristic of many societies outside the US, and reject their host culture's values of individualism and task-orientation. Bennett (1986) observed this to be the second of six stages of cultural sensitivity: defense against the differences. In this stage, cross-cultural novices sometimes defend the differences of their host culture, and express rejection of their home culture.

But the career missionaries I interviewed were able to be self-critical of their home cultures without idealizing the other or completely rejecting their home culture. Their tactic was not as much self-loathing, but instead to challenge the perception of US missionaries, or to distance themselves from that perception.

Challenge the Perception

A number of participants are painfully aware of the behaviors of "ugly Americans" and they challenge those images. Participants especially challenge the perception that US Americans are impatient or self-centered by building relationships and showing that they were genuinely interested in their hosts. If westerners are seen as above the law, missionaries take extra pains to follow the law, "even ones that the nationals disobey" like zoning and traffic laws. If westerners are thought of as pushy, missionaries are careful to listen better and seek consensus. If "ugly Americans" drive SUVs, these missionaries take the bus. If "ugly Americans" rush to the front of the line, they wait their turn. If the "ugly American" loses his patience in public, they keep their cool.

Well-trained missionaries challenge the perception that westerners are most comfortable in their wealthy enclaves. I asked a Cameroonian participant what caused certain US missionaries to be well received and others to be rejected. He said the well-received ones "learn the language. They are respectful of Islam in the way they dress." A missionary to Indonesia said that his mindfulness of the perceptions of US Americans as arrogant and self-serving compelled him to become part of the community. Whereas the expectation was that he, as a wealthy "patron," would not do manual labor or domestic tasks, he took part in road construction projects. "Indonesian patrons would never act like servants and make coffee or tea," he said, "so they were surprised when I made them tea."

In order to quash concerns about the temporariness of expatriate stays, missionaries challenge that perception by committing to work for the long haul. They challenge that notion in deeds, by marrying host country nationals or adopting children from there, or by building permanent homes. They also challenge the notion in word. Isaac, a missionary to Honduras, told me, "After teaching for a year, I walked into the classroom one day and the chalkboard said 'Missionary go back to Canada.' But I left the message there and wrote, 'I love Honduras.'" Isaac was not going home any time soon.

And some missionaries are challenging the notion of the sponsor or benefactor. If "ugly Americans" throw money at their problems, these participants challenged that image by looking to community action and cooperation, rather than to foreign money as the panacea.

Leverage the Perception

At times, it is more strategic to leverage perceptions of US Americans than to deny or challenge them. For example, in East Asia, English is valued (even if there is a stigma about nations where English is the first language). Missionaries in these regions capitalize on the interest in English as a way of building relationships. Where education in general is valued, missionaries often are highly educated, and are valued for that resource, even if their home country itself is not particularly respected.

The perception of US Americans as the benefactor can also be strategic. For example, the role of the "big man" in the Pacific requires leaders to distribute goods. Missionaries in the Pacific are automatically ascribed, perhaps as a legacy of colonialism, the status of "big man" (or "big woman"). But in order to legitimately fulfill the role, missionaries must have access to wealth that they can redistribute. This characteristic, recognized in the local cultural logic as generosity, is central to the status of leader. Missionaries from the Pacific indicated that they did not conceive of generous distribution as the focus of their work, but people in their host culture did key in on this role as central. So missionaries leverage their access to outside financial resources as a way of legitimizing their status as leaders. For example, when Roy and Jane lived at 7500 feet in Papua New Guinea, a frost destroyed the villagers' crops. As "big men" in the village, Roy and Jane recognized their role was to find food to alleviate the famine. "Part of the exuberant response to our Bible dedication later on," they said, "was due, in part, to the way we had helped bring food."

Also, two missionaries who served in the Pacific and later in Thailand recalled that they were often given a chance to speak "even at a random church simply by virtue of being a westerner . . . You have to have something prepared in advance, because you may be asked to speak, even if you have nothing to say." While missionaries often feel awkward (to use one participant's description) about this unmerited forum for public speaking, it would be disrespectful to decline the opportunity. Instead, one missionary explained, "Have something meaningful to say, and point to Christ rather than yourself." Having worked in the South Pacific, I noted that "big men" are often given the forum to speak, but leverage that opportunity to advance their own status as politicians or leaders. Missionaries stand in stark contrast when they decline to use the podium for personal gain.

A US American who teaches at a university in Southeast Asia said, "As a westerner, I am put on a pedestal, which goes against my grain" but this opportunity also gave him a platform of influence. He said, "People even come to me to ask for advice in their personal lives." Rather than decline the opportunity to influence his students' lives, he said that he tried to "use that as a way to speak truth into people's lives."

Purposeful Distancing from the Perception

Both negative and positive stereotypes are based on the assumption that every member of the exotic other's culture holds the same values and behaviors. Many participants said their strategy for cross-cultural work was to challenge this sort of essentialism—to show that *they* did not fit the stereotype. If they could be seen as individuals, rather than as "Americans-in-general" they would be immune from the attributions and stereotypes, and hence, the scrutiny.

Since the title "missionary" is controversial, missionaries around the world purposefully distance themselves from that name. A missionary to the Middle East told me that the term "missionary" in his host country connotes someone who will "steal your kids, take them to some camp and brainwash them, and return them, never able to fit back in to the family and social life." Missionaries from as far west as Ireland and as far east as Indonesia purposefully avoid the term "missionary" in order to disassociate themselves from negative images. A participant who works in Southeast Asia said that missionaries keep a low profile in Asia because host governments in those countries tend to be "pro-Muslim, pro-Buddhist, extreme-Hindu or pro-communist." So while western tourists may be welcomed, the Christian workers are seen as a threat to nationalistic movements that use religious identity as a unifying force.

The term "American" is also volatile. Some missionaries from the US have told me they tell people they are from Canada, "since people like Canadians more." And one missionary said he found it more expedient to tell people he was from California.

But the strategies of distancing go deeper than simply avoiding labels like "missionary" or "American." In fact, if anti-western sentiment is primarily a way for internationals to foster nationalism, as this research has suggested, then it is imperative for US missionaries to distance themselves from political discourse while overseas.

CONCLUSION

Cross-cultural workers are mindful that they "live in a fishbowl." Certainly natives of the countries that host them are prone to losing their patience, dressing immodestly, and exhibiting other "ugly" behaviors—but when expatriates violate cultural norms, people attribute these negative behaviors to their ethnicity or nationality. So there is a sense in which cross-cultural workers are simultaneously being evaluated as individuals (that is, interpersonally) and as ethnics (that is, inter-culturally).

This research has shown that anti-western sentiment does not debilitate western missionaries. Missionaries from all over the globe indicated that they enjoyed positive relationships in their host countries. But both negative and positive stereotypes of westerners do cause missionaries to be self-reflective about how they are being perceived. At times they challenge or distance themselves from those stereotypes, and at times they leverage them.

REFERENCES

Al Jazeera. 2013. "Iranians Cry 'Death to America' in Huge Rally," *Al Jazeera*, November 4. Accessed December 7, 2015. http://www. aljazeera.com/news/middleeast/2013/11/iranians-gather-anti -us-demonstrations-201311411503434943.html.

Bennett, Milton J. 1986. "Towards Ethnorelativism: A Developmental Model of Intercultural Sensitivity." In *Cross-cultural Orientation: New Conceptualizations and Applications*, edited by R. M. Paige, 27–70. New York: University Press of America.

Conn, Harvey. 1984. *Eternal Word and Changing Worlds: Theology, Anthropology, and Mission in Trialogue*. Grand Rapids, MI: Zondervan.

End of the Spear. 2005. DVD. Directed by Jim Hanon. Every Tribe Entertainment.

"Global Views of United States Improve While Other Countries Decline," 2010. *BBC World Service*, April 18. Accessed December 7, 2015. http://www.worldpublicopinion.org/pipa/pipa/pdf/apr10 /BBCViews_Apr10_rpt.pdf.

Goffman, Erving. 1958. *The Presentation of Self in Everyday Life*. New York: Doubleday.

Gray, Dennis D. 2014. "Chinese Tourists: The New 'Ugly Americans?'" *Seattle Times*, April 15. Accessed December 5, 2015. http://seattletimes .com/html/travel/2023382227_chinesetourismthailandxml.html.

Grisham, John. 1999. *The Testament*. New York: Doubleday.

Holliday, Adrian. 2011. "Small Cultures." In *The Language and Intercultural Communication Reader*, edited by Zhu Hua, 196–218. New York: Routledge.

Hussain, Murtaza, 2012. "The Roots of Global Anti-Americanism," *Al Jazeera*, December 11. Accessed October 1, 2014. http://www .aljazeera.com/indepth/opinion/2012/12/201212108205749534.html

Iyer, Pico. 1991. *The Lady and the Monk*. New York: Knopf.

Katzenstein, Peter J., and Keohane, Robert O. eds. 2006. *Anti-Americanisms in World Politics*. Ithaca, NY: Cornell University Press.

Kelly, William. 2008. "Applying a Critical Metatheoretical Approach to Intercultural Relations: The Case of US-Japanese communication." In *The Global Intercultural Communication Reader*, edited by Molefi Kete Asante, Yoshitaka Miike, and Jing Yin, 215–238. New York: Routledge.

Kerr, Alex. 1996. *Lost Japan*. Oakland, CA: Lonely Planet.

Kingsolver, Barbara. 1998. *The Poisonwood Bible*. New York: Harper Collins.

Lederer, William J., and Burdick, Eugene. 1958. *The Ugly American*. New York: Norton.

Machine Gun Preacher. 2011. DVD. Directed by Marc Forster. Beverly Hills, CA: Relativity Media.

Mclaren, Brian. 1998. *The Church on the Other Side: Doing Ministry in the Postmodern Matrix*. Grand Rapids, MI: Zondervan.

Pew Research. 2007. "Global Unease with Major World Powers: Rising Environmental Concern in 47-Nation Survey." *Pew Research*, June 27. Accessed October 30, 2013. http://www.pewglobal .org/2007/06/27/global-unease-with-major-world-powers/

The Inn of the Sixth Happiness. 1958. DVD. Directed by Mark Robson. Los Angeles, CA: Twentieth Century Fox Film Corporation.

Steffan, Melissa. 2013. "The Surprising Countries Most Missionaries Are Sent From and Go To," *Christianity Today*, July 25. Accessed October 27, 2014. http://www .christianitytoday.com/gleanings/2013/july/missionaries -countries-sent-received-csgc-gordon-conwell.html?paging=off.

The Mission. 1986. DVD. Directed by Roland Joffe. Burbank, CA: Warner Brothers.

The Other Side of Heaven. 2001. DVD. Directed by Mitch Davis. Burbank, CA: Walt Disney Home Video.

The Ugly American. 1963. DVD. Directed by George Englund. Hollywood, CA: Universal Studios.

TMZ. 2012. "Psy 'Deeply Sorry' for Singing about Killing Americans." Accessed October 27, 2014. http://www.tmz.com/2012/12/07 /psy-apology-dear-americans-killing-yankees/

CHAPTER 8

A CONTINUING ROLE FOR WESTERN BIBLE TRANSLATORS?

Dave Beine

INTRODUCTION

Citing a confluence of missiological factors, the largest global alliance of Bible translators—Wycliffe Global Alliance—is now promoting primarily a local and national translator model. The three North American members of this conglomeration—Wycliffe Bible Translators USA, The Seed Company, and Wycliffe Associates—have each adopted similar models that advocate increasing the number of local and national translators while decreasing the number of expatriate translators. In effect, these organizations are becoming Bible translation *facilitator* organizations rather than Bible *translator* sending organizations. What has precipitated this change and what are the overall implications? In this paper, I endeavor to answer these questions. I conclude that the wisest strategy would be a both/and strategy of Bible translation rather than an either (expatriate) / or (national translator) model.

HISTORY AND REFLECTION

In 1980, influential missiologist David Bosch described several complex historical and social elements that were shifting the center of world mission away from the West. He defined this shift in missions as a reaction to a "crisis in mission . . . more radical and extensive than anything the church has ever faced in her history" (Bosch 1980, 28).[1] Many missiologists have promoted this crisis narrative, claiming a significant

---

1. "Crisis in Mission" was the title of the first chapter of Bosch's influential book. He reiterated the theme in chapter 4 with the above quotation. Although this

impact upon western mission agencies and the western missionary workforce (Winter 1999, 258; Lausanne Committee for World Evangelization 2004, 9; Shenk 2006, 92; Charles 2009, 51; Olson 2010, 29).

In contrast to the crisis narrative, well-known mission historian and strategist Patrick Johnstone (2011) notes that the United States of America still tops the list of the "more significant missionary sending countries," sending out nearly 80,000 Protestant, Independent, and Anglican missionaries. India, the next country on the list, sends half as many as the United States, followed by South Korea and Canada, each with less than one quarter the number of American missionaries being sent today (Johnstone 2011, 225–229). In his 2011 treatise on the future of the global church, Johnstone traces the era of decline in traditional denominational missionaries through the nineteenth century, followed by "explosive growth" and expansion of the North American mission force in the twentieth century, even until 2010. He observes that "this has happened even as non-evangelical denominational missions collapsed, with a new wave of fervent evangelical missionaries more than replacing them" (Johnstone 2011, 228). Referencing a list of the top twenty missionary countries, from 1900–2010, Johnstone concludes:

> Anglophone countries dominated with nine in the top 20 and 80 percent of all missionaries. Britain was the largest sender of missionaries in 1900 but was soon eclipsed by the USA. The UK's numbers changed relatively little over the next 110 years. The US has headed the list ever since. (2012, 233)

I think it is premature to claim that North America has finished sending missionaries. I am not convinced of the veracity of the crisis narrative.

Some believe that in regard to Bible translation, in particular, "the number of people training in the West to do Bible translation is on

---

"crisis" narrative is still perpetuated today (see Fahlbusch, et al. 2003), Bosch's original conclusions are being contemporarily critiqued.

the decline" (Gravelle 2010, 13). Based on this belief, some western Bible translation agencies have adopted a "local translator" strategy. In a recent town meeting, the Chief Branding Officer of Wycliffe Bible Translators-USA (WBT-USA) highlighted:

> 1) Center of gravity shifted from North and West to South and East [local church taking leadership in BT movements]—the WHOLE church taking the WHOLE gospel to the WHOLE world. 2) Observing a philanthropic shift in the West away from charity giving (writing a check and disconnect) through generosity that includes advocacy (e.g. personal involvement and partnership). 3) SIL is in a process of reinvention itself and is emerging as a service organization (INGO). And so our response (after much prayerful consideration) is . . . the emerging model of Bible translation. (Wycliffe USA Town Meeting 2014)

The Chief Operations Officer for Wycliffe USA says, "the emerging model primarily follows a MTT [Mother Tongue Translator] model, so there is not likely to be many expatriate translators in it" (Hersman 2015). Wycliffe's two North American partners, the Seed Company and Wycliffe Associates, have also adopted local-translator-only strategies, becoming effectively Bible translation *facilitation* organizations rather than Bible translator sending organizations. I will address the possible dangers of excluding western translators.

THE FACILITATOR ERA?

Parish (2013) has added to Ralph Winter's (1999) famous three eras of modern mission with his proposal of a fourth era: the facilitator era.[2]

---

2. Parish (2013) characterizes this era as a time when the main mission agencies will be local church-based and local task-based organizations. The foreign missionary's main role is as a facilitator of local missionaries. Parish

Building on missiologist Tom Steffen's influential book *The Facilitator Era* (2011), Parish characterizes this era as a time when mission agencies are principally concerned with the facilitation of tasks that are accomplished by the local church, rather than by expatriate missionaries. The agencies that have historically led the Bible translation task worldwide have shifted to a facilitator model.

What could be the dangers of excluding westerners from Bible translation and other missionary endeavors? In a recent conversation with colleague Tom Steffen, I shared that my own mission shifted its emphasis to a MTT model and is no longer focused on sending westerners to do translation work. His response: "That is a huge misstep!" Although the focus of my question was on translation in particular, Steffen provided a bullet-point response of his view on the remaining role for westerners in the facilitator era. His points raise many important questions that should be answered by those advocating for a complete paradigm shift. I have tried to group these comments and questions into like categories below.

According to Steffen (2014):

- Providing administrators to aid locals is one thing; providing Bible translation teachers is quite another.
- Good teachers require more than cognitive book knowledge; they need practical experience that moves them beyond the abstract to the concrete. Good teachers teach out of experience.
- Good teachers not only require experience, they need cross-cultural experience. Cross-cultural experience allows the teacher to speak out of a wealth of concrete experience that says this works, this doesn't. Lose this and you lose any productive role in a short generation.

---

identifies the key leaders of this era as Rick Warren, David Garrison, David Watson, Neil Cole, and Alan Hirsch.

- Once you remove western personnel from the frontline, western creativity will virtually cease. And so much for your journal publications.
- Is this type of facilitation—"You come to our work-shops at the missionary center and we'll tell you what to do"—21st century paternalism? Don't you just love to listen to people without kids tell people with kids what to do?

The above comments relate mainly to the model of sending ex-patriate consultants, who have never had cross-cultural translation experience, as facilitators of local Bible translators. In regard to the impact of no longer sending western translators, Steffen suggests:

> When you stop sending western Bible translators, make sure you stop sending pilots, doctors, nurses, literacy workers, ethnodoxologists, anthropologists, dorm parents. And don't work with any agency in country that has expats to do the church planting, etc. To make sure that there is not a double standard, do not accept those from other countries to work in the home offices. And this will change your recruit-ment; no more incarnational model being promoted. And good luck raising funds for not doing Bible translation. (2014)

Steffen also addresses a hidden presupposition in this model when he contends that:

> "They can do it better" is sometimes a myth. Some-times we can do it better. In God's economy there is nothing wrong with being the best at something, in-cluding Bible translation. The US fighting forces are the best in the world because of practice, and they train a lot of other nations without losing that edge. (2014)

There are definitely gifted local and national translators! I have worked alongside some of these people. There are also some very gifted North American translators working in the world, and the people groups they are serving would lose something if they were not there. It cuts both ways. I will address this further in the coming pages.

Perhaps most importantly, Steffen uses the body analogy to point out that:

> Participation in all aspects of the Great Commission is *not* nation specific. The "body of Christ" calls for partnership at all levels, not just administrator roles. Learning will take place by all parties as all need each other. First century Paul teams were composed of multi-aged, multi-ethnic members using their specific gifts. (2014)

These concerns are not new. Missiologists have been discussing these topics for years. Eighteen years ago, Frank L. Roy (1997), quoting TV Thomas in *Missions Frontiers* Magazine, commented:

> I personally find it too simplistic and pragmatic a solution. "Nationals can do it best" and "Nationals can do it cheap" sounds inviting in the pressures of raising global missionary dollars. Christ's mandate for the church was not primarily to "give" but to "go." Our pragmatic approaches should not give the impression that Christ has retracted or revised His Great Commission mandates for the global church (Matt 28:18–20).[3]

---

3. Some of the shift may have to do with continuing to raise support for Bible translation in a changing North American church—changing to a mega-church model, just as Shaw (1994) predicted. As Priest, Wilson, and Johnson (2010) have demonstrated, American mega-churches are more financially supportive of the partnership-with-nationals model vs. the continuation of support for expatriate missionaries, particularly Bible translators. Mission agencies may feel

It might be good for today's western mission leaders to revisit Frank Roy's earlier writings and examine current practices in the light of his warnings. Steffen (2014) notes that, "One strong driver of facilitation is short-term missions." Mission agency leaders need to consider the strengths and weaknesses of applying the facilitator model in the long-term context. Steffen asked, "Does 'one-size-fits-all' work in all the countries where SIL works" (2014)? The short answer is no, but a facilitation model assumes it will. Finally, according to Steffen, if we fully embrace facilitation only, then "training centers, such as Biola, will no longer be recruitment centers" (2014).

THE CRISIS NARRATIVE

The crisis narrative—that the number of western translators is declining—contributes to the shift toward a primarily-local-translator model. Gilles Gravelle (2010) has done a masterful job explaining the rationale for the model of Bible translation now being used by the Seed Company and by Wycliffe-USA. The model uses MTTs instead of western translators. One justification for this approach, cited by WBT-USA, is a decline in the number of North American people training for foreign missions. Gravelle references such a decline at least three times in his article on the changing role of cross-cultural workers, in the Bible translation context.

Gravelle asks the question, "Why has interest on the part of the emerging western generation in doing Bible translation diminished?" (2010, 15). Although only anecdotal, interest in intercultural ministry at Moody Bible Institute remains strong. As of Fall 2013, there were 533 Intercultural Study majors, of which eighty were Applied Linguistics majors. Many students studying Applied Linguistics are interested in doing Bible translation. When I asked our former department chair, also a former Evangelical Missiological Society

---

obligated to change their product to meet the changing market, or risk losing funding.

(EMS) officer, whether he sees a crisis in Intercultural Studies departments across the country, he responded that he did not (Sisk 2014).[4] Interestingly, the president of Pioneer Bible Translators reports that they have doubled their career overseas missionaries over the past five years, and their organization is in a steady state of growth—around 12 percent annually (Pruett 2015). How do we explain these discrepancies in perception? Gravelle's observations pertained to a decline in WBT-USA membership specifically. Perhaps WBT-USA based their conclusions upon outdated information, and perhaps there is a recent rebound of interest in Bible translation. Maybe we are seeing a self-fulfilling prophecy, as fewer North American students come to WBT-USA because they have been told that there is no room for them. The reason for the discrepancy needs to be discerned.

A FURTHER EXAMINATION OF GRAVELLE'S PREMISES

I want to examine the premises upon which Gravelle's local-translator model is predicated. It seems that the changes being adopted by WBT-USA, The Seed Company, and Wycliffe Associates come from an application of Gravelle's local-translator model. If the premises which justify the model are questionable, then adopting the model might also be troublesome.

Gravelle's first premise is that mother tongue translators have an advantage over western translators. These MTTs are not trained in linguistic theories that are based on "western frameworks" and "influenced by western positivist epistemology" (Gravelle 2010, 17). The argument goes something like this: While western translators may be advantaged in the decoding stage of translation, MTTs have the advantage in the encoding stage of translation. MTTs know and use local conceptual frameworks. Western translators struggle to encode

---

4.   I asked him these questions in response to the claim, by a Wycliffe board member, that there is a crisis in North American missions today, as evidenced by a decline in students in intercultural study programs and the loss of jobs for intercultural professors at Christian universities across the country.

the message in a natural and meaningful way. Western translators are bound by their western cultural frames or are hesitant to use certain indigenous frames because of their western cultural biases. Therefore, Gravelle argues, the product of a MTT would be superior to that of a western translator. He then suggests a parallel between three stages of translation and Paul Hiebert's three historic periods of mission focus[5]—literal translation was first, followed by meaning-based translation (which is what western translators have been doing), culminating in "indigenizing" translation. In the indigenizing stage, Scripture is presented through local conceptual frames and worldview. Some believe that only MTTs can achieve this third stage.

I find Gravelle's premise problematic on several levels. First, while acknowledging that MTTs may have a disadvantage in the decoding stage, Gravelle does not address the obvious inverse: western-trained translators may have an *advantage* in the decoding stage. Second, as a professor of cultural anthropology, I am training students of various ethnic backgrounds to practice exactly what Gravelle denotes as the advantages inherent in the local translator. I teach my students to identify the emic. Whether a person knows something inherently (emically) or has learned it through anthropological analysis should make no difference in the translation process. Gravelle's argument seems a bit illogical to me. Third, his proposition suggests that westerners are biased and have consequently translated Bibles that represent western cultural frames. If this is true, then MTTs will also encode a message that represents their cultural frames. The truth, then, is that both groups are biased by their individual cultural frames and neither fully understands. Neither group is better able to fully unpack and repack the universal truth of the Bible. Mother tongue translators are just as ethnocentric as their western counterparts. Each of their translated frames is as culturally bound (biased) as the other. While the MTT's translation may better fit his or her culture, it may be just as far from

---

5. First is behavior focus, followed by belief focus, and finally a focus on worldview transformation.

universal truth as that of a western translator's versions. I contend that an anthropologically-trained translator, of any ethnic or national origin, can communicate the truth as well as a cultural native. The best scenario would be to translate the universal truth *together* rather than individually. I advocate both/and, not either/or.[6]

I also challenge Gravelle's premise that we must move beyond meaning-based translation.[7] Authors Arnold and Sanneh both reference the value of meaning-based translation. Arnold contends:

> We rightly display Bible Translation as a superior missionary strategy of indigenization and contextualization of the gospel in any culture. Hopefully the gospel will take root naturally in the form of a truly indigenous church. (1987, 116)

This has happened in many places around the globe where meaning-based translations were being done by westerners. Sanneh suggests:

> Often the outcome of vernacular translation was that the missionary lost the position of being the expert. But the significance of translation went beyond that. Armed with a written vernacular Scripture, converts to Christianity invariably called into question the legitimacy of all schemes of foreign domination—cultural, political, and religious. Here was an acute paradox: the vernacular Scriptures and the wider cultural and linguistic enterprise on which translation rested provided the means and occasion for arousing a sense of national pride, yet it was the

---

6. Even advocates arguing for "the apparent advantage" of native translators, over expatriate translators, have concluded that "this does not remove the need for an appropriate and reasoned theory of translation that has come from the West" (Franklin 2012). This seems to conflict with Gravelle's view that western linguistic theories hinder native translators, and should therefore be abandoned.

7. The translation stage that Gravelle refers to as the indigenizing stage in translation was not yet conceived at the time of these writings.

missionaries—foreign agents—who were the creators of that entire process. I am convinced that this paradox decisively undercuts the alleged connection often drawn between missions and colonialism. Colonial rule was irreparably damaged by the consequences of vernacular translation—and often by other activities of missionaries. (1987, 331)

Historian Mark Noll writes:

The translation of the Scriptures may be the most enduringly significant feature of the global expansion of Christianity . . . while the message of Christ that missionaries brought has been of great significance, even more important has been the message they left in the shape of vernacular Scriptures. When people hear the word of life in their own languages, salvation is no longer an offering from an alien culture but an offering from within the culture. (1997, 308–310)

Although Gravelle lends the voice of Kwame Bediako to his call for the new indigenizing stage of translation, Bediako's writings, on the value of vernacular Scripture, are explicitly tied to the meaning-based-era work done by western translators. In reference to the legacy of the modern missionary movement, Bediako writes:

The point I am making is this: African Christianity today is inconceivable apart from the existence of the Bible in African indigenous languages. By its deep vernacular achievement, therefore, relative to Europe's own missionary past the modern missionary movement from the West in Africa actually ensured that Africans had the means to make their own responses to the Christian message, in terms of their own needs and according to their own categories of thought and meaning. (Bediako n.d.)

It is clear, at least in this context, that Bediako is supportive of the meaning-based translation of the modern missionary movement, accomplished primarily by westerners. Gravelle's (2010, 13) citation of Bediako is taken from a book published in 2004,[8] a time when the idea of the "indigenized stage of translation" would have been only in its infancy, if it existed at all. I would like to have known Kwame Bediako's contemporary thoughts on the matter. Unfortunately, he died in 2008.

Given the positive evaluation of meaning-based translation, why is it essential that we do more than we have been doing? Gravelle suggests that more is accomplished in the indigenized stage. Could we potentially distort the Bible through indigenization? Perhaps the indigenization of the text should take place at the interpretation level, by local pastors during the exegetical process, rather than at the translation level. The best translation should not encode local interpretations of any kind.

I fully agree with the inherent value of including indigenous agency in translation work. The translation effort, however, should not be *just* a western missionary enterprise nor *just* an indigenous enterprise. We are enriched by the inclusion of wider perspectives. I would argue that there are still ways that cultural outsiders can contribute to translation and they may even do some things better.[9] I believe that the best translation model includes contributions from both indigenous translators and western translators. Bediako says that, "Christianity has become a non-western religion. This does not mean that western Christianity has become irrelevant; rather, that Christianity may now be seen for what it truly is, a universal religion" (Bediako 1993, 7).

---

8. Here Gravelle is citing Bediako's 2004 book, *Jesus and the Gospel in Africa: History and Experience.*

9. Unless of course indigenous translators receive the same training as westerners, then both would be on equal footing (minus the idea of an inherent gifting in linguistics, which could be recognized in an individual from any nationality).

Conceivably, Bediako might have been supportive of a both/and strategy of translation.

My final contention with Gravelle's premises regards funding. Gravelle uses different funding paradigms to justify a local translator preference. I challenge Gravelle's conclusion that western donors' preference for the results-oriented business model[10] should determine how we do translation (Gravelle 2010, 18). In regard to the influence of such efficiency models upon modern missions, Samuel Escobar has asked if we are "in danger of carrying on mission as a purely human enterprise" (2003, 25). Escobar suggests that some today might "[regard] mission as a manageable task that should be completed by a certain date, using appropriate technology, and following business principles of management by objectives" (Escobar 2003, 25–26). Bible translation is a spiritual enterprise, not a business transaction. I do not think it should be driven by donors and business models.

WHAT ARE THE UNDERLYING VALUES OF THE NEW PARADIGM?

As a cultural anthropologist, I am interested in examining the underlying cultural values that drive this paradigm shift in missions. David Smith, author of *Against the Stream: Christianity and Mission in an Age of Globalization,* has suggested that *all* of us in today's globalized world are being shaped by wider materialist and economic values (2003, 8). Yet, Smith suggests that theology and missions need to be countercultural in this respect. Are we overly driven by technological values? Smith writes:

> At the beginning of the twenty-first century, in a postmodern culture, transformed by the impact of new information technologies, the temptation to embrace every new scientific advance in an uncritical manner is vastly increased for Christians whose

---

10. Results-based comprehensive planning and participatory methods.

motivation in mission is related in a fundamental manner to the speed with which the task of world-wide evangelization can be completed. This explains the attractiveness of the media of mass communication for evangelicals. (2003, 91)

Here is a striking example. I recently received an email update from a media ministry that boasted, "We now have the technology to reach everyone on the earth" (Wilson 2014). Smith notes the American missionary optimism that "global evangelization might be completed before the end of the twentieth century" (2003, 92).[11] It has taken some time to realize that technology is a mixed blessing and that, "an increase in the speed of communication might be obtained at the huge cost of a loss of depth and that specific technological media possesses the power to shape both messages and messengers in ways that could be profoundly harmful to the gospel of Jesus" (Smith 2003, 92).

Samuel Escobar echoed Smith's warning, cautioning us against "an uncritical acceptance of modernization and globalization as supreme values," concluding that the modern values of efficiency, innovation, and technical rationality, if not kept in proper perspective, can actually inhibit us in our missions (2003, 57–59). He contends that "the culture of globalization creates attitudes and a mental frame that may be the opposite of what the gospel teaches about human life under God's design" (Escobar 2003, 59). Escobar further cautions us against "the total identification of modern western values with the gospel" which is being "propagated by many missionary organizations in the name of Christian mission" today (2013, 59). He counsels us against turning our mission into an industry that packages and markets a product, using the latest cultural innovations to do so and reminds us that "foreign missionaries must always be aware that they may be carriers of the material tools or the intellectual vehicles of the globalization process" (Escobar 2003, 62).

---

11. Although this book was published in the twenty-first century, this quote comes from a lecture given at the end of the twentieth century.

Regarding Bible translation in particular, Escobar notes that circa 1960, specialized agencies for Bible translation emerged in the United States. Alongside these, other agencies developed that specialized in the "transportation of missionaries, broadcasting media, health services, [and] mass evangelism" (Escobar 2003, 24). Note the technological focus. Escobar observes that, "their missionary concepts and methodologies, which reflected American cultural values and mores, became influential around the world" (2003, 24). Furthermore, he reminds us that missionaries must be concerned not only with orthodoxy—"concern for the integrity of the gospel"—but also with orthopraxis—"concern for the way in which the missionary practice is carried on" (Escobar 2003, 25).

Are these warnings from Smith and Escobar being considered by North American Bible translation organizations today? Are the cultural forces noted above driving the shift in the translation paradigm today? On January 21, 2015, the president/CEO of Wycliffe Associates emailed the organization's entire donor list with this claim: "For just $19,500, we can launch a full team of twenty-six translators into immediate action . . . to cut Bible translation time from years to weeks! . . . With your donation you can help national believers translate the *entire* New Testament in as little as *two weeks!*" (emphasis theirs). In an email to all staff worldwide, the president of WBT-USA commented that "cheaper, faster, and better quality" is one of his "favorite ways to describe Vision 2025 strategies for Bible translation."[12]

Escobar's concern seems appropriate to repeat here. He wonders if we are "in danger of carrying on mission as a purely human enterprise," suggesting that some might "regard mission as a manageable task that should be completed by a certain date, using appropriate technology, and following business principles of management by objectives" (Escobar 2003, 25–26). One might be tempted to conclude that I am anti-technology; I am not. However, I believe that some

---

12. As I read through Gravelle's (2010) article I could not help but notice the emphasis on similar values, particularly speed and efficiency.

might be overselling the benefits of technology without counting the associated costs. Media is a *tool*, not the message (Smith 1992), a means to an end rather than an end in itself. I encourage mission leaders to reflect on Escobar's conclusion:

> A great challenge to Christian missionaries in the coming years will be how to remain first and foremost messengers of Jesus Christ and not just harbingers of the new globalization process. They will have to use the facilities of the system without being caught by the spirit of the system. This is a question not only for the missionaries from affluent societies but also for those from poorer societies who are tempted some-times to rely mainly on the economic facilities and the technical instruments available to them. (2003, 63)

I concur! Sometimes mottos like "cheaper, faster, and better" become our mission mantras, as if time, money, and technology comprise the silver bullet of missionary success.[13] It may be time to "examine and revise our present models" (Escobar 2003, 25). My hope is that critiques such as this one might provide discussion points for mission leaders in today's technology-centric mission world.

CONCLUSION

It is clear that the pendulum is swinging within these three North American Bible translation organizations. It is swinging away from the use of western translators toward a primary use of national and local translators. While an inclusive corrective was much needed and will certainly benefit the wider Bible translation endeavor, there is

---

13. Some mission authors today seem to be overselling technology as a kind of "silver bullet" (e.g. Boehme 2011), while other writers seem to be more realistic (i.e. realizing that bullets, silver or not, can kill people). The latter fairly address both the positives and negatives associated with the use of modern technologies in missions (e.g. Pocock, Van Rheenen and McConnell 2005).

also the danger of the pendulum swinging too far, to the exclusion of all expatriate Bible translators.

"Passing the torch" was the title of a 2009 letter from the Wycliffe president to all WBT-USA staff, worldwide. "Passing the torch" would be a natural response to a crisis in missions—a declining interest in Bible translation, decreased funding for western missionaries, a belief that nationals can do it better, etc. Perhaps it would be most beneficial to carry the torch together. I have discussed some of the premises underlying a shift to a local-translator-only model, by three translation organizations. I have questioned the accuracy of these premises. We North Americans should not "outsource the mission of God" (Stetzer in Escober 2003, 120). Neither should we outsource Bible translation. The quality of translation will suffer, just as it would if we did not involve locals in the process.

I want to emphasize that I am not advocating a western-translator-only model, but rather a both/and strategy. While I understand the impetus of these organizations to shift toward the local-translator model, I encourage them to make haste slowly (see Smith 2011). In the introduction to *Finish the Mission: Bringing the Gospel to the Unreached and Unengaged* (Piper and Mathis 2012), David Mathis comments that "This amazing trend [the growth of the Global South] raises the question for some as to whether the West is done sending missionaries. Will it not be left to the Global South to finish the mission? The clear answer is no" (22). In the same tome, Michael Oh adds, "*Every* nation is a mission-sending nation" (2012, 87, emphasis his). We should not be only Bible translation facilitators, nor should we be only Bible translators. We should be both, alongside our local partners.

As an expatriate missionary, I am inspired to think about the rich opportunities of working alongside an ever-increasing multinational and multicultural workforce. As an anthropologist, I am interested in the depth of understanding and cultural creativity that diversity will bring to Bible translation. Again, Bible translation should remain a both/and, not an either/or, endeavor.

Finally, we must remember that paradigm shifts are never total. Some remain advocates for a minority opinion despite major paradigm shifts, and these are usually the harbingers of subsequent paradigm shifts (often corrective). In this case, there are other North American Bible translation organizations that continue to include western translators. I am encouraged to know that Bible translation is God's endeavor, not just man's. God will see it through to its completion.

REFERENCES

Arnold, Dean E. 1987. "Anthropology and the Future of SIL: What Her Critics can Teach Her." In *Current Concerns of Anthropologists and Missionaries,* edited by Karl Franklin, 113–122. Dallas, TX: International Museum of Cultures.

Bediako, Kwame. 1993. "Cry Jesus! Christian Theology and Presence in Modern Africa." *Vox Evangelica* 23: 7–26.

———. n.d. "The Role And Significance of The Translation Of The Bible," Accessed February 17, 2015. http://www.wycliffe.net/resources/missiology/globalperspectives/tabid/97/Default.aspx?id=1105#sthash.F00g3GLW.FtCfQ07I.dpuf.

———. 2004. *Jesus and the Gospel in Africa: History and Experience.* Maryknoll, NY, Orbis.

Boehme, Ron. 2005. *The Fourth Wave: Taking Your Place in the New Era of Missions.* Seattle, WA: YWAM Publishing.

Bosch, David. 1980. *Witness To The World: The Christian Mission in Theological Perspective.* London: John Knox Press.

Charles, J. P. 2009. "Global Christianity: Trends in Mission and the Relationship with Non-Western Missionaries Working Cross-Culturally in Thailand." MTh thesis, South African Theological Seminary.

Escobar, Samuel. 2003. *The New Global Mission: The Gospel from Everywhere to Everyone.* Downers Grove, IL: IVP Academic.

Fahlbusch, Erwin, Jan Milič Lochman, John Mbiti, Jaroslav Pelikan, and Lukas Vischer, eds. 2003. *The Encyclopedia of Christianity,* Volume 3 (J-N). Grand Rapids, MI: Eerdmans.

Franklin, K. J. 2012. "The Wycliffe Global Alliance—From a U.S. Based International Mission to a Global Movement for Bible Translation," MA (Theology) thesis, University of Pretoria. Accessed March 2, 2015. http://repository.up.ac.za /bitstream/handle/2263/32974/Franklin_Wycliff_Global_2012 .pdf?sequence=1.

Gravelle, Gilles. 2010. "Bible Translation in Historical Context: The Changing Role of Cross-Cultural Workers," *International Journal of Frontier Missiology* 27, no. 1: 11–20.

———. 2013. "Literacy, Orality and the WEB," *Orality Journal* 2, no. 1: 11–26. Accessed February 18, 2015. http://orality.net /literacy_orality_and_the_web.

Hersman, R. 2015. Personal communication with author, Jan. 12.

Lausanne Committee for World Evangelization. 2007. "The Two Thirds World Church." Lausanne Occasional Paper no. 44. Accessed February 1, 2015. http://www.lausanne.org/wp -content/uploads/2007/06/LOP44_IG15.pdf.

Noll, Mark. 1997. *Turning Points: Decisive Moments in the History of Christianity.* Grand Rapids, MI: Baker Academic.

Oh, Michael. 2012. "From Every Land to Every Land: The Lord's Purpose and Provision in the Lord's Prayer." In *Finish the Mission: Bringing the Gospel to the Unreached and Unengaged,* edited by John Piper and David Mathis, 83–109. Wheaton, IL: Crossway.

Olson, J. 2010. "Rethinking Missions: A Pathway for Helping the Next Generation to Fulfill Christ's Great Commission." DMin thesis, George Fox University.

Parish, David. n.d. "The Fourth Era of Modern Missions" Accessed February 1, 2015. http://worldmissionsevangelism.com/the-fourth -era-of-modern-missions-2/.

Piper, John, and David Mathis, eds. 2012. *Finish the Mission: Bringing the Gospel to the Unreached and Unengaged.* Wheaton, IL: Crossway.

Pocock, Michael, Gailyn Van Rheenan, and Douglas McConnell. 2005. *The Changing Face of World Missions. Engaging Contemporary Issues and Trends.* Grand Rapids, MI: Baker Academic.

Priest, Robert J., Douglas Wilson, and Adelle Johnson. 2010. "U.S. Megachurches and New Patterns of Global Mission," *International Bulletin of Missionary Research* 34, no. 2. Accessed December 7, 2015. http://www.internationalbulletin.org/issues/2010–02/2010–02–097-priest.html.

Pruett, Greg. 2015. Personal communication with the author, February 10.

Roy, Frank L. 1997. "Proceed with Caution; Part One," *Mission Frontiers* (January-February). Accessed December 7, 2015. http://www.missionfrontiers.org/issue/article/proceed-with-caution-part-1.

Sanneh, Lamin. 1987. "Christian Missions and the Western Guilt Complex," *The Christian Century* (April 8): 331–334.

Shaw, R. Daniel. 1994. "Social Profiles: Religious Views/Structures," Social Anthropology Course Syllabus and Lecture Notes, Fuller Seminary, Pasadena.

Shenk, Wilbert R. 2006. "Three Studies in Mission Strategy," *Mission Focus: Annual Review* 14: 90–122.

Sisk, Tim. 2014. Personal communication with author, November 26.

Smith, David W. 2003. *Against the Stream: Christianity and Mission in an Age of Globalization.* Leicester, UK: Intervarsity Press.

Smith, Donald K. 1992. *Creating Understanding: A Handbook for Christian Communication Across Cultural Landscapes.* Books on Creating Understanding.

———. 2011. *Make Haste Slowly: Growing Effective Intercultural Communication.* 2nd ed. Books on Creating Understanding.

Steffen, Tom. 2011. *The Facilitator Era: Beyond Pioneer Church Multiplication.* Eugene, OR: Wipf & Stock.

———. 2014. Personal communication with author, November 22.

Wilson, W. 2014. Personal communication with author, April 22.

Winter, Ralph D. 1999. "Four Men, Three Eras, Two Transitions: Modern Missions." In *Perspectives on the World Christian Movement: A Reader*, edited by Ralph D. Winter and Steven G. Hawthorne, 253–261. Pasadena, CA: William Carey Library.

Wycliffe USA Town Meeting. 2014 (video file). Accessed February 1, 2015. https://unity.insitehome.org/Executive/TownMeetings /default.aspx.

CHAPTER 9

UP FROM THE PIT—IMMIGRATION, DEPORTATION, PAIN, AND HOPE
Miriam Adeney

We hold these truths to be self-evident,
That all men are created equal.
That they are endowed by their Creator
with certain inalienable rights.
That among these are life, liberty,
and the pursuit of happiness . . .

When Thomas Jefferson wrote those words in our Declaration of Independence, he did not apply them to women or to nonwhite men who were slaves. A black woman, Sally Hemmings, gave birth to six of Jefferson's children, according to DNA and other evidence. Sally had no choice. She was his slave.

Nor did Jefferson's words on equality apply to those local residents who were considered "uncivilized tribes." For thousands of years Native Americans had been living on this land when Europeans first stepped ashore. Then, like the diminishing thunder of the bison, the thrum of the drums receded westward region by region. Those drums signaled not only violence but also peace, feasts, family, elders, marriages, births, creativity, bravery, and skill. Pulsing like the heart of the earth, their rhythms had reinforced order and coherence in communities. Increasingly they were silenced. Overall, our encounters with Native Americans constitute a sad, shameful chapter in our history, full of repeated betrayals, greed, and violence.

Were Jefferson's words hypocritical? Somewhat. Yet, however poorly they may have lived it out, Jefferson and his fellow writers glimpsed a truth: All people are created in the image of God, and all people have rights (cf. Fukuyama 2011).[1] That conviction helped fuel the subsequent American fight against slavery and the movement for women's suffrage. It motivated reformers to "struggle for America, for she is our unfinished dream," in the words of Carlos Bulosan, a Filipino migrant laborer and writer, in his autobiography *America Is in the Heart* (1943, 312).

Those ideals also attracted immigrants, as reflected in the renowned poem associated with the Statue of Liberty (1886):

> Give me your tired, your poor, your huddled masses
> yearning to breathe free
> The wretched refuse of your teeming shores.
> Send them, the hungry, tempest-tossed to me.
> I lift my lamp beside the golden door.

Gustav and Emma Fleischmann, my mother's parents, heard that call. They immigrated from Germany to Oregon's lush green Willamette Valley. Here on this rich soil hard work was rewarded. Farmers toiled, and the earth responded. Like Gustav and Emma, their neighbors up and down the road spoke German. That was the language of their Baptist church and their one-room schoolhouse. Only after the government took their farmland for an artillery practice range during World War II, and dispersed them, did English become their everyday tongue. Most Americans are descended from immigrants like these.

Yet today, eleven million people live in this land illegally. According to the law, they have no right to be here because they lack

---

1. Fukuyama (2011, 445) writes, "One of the most important changes in values and ideology that define the modern world—the idea of the equality of recognition—has deep roots; writers from Hegel to Tocqueville to Nietzsche have traced modern ideas of equality to the biblical idea of man made in the image of God. The expansion of the charmed circle of human beings accorded equal dignity was very slow, however, and only after the seventeenth century came eventually to include the lower social classes, women, racial, religious, and ethnic minorities, and the like."

residency documents. Nevertheless, more continue to slip across our borders, including tens of thousands of children, who pushed up from Central America in 2014.

This mobile population represents one of the great issues of our time. What is justice in relation to these people? What is mercy? How do we balance safeguarding our communities, upholding the law, and loving our neighbors? Furthermore, when we encounter migrants who are believers, how do we partner together in the new arenas of cross-cultural mission and ministry that are opening? These questions echo not only in America but worldwide as diasporas ebb and flow across many nations.

This paper focuses on the federal Northwest Detention Center, a 1500-bed facility south of Seattle housing people scheduled for deportation.[2] The detainees range from hardened criminals to those who have overstayed their student or work visas to others who lack complete papers simply because of irregularities in their journeys. For example, they may have no birth certificate because they were born in the middle of a war, and their non-English-speaking parents did not explain this.

Whatever the reason, when the gates clang shut, the words over the entry to Dante's inferno reverberate: "Abandon hope, all you who enter here." Suddenly a man loses his income, his long-term goals, and maybe even his spouse and children. Most detainees do not have attorneys. If they do not speak English, they may not understand what is happening. Most likely they will be dumped back in the land of their ancestors with or without money, or language, or family or friends. If that country has political or religious prejudices, they may undergo torture. Dante's warnings ring loud.

Yet a surprising and fruitful ministry with international reverberations has developed in the detention center. This paper briefly narrates that story. Several missiological themes appear:

---

2. The data for this paper was collected by Miriam Adeney between 2001–2015.

- Theology of culture and nation, of migration and exile, of justice and shalom
- Global diaspora movements: scope, causes, and mission opportunities and strategies
- Ethnic churches in the U.S.: vision, outreach, and possibilities for partnership
- Ministry within the U.S. government's legal restrictions

Each of these themes deserves to be studied at much more length. Hopefully future research will continue this.

THE CHINESE STORY

One morning in 2000 Jonathan and Sherry Soepardjo were enjoying coffee and flipping through the Seattle newspaper. Suddenly Sherry stabbed her finger on a news item. "Look at this, Jon. 'Chinese die in ship containers'!"

It turned out that several dozen Chinese had smuggled themselves into ship containers while the ships were loaded in China. Tragically, some had died during the voyage. The others were taken to a hospital, and then to the Northwest Detention Center.

"Why were they so stupid?" Jonathan grimaced. "Stowing away in a ship container! What were they thinking? It makes all of us Chinese look bad."

A few days later the phone rang. "I understand that you're the coordinators of a monthly prayer meeting that brings twenty Chinese churches together," the caller said. "Would you be willing to convene a meeting of local Chinese Christians? We want to explore the possibility of ministry to the Chinese who smuggled themselves here in ship containers. Everyone I contacted said, 'Call Jonathan and Sherry.' You are the ones who can coordinate a team of Chinese volunteers, they said."

What impacted Jon, however, was the way the caller had identified himself: "Hello, my name is Cal Uomoto . . ."

"A *Japanese* is more concerned about these Chinese than we are?" Jon thought. So challenged, the couple began a ministry that now has continued for fifteen years. Jon and Sherry have listened, cried, counseled, advocated, networked, witnessed, discipled, schlepped innumerable armloads of jackets and jeans and Bibles and study books to those who need them, housed ex-prisoners, been investigated by the FBI, trained teams of volunteers, visited deportees back in China, helped deportees plant churches in other countries—and they continue to this day weekend after weekend after weekend. "I have developed a profound respect for Jonathan and Sherry," says one colleague. "As far as I'm concerned, they're angels. You just can't see their wings."

To get volunteers for the ministry, Jon and Sherry tapped into twelve local Chinese churches. These included Taiwanese, mainlanders from the Peoples Republic of China, Southeast Asians like Sherry and Jon, and members of various denominations. That variety impressed the prisoners. "You guys are strange. You have communists and KMT people all together!" one detainee observed.

For the first worship service in 2000, about twenty-five prisoners showed up. Though suspicious, over time they thawed. Eventually many of them would trust God and commit themselves to Jesus as Lord, and would experience significant changes in their spirits. Like Dante's traveler, they had abandoned hope. Like the psalmist lamenting in Psalm 40, they had fallen into a pit. But, just as the psalmist testified, the Lord lifted them up, and put a new song in their mouths (Ps 40:2–3). Now, week-by-week, when an officer shouted "Chinese church!" detainees streamed in for worship, men for one hour and women the next. They learned to pray with power. One woman composed a song that was recorded onto a CD of Chinese Christian music. This was a source of great pride for the detainees. When some were transferred to other deportation centers, they viewed the move as a missionary journey, a chance to share the gospel in a new place.

Eventually the new Christians asked if they could be baptized. If they were deported, they wanted to go home as baptized believers. So volunteers tried to disciple them, and baptisms were arranged.

This was a challenge because each week some were deported and no one knew who would be next. It seemed wrong to postpone baptism for any sincere believer, but in the short period of time allowed for the worship service it was hard to include all who were asking for it. Quite a few were shipped out unbaptized, even though they had been scheduled for the rite.

In 2002, I was attending a gathering of ethnic ministries in the Seattle region. A Hispanic pastor had just reported on a network of Spanish-speaking churches. He sat down, and Jonathan Soepardjo rose to bring us up to date on ministry among the Chinese in the detention center. Midway through his report, Jonathan paused. Then he continued thoughtfully. "You know, the Chinese are not the major population in our deportation jails. It's the Mexicans. And lately the Mexicans have been coming to our Chinese services. We can't speak Spanish. They can't speak Chinese. But they sense that God is in the room. And they're so desperate that they come and wait for some crumbs to fall from the table." Jon looked at the Mexican pastor sitting right in front of him and said, "Brother, come over and help us!"

That opened a new chapter. Today there are six services every weekend attended by people from multiple nations. More intriguingly, volunteers *from* various nations have come forward. A team of Hispanics minister to Hispanics inside the jail. Russian-Americans reportedly have created a unique rehabilitation program for Russians who are out on bail awaiting sentencing. A Korean-American has an extensive multifaceted ministry. An Eritrean-American coordinates logistics. Chinese-Americans continue faithfully. Behind it all is the vision of the Japanese-American man who first telephoned Jonathan and Sherry.

The richly diverse church in America is represented by these volunteers. While they have neither great wealth nor education nor power in society, they do have the love of God and the rejuvenating experience of the Holy Spirit. They also have compassion for those in trouble, because they themselves have gone through hard times either in their homelands or in adjusting to a new country. For them, loving

God leads naturally to loving their neighbor. Even those who are poor will share out of their poverty, praying that God will multiply their resources like Jesus did the loaves and fishes until there is something for everybody.

Dreaming bigger, they hope to be channels of grace to the church as a whole in the United States. "Many Hispanics sincerely believe that God has led them here for a purpose: to play an important role in a revival of the Christian faith in this country," says Daniel Carroll-Rodas, professor at Denver Seminary (2008, 61). "Hispanic immigrants stand poised to change the Christian experience by broadening the evangelical agenda, incorporating a transformational missiology, reigniting a prophetic socio-political movement, and globally serving as ambassadors of a Kingdom cultural ethos that reconciles righteousness and justice," adds Samuel Rodriguez (2009), president of the National Hispanic Christian Leadership Council representing 40,000 Spanish-speaking congregations in the U.S. The jail volunteers and their ethnic churches represent humble immigrants who refuse merely to grab benefits from America. They are impelled to "give back," especially when they see compatriots in need. In so doing, they model service for all Christians in the United States.

THE SRI LANKAN STORY

After a cruel and bitter war shattered the nation of Sri Lanka, Fernando joined seven other men seeking their fortunes in fish canneries in Alaska. Each man signed a contract in which he pledged to pay $8,000 to the recruiting company out of his future earnings.

Seattle was a way station, a transit stop. As soon as their visas were stamped, they would board one more plane. So after the long transoceanic flight they disembarked blearily at Sea-Tac airport and took their places in line, holding papers to present to the officials.

Then the nightmare began.

"You have no valid entry documents," the official said.

Perplexed, they pressed forward, mustering the limited English language at their command. "Sir, these papers are for entry into the U.S. for two years. They are for our visas."

"Those papers are no good."

Perplexity changed to alarm. "But sir, we have each signed contracts for these papers. Each of us owes $8,000. We cannot back out. We were guaranteed entry."

"The 'company' that guaranteed these does not even exist. Step over to the side, please." Already the official was signaling a guard.

Hours of interrogation followed. Then they were corralled and herded into a van. "Where are we going?" they whispered to each other. They would not have long to wait. They were delivered to the Northwest Detention Center and slated for deportation.

Then, as it turned out, there was a block. Just a month before the men had embarked on their journey, Southeast Asia had been ravaged by a horrific tsunami. To keep from making matters worse, the U.S. government had issued a "Stay of Removal" order which postponed deportations to the most damaged nations, including Sri Lanka.

So the men phoned their families and told them, "We're not going to be able to work for a while, so we won't be able to send money." They didn't tell the whole truth, so as not to worry their families. But they could picture what was happening back home. In the months that followed, while they remained in limbo, they knew the recruiters would visit their families and demand interest payments. Threats would escalate. Violence would begin. In fact, one man's wife was beaten so badly that she miscarried her baby. Another whole family went into hiding.

Meanwhile, in the detention center kitchen there was an Indian worker who had been incarcerated for four years. One day he reached out to Fernando. "Here is a book that might help you," he said.

"What is it?"

"The Psalms from the Christian Scriptures."

Fernando shrugged. "Thanks."

The Indian offered something more. "If you're interested, there are worship services here every weekend . . ."

Soon all the Sri Lankans were attending the Sunday night services.

After eight months in detention, the Sri Lankans were offered the opportunity to live outside while awaiting sentencing. Some detainees are allowed to do this if someone will provide housing and food. It reduces the jail population. The parolees must report in to the office weekly.

Never having spent a day in America, the Sri Lankans knew nobody. However, at the jail worship service, they had met a volunteer named Sigrun, a professional social worker who was touched by their plight. Sigrun found a place for the men in a halfway house for ex-prisoners, and also found donors to pay the minimal rent. One room was unfurnished, so Sigrun and her husband went to IKEA and bought two bunk beds and bedding with their own credit card.

Sigrun helped the men find a food bank. Rent and living expenses totaled $2000–3000 per month, including bus fare and phone cards. The men did not qualify for benefits such as health care because they had no legal status. Nor could they work legally, even to earn money for basics like toothpaste.

The first week out, one man's dentures broke. "What are the resources in the community for this?" Sigrun asked. She found Bates Technical College, where dental students fixed the man's dentures free of charge.

One step at a time, needs were met. Sigrun went to churches, and took the Sri Lankans with her. Money came in steadily in small increments. She went to book clubs, and college students, and the Sons of Norway. The after-school program for the "21st Century Learning Center Grant" had drawn together many people who sponsored enrichment programs—Girl Scouts, local artists, 4-H clubs, university students. Now Sigrun presented the Sri Lankans' needs, and people responded, $5 here, $20 there.

Fernando saw that there is a heavenly Father who loves us. He began to write Bible verses on little pieces of paper and stick them on the wall next to his bed so he could see them when he fell asleep and when he woke up.

Victory Outreach Church is a congregation pastored by Isaiah Washington in the rough Hilltop neighborhood of Tacoma. This church runs a home for men who are leaving alcoholic patterns of life. The Sri Lankans started attending Bible studies there. Men in this program helped the Sri Lankans find informal work as day laborers in construction projects. These alcoholics also prayed for the detainees and witnessed to them.

Other people invited the men for Thanksgiving dinner. College students had a Christmas party for them. In their gift bags were stamps and phone cards and other practical things, because people were attentive to their needs. "We made ourselves available to them and to the Holy Spirit so when a question arose we were there, and not far away," Sigrun says.

One autumn day, for example, Sigrun dropped off packages of toilet paper. As she was opening her car door in order to leave, Fernando asked, "What does God's eternal Kingdom mean? What does it mean that Jesus is coming?" For half an hour, while the fall sun shone over the parking lot, Sigrun stood with her keys in hand and talked about Jesus the king. Through such small events discipleship occurred.

In January the men had been detained. In September they were released temporarily, pending a final decision. In December, the U.S. government lifted the "Stay of Removal" ban and prepared to deport them. Four absconded immediately, fearing death from the recruiters if they arrived home penniless.

Following a volunteer attorney's advice, Sigrun collected letters from the community to request that the remaining men be allowed to stay for six months in order to earn enough to pay off the recruiters. The letters helped to build their case.

Every week they reported to the government office. As Sigrun drove them to the appointment, they enjoyed an informal Bible study in the car. At the office the men would go upstairs and she would wait in the lobby. One morning she waited and waited. What was happening? She had a job, and needed to get to it. Then an official strolled in. "Miss Freeman, the request for the 'Stay of Removal' has been denied. We have rearrested the men. They will not be returning to the outside."

Fernando telephoned her cell phone from upstairs, where he was shackled hand and foot. His first words were, "This is God's will. We have been praying. This is what God has allowed."

The following Tuesday they were deported.

The U.S. government doesn't inform relatives when it deports people. The men's homes are many hours up in the mountains in their homeland. Sigrun called Fernando's wife so she could mobilize someone to meet them.

Once back home, Fernando found a job as a shuttle van driver. He also began a weekly Bible study in his home, and now serves as a leader in a men's fellowship. As well, he and his wife help out in a home that houses twenty orphan girls. Following the war and the tsunami, a local church had created this group home. Fernando's wife sews, cooks, and does domestic management, while Fernando helps with paperwork and administration. He also shares the gospel in hospitals, prisons, and general outreach. "It was God who brought me to the shores of America, spoke to me through the detention center ministry, and then took me back to my country of origin to be a witness," he says.

But the men did not step back onto Sri Lankan soil with a blank slate. Worse than empty-handed, they were deep in debt. High interest had been accumulating on their loans. Each man now owed $10,300, and there was no way they could work this off. It was close to ten years' income.

"This would not let me go," Sigrun said. "I sought the Lord's face."

Up to this point, the men had been blessed by a network of Christians. "This work could not have been done without a community of believers," Sigrun says. "So now I went back to that same extraordinary community and started raising the money for their loans, which totaled $30,900." Quite soon $20,600 was raised.

Sigrun made a proposal to Fernando. "Why don't you take this money and pay off Udea's and Ebert's loans completely at once?"

There was a risk. If Fernando did not pay anything on his own loan, he and his family were in danger. However, it made sense to stop the interest on two loans. He agreed. Sigrun continued raising money. By Memorial Day the final loan—Fernando's—was paid off in full.

"Here the gospel was lived out," Sigrun says. "Men who owed a debt that they could not pay saw it paid off by people who did not owe that debt. This is just what Jesus has done for us."

In Fernando's last letter from the detention center as he was just about to be deported, he wrote, "We had the idea of raising our heads and had just started, when everything went the other way. But I am happy, because that is God's will. I obey him. Still I have faith, trust, and believe in him. Mostly I love him. I have not given up. He has given me strength and courage to overcome my burden." Later in Sri Lanka he prayed, "Gracious Father, we thank you for those who have loved us enough to show us your way. Help us to pass on the message to those who are part of our lives now."

Fernando's story shows detainees' physical and social needs, which can be very basic. Sherry and Jon Soepardjo remember passing a Greyhound bus station where they saw a man juggling documents and bags of clothes and looking confused. "That guy must have just been released from the Center," they said to each other. They stopped, and asked the man, "Do you need help?"

"Yes, I'm going to Seattle but I don't know how to take the bus," he answered. They gave him directions, some food, a little money, and a jacket. He took Jon by the shoulders and looked him in the face, and tears trickled down his cheeks.

During the drive home, Jon cried too.

Volunteers also sometimes arrange rides to the airport, and gather gifts for the detainees' children at Christmas. Clearly the extent of community outreach to the Sri Lankan men's needs cannot be replicated for every detainee. But some degree of compassion, reflecting the God who loves, can be shown.

The logistical structure of this detention ministry has evolved over time. While grace-propelled volunteers constitute the core, the local World Relief office has stepped up to provide some oversight, funding a Honduran-born discipleship coordinator and a part time logistics coordinator who is Eritrean. A credentialed volunteer chaplain has become part of the team. A small government-vetted team of volunteers minister at the worship services inside the center, and others minister "at the window" outside, talking and praying with detainees one on one. The government requires the two teams to be separate completely. Other outsiders write encouraging letters to the detainees. Hispanic churches in the area are involved in the letter-writing ministry. World Relief has produced a twenty-page handbook in English and Spanish to guide the volunteers.

While giving Bibles to the detainees was prohibited in the early years, it is allowed now. With these Bibles, detainees themselves run daily Bible studies in all eighteen pods of the center. The worship team offers a little discipleship training to the leaders, squeezing in a few minutes here and there. Several incarcerated Hispanic women confess that leading Bible studies here fulfills a lifelong dream: "All my life I wanted to be a minister or missionary, and now at the center, I am!" Today baptisms are quarterly. In the past twelve months, 1,534 detainees have been baptized. At the most recent baptism, 260 people were baptized.

As for Fernando, compassionate mercy changed him so much that when he was deported back to Sri Lanka his daughter exclaimed, "I got a new Dad. He went to the U.S. one way and came back a different man." Recently she wrote to Sigrun, "I can't imagine this—the way Daddy is reading the Bible. I was shocked to see him in church, and the way he worships God. Every morning when I get up from my bed, my day begins with watching him praying to God. Oh what a wonderful thing it is. And now I see my little family as God's family. Not only Daddy's life was changed. Even I am reading the Bible and worshiping God."

THE LAOTIAN STORY

Lo was sentenced to fourteen years in a U.S. prison. His story introduces the heart-wrenching dilemmas that surround immigrants who are children.[3] Lo's family are Mien, a farming people in Laos. During the Vietnam War the CIA employed Mien as guides. After the war, the communist government of Laos retaliated against the "collaborators." Soon there was a spate of tribal people gushing down the mountains, through the jungles, and into refugee camps. Lo's family was part of this flood. It was in a camp that the family heard the gospel, and responded. Eventually they were repatriated to Seattle where Lo's mother got a job as a janitor, and his father was hired to do electrical work. They joined the local Mien church.

When they arrived, Lo was twelve years old. He could not read English, and found school frustrating. Like any teenager he wanted to belong. His parents also were new to the English language and American culture, and their child raising style was traditional and authoritarian. In the neighborhood were gangs—Black, Mexican, Vietnamese, Cambodian, and Laotian. Even boys who did not intend to join sometimes got slotted in. Lo drifted into that network. Before he knew it, he was packing a gun as a safety measure.

One evening shortly after Lo graduated from high school, he went out with some friends to eat noodles. Members of another gang showed up at the *pho* shop. Suddenly a fight erupted. In the melee Lo pulled out his gun and shot someone three times. Because of that, Lo

---

3. Much of this story was gathered by Laura Wright when she was a student at Seattle Pacific University.

was charged, convicted, and sentenced to fourteen years in prison. The first stop was three years in the maximum-security prison in Walla Walla, in a place called "blood alley."

His father counseled him, "It will be like sheep and wolves in there. Don't show your fear."

Whatever horrible things happened, Lo kept it all inside. Although raised in a Christian home, he did not reach out to God. He did not go to the chaplain. That was seen as weak, and weak people were prey. He tried to be as inconspicuous as possible. The prisoners divided racially. Some of the Asians had forty or fifty year sentences. As a group, they were known for their toughness and dangerousness, so other prisoners often left them alone.

When the prison got crowded Lo was transferred to Pueblo, Colorado, where it was boiling in the summer and freezing in the winter. Here, finally, he started to go to prison church services. As much as anything, he went so he wouldn't have to keep lying to his mother.

But he found more than he had expected. Strong Christians took an interest in him and mentored him.

One day in a pitch black room Lo found himself at the foot of the cross, suddenly illuminated by light. A hand reached into his chest and tore it open. He felt he was washed clean. Christ was real, and life in Christ was real. He could feel it, see it, hear it. Now he had an appetite to read the Bible and to pray. Before long, he was leading Bible studies.

Thirteen years passed. In the world outside, Lo's friends got married and started having children. His brothers and sisters grew up. Some got good educations and good jobs. Technology evolved. Meanwhile, Lo did not even know how to turn on a computer. He read at a sixth-grade level.

Finally he completed his sentence. What joy! And then—what horror! Lo was rearrested immediately and transferred to the Northwest Detention Center to be deported.

Why? Lo is not a citizen. He is an alien who committed a crime and lost the opportunity to stay here. When Lo's parents first arrived in America, they were told that their children could apply for citizenship when they became adults. Yet before Lo was old enough to apply, he was in prison. Now, with a criminal record, he would be sent to a land where he had no family and no connections and a government ready to punish him for what some Mien had done a generation ago.

Outside the jail, Lo's Mien church lifted him up to God in prayer.

The deportation center seemed like jail all over again except that there were bigger cells with more people and no yard for exercise. In Lo's section there were Russians. "Watch out. They might cause you trouble," someone warned him. So he was careful.

One night he overheard something strange. The Russians were singing songs, and Lo knew the tunes. No question about it, those were worship songs. How could that be? Cautiously Lo approached the Russians.

"Are you Christians?" he asked hesitantly.

"Yes, we are."

Then Lo introduced himself. "I'm a Christian, too."

The Russians became his friends, his brothers. They experienced the power of the gospel. "There is neither Jew nor Greek, male nor female, bond nor free, but all are one in Christ" (Gal 3:28). From a human perspective, Russians and Mien have little in common. They are so far apart that they are not even enemies. Yet in Christ they came together. In the place where they had lost everything, where they might have defensively guarded what little space and rights they had, they became true friends.

Like Fernando from Sri Lanka, Lo has been let out on parole while his case is pending. He reports to the Department of Corrections every week. The reason he has not yet been deported is because Laos refuses to receive people in his category. If that changed, Lo would be shipped off.

He cannot get a regular job because he has no legal papers. Old gang friends placed a running bet on who would be the first to "bag him a girl," but Lo did not want to be part of that any more. A woman in the church was willing to take a chance on him, and they got married. Recently they had their first baby.

When Lo thinks about his parents growing older, he feels an obligation to help them financially. For a long time his brothers and sisters shouldered that responsibility. Now it's his turn, he thinks. The family has a garden, and he dreams of finding some farmland where they could grow more food. In prison he learned to do beautiful woodwork, and he dreams of a wood shop. Meanwhile he volunteers at the local food bank and in lots of church activities.

In particular he is learning to help the church in its IT needs.

Second-generation migrants present special challenges. Some Russian and Ukrainian young men have fallen into Lo's predicament. Although children of strong believers, they incurred DUIs or similar charges. Not yet citizens, they are slated for deportation, even though all their family is in the U.S. To meet this challenge, Russian Christian volunteers reportedly have developed a rehabilitation farm where deportees can live together in wholesome community away from vices and temptations while they await their sentencing. Here they can develop new habits. Then, when their cases are considered, it can be argued that they have something positive to offer to American society.

IMMIGRATION AND THE LAW

Lo broke the law. So did Fernando. So did the Chinese who arrived in ship containers. This is serious. Law matters. We must be able to trust people to tell the truth and honor agreements. Otherwise, our society will fall apart. We also need secure borders. New people are welcome, but must be integrated in ways that increase *shalom* in our communities.

Yet human laws are not eternal. In particular, U.S. immigration law is flawed. Both Democrats and Republicans agree on that.

Multiple theological implications are present in the previous two paragraphs. Other relevant theological motifs include these:

- All persons are made in the image of God and must be honored as such (see Gen 1:26; Lev 19:34; Deut 10:19).
- Movements of people are common in Scripture and in history. Consider for example, Abraham; Jacob and his sons; Moses; Ruth; David among the Philistines; Daniel and all the displaced Jews in the Babylonian and Persian periods including Jeremiah, Esther, and Nehemiah; Philip and other Christians who were scattered; Paul and his missionary companions from Barnabas to Luke to Priscilla and Aquilla; John in Ephesus and Patmos; and Jesus and his family fleeing as refugees to Egypt.
- God hears the cries of the needy, and models and mandates compassion for them. Consider Isaiah 58; Hannah's prayer; Mary's prayer; Amos; and thousands of other verses.
- God's Kingdom society embraces a diversity of cultures (see Pss 67, 100; Is 60; Rev 5, 7).
- Brothers and sisters in Christ are particularly close to our hearts and welcome in our homes (Matt 25:31–46; Gal 6:19; Heb 13:2).

Clearly, keeping the law is one of several significant mandates surrounding immigration issues. At the practical level, compassionate investigation may reveal that some detainees' cases should be reconsidered because these persons would face persecution back home. Others may have begun legal residency processes in good faith, but lost papers along the way. Yet others do merit deportation, even our brothers and sisters in Christ. Empathetic accompaniment can smooth this process. As the next section shows, good may come from such deportations.

PLANTING CHURCHES GLOBALLY

"Now I know why I came to America—so that I could be deported and go home with the gospel for my people." This is the testimony of some deportees.

Wang was converted at the Northwest Detention Center, discipled, and then deported back to China. But the region to which he returned was just as poor as when he left. Then an uncle working in Ecuador wrote to Wang. "You want to make money? Come over here. We have a shrimp-fishing village—totally Chinese—and we're doing well."

So Wang travelled to Ecuador, and began to make good money. Soon, however, he was sending pleas to his Christian friends in Seattle. "There's no church here. I'm a young believer. I don't know enough to run a church. Come down and help me start one."

"Oh, I don't want to go there," Sherry thought. "The challenges *here* are enormous. The demands on our time are crushing. What do we know about Latin America? Or even about church-planting? No, that's not our call. Somebody else will have to do that."

But Wang kept on phoning.

"Surely there are churches closer than Seattle!" Sherry reasoned. "Ecuador is supposed to be a Christian country."

"Yes, but the churches are Spanish-speaking, and not adapted to our culture. They have no appeal," Wang insisted. For two and a half years Wang pleaded. One day he said, "I'm not going to hang up the phone until you give me a date."

Jon and Sherry had been challenging Chinese senior citizens who had money to go on short-term mission trips. Now they invited their retired friends, "Would you like to go to Ecuador?"

People from four Chinese churches formed a team.

Once in Ecuador, they drew a map of the village and went door to door to all the homes and shops, inviting people to a Christian worship service. Thirty Chinese showed up. Eight were already prepared for baptism, so they went to a swimming pool and a lay pastor baptized them.

When Sherry saw how spiritually needy the people were, and how eagerly they responded, she repented that she had not gone sooner.

Since then, several Chinese churches across America have sent teams. As one team was preparing, the Ecuadorian-Chinese church representative quizzed the American-Chinese pastor. "OK Pastor, we'd love to have your team come. Can they sing?"

"No, not really," the pastor confessed.

"Can they preach?"

"No, I'm sorry."

"But what can they do?"

"Well, they're all high tech."

"OK, you can be a computer team. Everybody here has a broken computer at home. They're all made in China, and the Ecuadoreans cannot fix them."

Other popular teams have been comprised of acupuncturists. Another team conducted an English camp for the Chinese kids. "One of the very beautiful things is to see the different churches working together," Sherry says. "Before, we were all separate. Now it's like we belong to one family."

For a few years, the Ecuadorian church received sermons on Skype from a rotating group of pastors and speakers, including Jonathan. A Chinese woman missionary from San Francisco who was already in Ecuador helped out. Now the church has hired their own pastor, a Chinese businessman-turned-pastor from Argentina.

There are tensions between Taiwanese and mainland Chinese in this village, but the church is building bridges, reaching out to new arrivals, orienting them and sharing insider knowledge. "Even our own people would not tell us the ropes. But you share product knowledge, brands, techniques," the newcomers marvel. This draws them to Christ, and to each other.

Wang was deported to bless Ecuador—and China. Fernando was deported to bless Sri Lanka. This has been repeated in several countries. In the words of the man with the original vision, Cal Uomoto, "The Holy Spirit goes ahead of us, and God's witnesses move from the jail to the ends of the earth."

UP FROM THE PIT

Immigration is one of the large issues facing Americans today. Christians in the United States are serving migrants in a variety of ways.

This paper explores one ministry. The cases in this study put faces on the issue, faces of migrants and also faces of those who bless them.

Through these stories, we have noted some of the economic and political impetuses to global migration. We have observed U.S. Christians responding, particularly members of ethnically-specific churches. We have glimpsed strands of theology of immigration, of justice, and of culture. We have seen cooperation between groups of volunteers. Admittedly, their power is fragile. Many of them are among the weaker people in our society. Discipling in the detention center remains a big problem due to the shortness of time and the linguistic and cultural challenges even in procuring language-appropriate materials. However, daily Bible studies led by the detainees themselves offer grassroots accountability. In this case a weakness—the volunteers' limited access, equipment, and training—may have propelled the inmates to develop leadership skills and take responsibility. Clearly some have grown in Christian maturity, even planting churches in other countries.

The Spirit-inspired creativity of volunteers from diverse ethnic communities and their interethnic cooperation is a shining strength in this ministry. Because of their perseverance, detainees learn not to abandon hope like Dante's traveler. They are not left in the pit, but lifted up with a new song, like the psalmist (Ps 40:1–3). They go home not as felons but as ambassadors of reconciliation (2 Cor 5:18–20).

REFERENCES

Bulosan, Carlos. 1943. *America Is in the Heart: A Personal History.* San Diego, CA: Harcourt, Brace and Company.

Carroll-Rodas, Daniel. 2008. *Christians at the Border.* Grand Rapids, MI: Baker Academic.

Fukuyama, Francis. 2001. *The Origins of Political Order: From Prehuman Times to the French Revolution.* New York: Farrar, Strauss, and Giroux.

Lazarus, Emma. 1886. "The New Colossus." Plaque installed on the Statue of Liberty.

Rodriguez, Samuel. 2009. "Kingdom Culture Christianity: The Hispanic Transformation of American Evangelicalism," Paper presented to the Annual Meeting of the National Association of Evangelicals, Orlando, FL.

PART THREE   The Practice of Mission

CHAPTER 10

THE NECESSITY FOR RETAINING FATHER AND SON TERMINOLOGY IN SCRIPTURE TRANSLATIONS FOR MUSLIMS

Mark Hausfeld, Ben Aker, Jim Bennett, Jim Hernando,
Tommy Hodum, Wave Nunnally, Adam Simnowitz

INTRODUCTION

This paper will address the necessity of retaining Father and Son terminology in Scripture translations due to the missiological implications. In addition, it will discuss the language of sonship in Intertestamental literature, as revealed in the Dead Sea Scrolls and Rabbinic texts. Finally, it will illustrate the familial language and the Christology evident in the New Testament.

MISSIOLOGICAL IMPLICATIONS

The past two decades have witnessed the birth and proliferation of specialized Scripture translations for Muslims that remove from the text and/or redefine the divine familial terms Father, Son, and Son of God with the substitution of alternative terms such as "Guardian" for Father and "Caliph of God" or "Beloved of God" for Son. While this is not the only feature of such translations, it is the feature to which this paper is confined. Of special concern are the consequences this practice sets in motion, especially regarding textual corruption and the promotion of heterodox views regarding the nature of God, the deity of Jesus, and the Trinity.

From the standpoint of Christian mission, this goal of removing offensive language from the biblical witness is a long-standing issue of considerable importance. There are innumerable occasions where members of the ancient receptor culture (religious, social, civil, etc.)

found the gospel offensive; however, there is no evidence that the Christian church made accommodations to remove the offense (Gk. *skandalon*) of the cross to Judaism or Greco-Roman paganism. In fact, Paul exalts such teaching as the "wisdom of God" (1 Cor 1:21–24).

The Romans of Jesus and Paul's day were involved in the worship of Caesar and to declare "Caesar is Lord" was an act of civil loyalty to Rome. The Christian declaration of faith that "Jesus is Lord" flew in the face of Rome's emperor cult worship. Moreover, Christian commitment to *one* God was an offense to the polytheistic Romans who regarded them as virtual atheists, according to Pliny the Younger (*Ep.* 10.96).[1] Nevertheless, Christians did not budge from their Trinitarian monotheism, even though a tri-theism would have been much more palatable to the prevailing religious culture.

More to the issue at hand, it is patently clear that Christianity was at odds with Judaism's monotheistic claims when it proclaimed that Jesus was the Messiah, Son of God, yet they did not remove this offense. We know that it was indeed an offense, because on at least one occasion the Jews sought to kill Jesus for saying "I am the Son of God" (John 10:32–36; 19:7). One would think that the Apostle John, knowing the hostility of the Jews toward this proclamation, would have mitigated the controversy by avoiding the phrase. Instead, the phrase appears more often in his gospel than any other.[2] Again, one might think that John, a Jew, would have understood the scandal of Jesus' divinity before a Jewish audience and sought to lessen the offense if he thought it was necessary to build a bridge to the Jews. However, nowhere in John's Gospel, or any other of his writings, is

---

1.   The charge of atheism is confirmed by Athenagorus who listed it among the three most common charges against Christians. It meant that Christians did not pay homage to the state gods of Rome, nor the pagan gods, in *Plea* 3 (cf. Ferguson 1993, 558–559).

2.   John uses the term nine times as compared with seven times in Matthew, three times in Mark, and six times in Luke.

there evidence that the evangelist avoids calling or identifying Jesus as the Son of God.[3]

This leads us to ask why the church has only now seen it necessary to accommodate Muslim sensitivities and has ignored very similar ones within Judaism, and done so for two millennia. If such accommodation is carried further, will we begin to create translations that remove the offense to sects within Judaism? Should we now create translations to accommodate, select groups within Hinduism, Buddhism, Jainism, Sikhism, Lamaism, Taoism, Confucianism, and Zoroastrianism, not to mention the innumerable current folk religions? If this strategy, indeed, removes obstacles to evangelizing these religions, why has the church not used such accommodations long before now, especially considering that formal Bible translation has been going on almost as long as the church has been in existence, at least from the time of Origen (185–254)?

We believe that the biblical witness of saving faith in Jesus Christ is inextricably tied to the belief in and confession of Jesus *specifically being the Son of God.* We further understand that the witness of the Holy Spirit within the believer, the presence of God in the believer's life, overcoming the world, having genuine belief in Jesus Christ, possessing eternal life, and enjoying a relationship with God the Father are all contingent on the belief, acceptance, and confession of Jesus Christ *as the Son of God* (John 20:31; 4:15; 1 John 5:10–12; 2:22–23).

What is being proposed is *not* simply a matter of producing a better contextualized translation for use within a global language or ethnic group, but a removal of familial language from the biblical text—language that is not only relevant but essential to the biblical witness concerning Jesus Christ and His relationship to God, His Father. This analysis and critique is organized around two fundamental questions: *Can the gospel of Jesus Christ be properly understood apart from*

---

3.   For a fuller look at the familiar witness of the Johannine corpus, see the expanded edition of this paper available at FatherSon.ag.org.

the use of familial language? Was Jesus' identity as the Messiah intrinsically bound to His filial relationship as a Son to God, His Father?

Muslims, due to false teaching from their holy book, the Quran (Arberry, 1996),[4] reject Jesus as the Son of God (cf. Sura 2:116; 4:171; 9:30; 10:68; 19:88–93; 21:26; 23:91). Proponents of specialized translations argue that the phrase Son of God and the related terms of "son" and "father" must not be literally translated in the Bible, since to do so conveys incorrect and inaccurate meaning to Muslim readers. Instead, meaning-based equivalents from their natural or heart language must be substituted in order to communicate the accurate or properly intended meaning behind this terminology. There are a number of errors with this argument, of which we highlight the following:

- It denies that Father and Son terminology are divinely inspired. This is related to the linguistic fallacy that meaning is not and cannot be communicated by specific words.
- It presupposes that the text of the Bible does not provide sufficient context for a person to understand the meaning of Father and Son terminology within its pages.
- It implies that Muslims are intellectually inferior people who cannot understand language in its context.
- It ignores the role of God the Holy Spirit to give proper understanding of Scripture.
- It makes relative all biblical doctrines drawn from Father and Son terminology, such as the adoption of believers as sons and children of God.

The lack of uniformity regarding what constitutes non-literal equivalents that accurately convey the meanings of Father and Son terminology engenders confusion for Muslims. Will Muslims see Jesus as "Caliph"—which for them is the historical representative of

---

4. All Quranic quotations and/or references are from Arberry (1996).

Islam entrusted with its promotion and defense by physical force, or will they see Jesus as the "Beloved Messiah"?

Other practical missiological ramifications that are relevant but beyond the scope of this paper are:

- Exposing Christians to the charge of being misleading
- Damaging the reputation of Christians for having corrupted the word of God
- Bringing confusion on numerous levels to both Christians and non-Christians
- Confirming the mistaken views that Muslims have about Son of God
- Strengthening the Islamic view that Christianity (i.e. the message of the Bible) is false, that Christians cannot be trusted, and that Islam is true.

Thus, specialized Scripture translations that remove Father and Son terminology ultimately hinder evangelism among Muslims.

In recent years, deconstructionists have argued that meaning, like beauty, is very much in the eye of the beholder and, thus, it is important to shift the authority for determining the meaning of a text from the author to the *reader*. Another factor is the issue of syncretistic accommodations in Muslim evangelization. Such syncretistic accommodations may include providing natural language Scripture translations for Muslims who acknowledge Jesus as Messiah and may be encouraged to identify themselves as Muslims, or who consider the Quran as authoritative and practice the five pillars of Islam, including the affirmation that "there is no deity except Allah, and Muhammad is his messenger."

An increasing number of national constituencies, Bible Societies, and former Muslims have expressed alarm about the proliferation of specialized Scripture translations for Muslims in their countries. Especially given our privilege to partner with national churches around the world, it is our belief that their position on this issue should be honored.

THE PRIMARY CONCERN

At the heart of this issue is whether familial words in the biblical manuscripts are divinely inspired terms or terms that can be replaced with alternative, non-literal renderings. First, consistency with the verbal inspiration of Scripture requires that the *nouns* Father and Son, as they are used in the biblical manuscripts, can *only* be accurate when literally translated in order to convey the meaning that God intended.[5] The verbal inspiration of Scripture includes the specific words themselves[6] and we are warned against changing any of God's words: "Every word of God is tested . . . He is a shield to those who take refuge in Him. Do not add to His words lest He reprove you, and you be proved a liar" (Prov 30:5–6, NASB). Jesus himself stated: "And the Scripture cannot be broken" (John 10:35, NIV). When Jesus made this statement, He neither acquiesced to a hostile audience, nor hesitated to quote a passage of Scripture from the Old Testament that could be easily misunderstood. Instead, He affirmed the verbal plenary nature of divine revelation (i.e. God's Word) (see Ps 82; John 10:30–39).

Second, biblical scholars concur that throughout Scripture, God confirms specific truths on the basis of repetition (Gen 41:32; Deut 19:15; 2 Cor 13:1). In the Greek manuscripts of the New Testament, Father (*pater*), in reference to God, appears 260 times; Son of God (*huios tou theou*), in reference to Jesus, appears 45 times; and Son (*huios*), in reference to Jesus, appears 79 times.[7] Because of the sheer

---

5.   Father, Son, and even God are all nouns that can be literally translated into other languages—the only way to accurately convey their meanings as used in the biblical manuscripts. This is due to the fact that fathers and sons exist in all cultures, providing the confirmation of the witness that humanity has been created in God's image (Gen 1:26–27; Jas 3:9).

6.   For example, see "seed" in Gal 3:16 where Paul quotes from language spoken to Abraham. Understanding this as a prophecy of Jesus is dependent on the grammatical form of the word.

7.   The figures for Father were exported from Logos Bible Software 4 and the figures for Son and Son of God were exported from BibleWorks 9.

volume and repeated use of the terms Father, Son of God, and Son, any alteration to just one of these terms introduces serious change that undermines the integrity of the divine message of salvation found in the Bible.

Third, the argument that the literal translations of Father and Son terminology communicate incorrect, inaccurate, and wrong meaning because they imply biological or sexual connotation, is misleading. For example, the Arabic *ibn Allah* refers to Son of God. Since *ibn* is the most natural way that any father would refer to his son in Arabic, this is the accurate translation of the Greek, *huios* (Son).[8] As in all languages, the context in which *ibn* is used determines whether or not it refers to a son that has resulted from a biological relationship. Native Arabic speakers overwhelmingly insist that *ibn* is the correct word to use when translating the Greek phrase *huios tou theou* (Son of God) and that the context clearly explains that no sexual meaning is implied. Nowhere in Scripture does *ibn* imply a physical relationship between God the Father and Mary. For example, Luke 1:34–35 and Matthew 1:18–25 make it clear that no sexual relations were involved in the case of Jesus' conception. In these passages, *ibn* is used to describe the *son of a virgin* (also in Isa 7:14).

Samuel Zwemer, known as the "Apostle to Islam" and one of the most astute observers ever of Islam, provides further insight:

> Even though we [stop] the confusion concerning this expression ("Son of God") and we dispel from their understanding the clouds of bias and error, we say to our Muslim neighbor that the Book of God, the

---

8.   This is easily confirmed by native Arabic speakers, Arabic dictionaries, and Arabic translations of Scripture from at least the ninth century until the present. The following is a partial list of these translations, all of which use *ibn* (son) for *huios* whether for human sons, as well as the Son and Son of God in reference to Jesus Christ: Vatican Arabic MS 13 (c. 9th century), Mt. Sinai Arabic Codex 151 (c. 9–11th centuries), Roman Catholic (1671), Van Dyck (1865), Jesuit version (1880), Kitab Al-Hayat (1988), Jesuit, revised (1988), Today's Arabic Version (1992).

New Testament, does not say even once in its description of Jesus as the only Son of God, that God, the strong and glorious, is a [biological] father (Arabic *waalid*) but always uses, to His glory, the word, "Father" (Ar. *ab*) in a general, spiritual sense. There does not appear in the New Testament, regarding Jesus, that He is the [biological offspring] (Ar. *walad Allah*), that is, a [biological] son [physically] begotten from God. What appears, instead, is that He is the "Son" of God (Ar. *ibn Allah*) and the differences between the two expressions are as clear as the [shining] sun to him who has eyes! An adopted son is called, by common convention, "a son" (Ar. *ibn*) [as opposed to] a [biological] son (Ar. *walad*). What is a [biological] son (Ar. *walad)* but one born from a [physical] birth to two parents, from a real, natural birth? The Arabs [also] commonly use the word, "father," in a spiritual sense, as well as in a general sense. They [often] say, "father of mercy" (*Abu Al-Rahma*), "father of truth" (*Abu Al-Haqq*), "father of encouragement" (*Abu Al-Shujaa'a*), "father of generosity" (*Abu Al-Fadl*), etc. (Zwemer 1906, 78)

Given that in every language the word(s) for son or father (without any context) normally implies biological relationship (since most sons are a result of such relationships), there is no language where son could be used without *any* possible implication. That is, there would always be the slight chance that some people (in any language) might hear the term Son of God before they hear the explanation of what that means from the birth narratives in Matthew and Luke (which clarify that there was no sexual activity) and thus they might think God had a sexual relationship with Mary, especially in societies that have no prior biblical knowledge or where they have been taught false information about the Bible. Even in English, the phrase Son of God has the possibility of having this implication. It is better to translate the Bible accurately, using Father-Son terms as the Holy Spirit did, and then teach people the context so that everyone understands God's message accurately.

The command to teach is central to the mandate the church has received from Jesus (Matt 28:18–20). Further, Paul, in writing to the Ephesians about Christ giving individuals to the church, listed *teachers* as key personnel with great responsibility "for the equipping of the saints for the work of service, to the building up of the body of Christ; until we all attain to the unity of the faith, and of the knowledge of the Son of God, to a mature man, to the measure of the stature which belongs to the fullness of Christ" (Eph 4:12–13, NASB). This emphasis on our responsibility to teach in no way nullifies or diminishes our steadfast belief that a full understanding of Jesus only occurs through the work of the Spirit of God (Matt 16:13–17; John 16:13–15). Myer Pearlman states:

> The Holy Spirit is the Interpreter of Jesus Christ. He does not bestow a new or different revelation, but rather opens the minds of men to see deeper meaning of Christ's life and words. As the Son did not speak of Himself, but spoke what he had received from the Father, so the Spirit will not speak of Himself as from a separate store of knowledge, but will declare what He hears in that inner life of the Godhead. (1937, 287–288)

A faithful teacher of the Bible requires the tool of translations that include the divine familial terms of Father and Son and a steadfast belief in the Spirit of God to convince men of this truth.

THE LANGUAGE OF SONSHIP IN INTERTESTAMENTAL LITERATURE:
THE DEAD SEA SCROLLS AND RABBINIC TEXTS

At Qumran, a number of passages clearly refer to a coming figure that is stunningly close to what we see in later New Testament texts. These texts have revolutionized our understanding of pre-Christian Palestinian Jewish messianic speculation and spells the death of the thesis that Jesus' filial/divine messianic identity derived from Hellenistic Christianity borrowing from Greco-Roman paganism.

Among the terms that appear in the Dead Sea Scrolls is "the Messiah of Israel" who is "begotten" by God (1Q28a). Elsewhere, He is referred to as "your [David's] seed," as the "Branch of David" of whom God says, "I will be a father to you and you will be a son to me" (4Q174). In 4Q246, He is called "Son of God" (cf. Luke 1:35) and "Son of the Most High" (cf. Luke 1:33). 4Q369 declares, "You [God] made him for you a first-born son . . . to be a prince and a ruler in all [the] inhabited world" upon whom is placed the "divine/heavenly crown." In 4Q534, it is possible that the Messiah is described as omniscient and as "the elect of God" from whom is "His birth and the spirit of His breath." Lastly, the Melchizedek figure is presented in 11Q13. He is a priestly-messiah who comes from heaven in the last days to defeat Satan, judge the wicked, and exalt the righteous. He is further identified as "The Anointed/Messiah of the Spirit about whom Daniel spoke—an anointed, a prince" who announces "the year of God's grace," and who is declared divine three different times. As noted in the discussion, although the specific term son does not appear here, the context of sonship is clearly in view, as evidenced by the appearance of "inheritance" twice and by His status as leader of the "sons of the Most High."

This evidence demonstrates that the ideas of Messiah as son and as divine have developed far beyond their Old Testament moorings. It also demonstrates that various apocryphal and pseudepigraphical texts employing similar language, which were previously dismissed as later

Christian interpolations, should now be considered as legitimate parallels with the Qumran material and as precursors to New Testament usage. Lastly, it is quite evident that the Bousset-Bultmann thesis of paganistic origins for Jesus' divine sonship should be abandoned.[9]

Rabbinic evidence is scant, but Qumran has made clear that the rabbis were not unfamiliar with the concept of divine sonship. Probably in reaction to Christian interpretation, near-complete avoidance of language suggestive of sonship and deity is obvious, including contexts where interpretation of Old Testament texts provide ample opportunity (e.g., 2 Sam. 7; Ps 2, 110, etc.). Nevertheless, at least one text has survived (*Midrash Tehillim* 2:9) that explicitly weds messianic, filial, and divine language. Other rabbinic texts clearly identify specific individuals who enjoy especially intimate relationship with God as son.

That the Qumranic and rabbinic materials did not come into existence in a vacuum is evident from similar language in the Apocrypha, the Pseudepigrapha, Philo, the New Testament, and even Josephus. Messianic speculation was diverse in the period preceding the advent of Jesus and Christianity, but can clearly be said to have included messianic sonship *and* messianic deity in at least some circles. These ideas were neither new with, nor restricted to, the authors of the New Testament. Therefore, to better understand the person of Jesus of

---

9. The construct championed by W. Bousset and popularized by Rudolf Bultmann, that Jesus' divine sonship derives from pagan notions of sons of gods (Bultmann 1951, 1:128–29), must be abandoned in favor of sources ideologically, linguistically, and geographically closer to Jesus and the movement He spawned. More than a half-century ago, Nock (1963, 45) inveighed, " . . . attempts which have been made to explain [Jesus' divine sonship in early Christianity] from the larger Hellenistic world fail." More recently and in light of even more evidence from the Intertestamental Period, Neufeld (1997, 140) has observed, "Labels such as 'Son of God' and 'Son of Man' cannot be removed from Jewish messianism and relegated to later, Hellenistic Christianity. The title 'Son of God' is not the product of a church that arbitrarily changed 'Son of God' from designating a messianic king to denoting a figure of heavenly origin . . . A heavenly, transcendent Messiah was not a unique invention of the Christian community but the outgrowth of reflection that had its roots in Judaism."

Nazareth, we must be willing to do three things: (1) embrace the titles ascribed to Him in their original contexts; (2) recognize their textual origins in the Hebrew Bible; and (3) be willing to follow the development of these messianic concepts throughout the relevant literatures that connect the two Testaments.

FAMILIAL LANGUAGE AND NEW TESTAMENT CHRISTOLOGY

Careful study of the New Testament makes abundantly clear that the familial language of Son/Son of God and Father is not only pervasive but inextricably woven into the fabric of New Testament Christology. In fact, familial language demands our theological reflection because of its strategic placement alongside and inter-connection with the doctrines of God, the Messiah/Christ, and salvation itself.

The doctrine of Christ, as we have seen, is an eschatological advancement in the revelatory self-disclosure of God (Heb 1:1). To be precise, we can declare, in concert with the Apostle John, that we cannot truly know God apart from the revelation He has given in the person of His Son Jesus, the Christ (1 John 5:20; cf. 2:13). This revelation, as Hebrews 1:1 states, is the culmination of salvation history, and this culminative expression is conveyed through one whom God identifies as His Son. Therefore, sonship is not incidental or peripheral, but an essential feature of that eschatological revelation. While the titles, Son and the Son of God find location in messianic contexts, they are not simply equivalent and alternative references to the title of Messiah. That is, identifying Jesus as the Son of God says something more about the Messiah than Judaism understood or expected from their reading of the Old Testament. That *something more* came through a special revelation of God—the incarnation of the Word (John 1:1, 14). This revelation is presented and interpreted throughout the New Testament. The corporate witness of the New Testament establishes that Jesus, the Christ of God, bears a unique filial relationship to God, His Father. That relationship is without precedent or true analogy. He is uniquely the Son of God!

Moreover, our examination of the New Testament has shown that this identity is indispensable to the gospel. To preach the true apostolic faith (Jude 3) is to preach the divinely revealed identity of Jesus Christ. To repeat the sobering assessment of Bruce Waltke, "It is inexcusable hubris and idolatry on the part of mortals to change the images by which the eternal God chooses to represent himself" (2007, 244).

THE WITNESS OF THE PAULINE CORPUS

The Testimony of Paul's Damascus Road Experience (Acts 9)

Luke's record of Paul's so-called conversion on the road to Damascus presents an almost unbelievable account when we know the background of the apostle, who and what he was within Judaism, and what he believed. He was a monotheistic Jew. In fact, he was a Pharisee zealously committed to following Mosaic Law and did so through Jewish tradition handed down by his rabbinic forefathers (Gal 1:14). He became a brilliant rabbi under the tutelage of the renowned Gamaliel (Acts 22:6) and a passionate defender of Mosaic Law and rabbinic tradition. His zeal, as Paul admits (Phil 3:6) and Luke recounts (Acts 8), led him to persecute Christian believers in the church resulting in their imprisonment and death (Acts 22:4). Acts 9 tells us of his encounter with the risen Christ on the Damascus road, one which left him blind and certainly bewildered. However, God directs Ananias to lay hands on him to regain his sight, and something more than physical healing takes place. He is "filled with the Holy Spirit."[10] Just like Peter on the Day of Pentecost, Paul's Spirit-baptism results in an immediate boldness to preach about Jesus Christ. After a few days of regaining his physical strength, we find him preaching about Jesus in

---

10. The words are reminiscent of Acts 2:4. The verbs (*pimplēmi* and *plēroō*) are not identical but clearly cognates, both bearing near identical meaning—"to fill" or "be filled." The genitive of content for each verb is identical—*pneuma tou hagiou* with the Holy Spirit.

the synagogues. What he preaches is nothing short of incredible if not blasphemous for an orthodox Jew. In reference to Jesus, he preaches "that this one is the Son of God" (Acts 9:20).

Placed alongside this background, what Luke describes is not only shocking but also incomprehensible apart from divine revelation. The Christophany, as recorded in Acts 9, is clear enough, but the compressed narrative recounts an impossible paradigm shift. Paul, the fanatical *persecutor* of the Church, became Paul, the *preacher* of the gospel of Jesus Christ (see also Acts 9:22; Cf. Gal 1:23.) Here is one of the first two Christological confessions of faith (Acts 8:37 and 9:20) recorded by Luke and both profess Christ as "the Son of God."[11]

The Testimony of Paul in Galatians 1

The relevance of Paul's letter to the Galatians to our thesis is demonstrated on two fronts: Paul's defense (*apologia*) of the true gospel contra the Judaizers who "trouble" (*tarasso*) the church by their errant gospel. Paul wastes no time in condemning them for abandoning the "grace of Christ" for "another gospel," which he emphatically explains is not another gospel at all but a perversion of it (Gal 1:6–7). His ire is so great that he anathematizes anyone who would propose a gospel different from the one preached by him and the other apostles (Gal 1:8–9). He explicitly refers to his gospel as "the gospel of Christ."

What follows is a fascinating biographical account of how he became an apostle—a steward of this gospel. He first makes it clear that his gospel is not a second-hand version. That is, it is not *kata anthropon* ("according to man"), nor did he receive it *para anthropou* ("from man"), nor was he "taught" it. The last two phrases deny that his gospel is owed to human tradition. Rather, Paul's gospel came via a "revelation of Jesus Christ" and this accords quite well with what Luke describes in Acts 9:3–8.

---

11. Some will object to Acts 8:37 because the Greek text of 8:37 is suspect as to its authenticity. However, the numerous variants of verse 37 testify to the church's attempt to make explicit what was universally understood. To preach Jesus (v. 35) was to preach Jesus as the Christ *and* as the Son of God.

Combined with Acts, we have the earliest account by Paul's own hand of his conversion and call to apostleship, a call to preach the gospel. To emphasize how remarkable his present ministry is, Paul recalls his former life in Judaism, a life not without prominence and reputation among the faithful in Judaism (Acts 1:14). Note Paul's own words as he chronicles the dramatic transference to becoming a follower and apostle of Christ:

> But when He who had set me apart, *even* from my mother's womb, and called me through His grace, was pleased to reveal His Son in me, that I might preach Him among the Gentiles, I did not immediately consult with flesh and blood, nor did I go up to Jerusalem to those who were apostles before me; but I went away to Arabia, and returned once more to Damascus. (Gal 1:15–17)

It is extremely hard to miss the fact that in Paul's words we have a reference to Paul's revelatory encounter with Christ. It came via God's grace and at his pleasure to reveal "His Son" in and through the life of Paul.[12] The sonship of Jesus Christ lies at the heart of God's revelation and it was this sonship that Paul immediately began to preach (Acts 9:20) as an essential part of his gospel.

---

12. Paul's choice of words is significant and suggests more than that God's Son was revealed to Paul who, in turn, preached Him through the gospel. This conclusion is strengthened by two observations. First, if Paul merely intended to convey his agency (indirect) or instrumentality in preaching the gospel, he certainly could have done so less ambiguously by simply writing *dia emou*. His choice of the preposition *en*, while it can certainly express agency, can also serve as a marker denoting the object in which something shows itself, or by which something is recognized (Danker, 2000, p. 328). Thus, it is *in Paul* that God's Son is revealed. Second, if Paul meant to say that God was pleased to *reveal* his Son *to* Paul, he could have simply dropped the preposition *ein* and simply used the dative of indirect object *emoi* as he does with the verb "to reveal" (*apokaluptō*) in Phil 3:15. Unless this is the sole exception, I know of no instance of *en emoi* as referring to the indirect object of a verb in Paul's writings.

The Testimony of Romans 1:1, 7–9

Paul's magisterial epistle to a church he had, up to that point in time, never visited holds another compelling piece of evidence for the thesis that familial language is indispensable for the preaching of the apostolic gospel. The apostle is clearly writing a letter that is unique among the corpus of his writings. Clearly, he labors to carefully and systematically lay out his understanding of God's salvation in Christ. That salvation is made known and declared in the preaching of the "gospel."

Romans also serves a practical purpose. Paul, the missionary, has plans to take the good news beyond Rome to Spain and he views the Roman church as a potential missionary sending agency providing support for his evangelistic enterprise. To garner their support, it is crucial that Paul establishes good will with this church and wins their confidence that he is a trustworthy bearer of the true gospel. The opening of this epistle holds insight and weight for our thesis:

> Paul, a bond-servant of Christ Jesus, called *as* an apostle, set apart for the gospel of God, which He promised beforehand through His prophets in the holy Scriptures, concerning His Son, who was born of a descendant of David according to the flesh, who was declared the Son of God with power by the resurrection from the dead, according to the Spirit of holiness, Jesus Christ our Lord. . . . First, I thank my God through Jesus Christ for you all, because your faith is being proclaimed throughout the whole world. For God, whom I serve in my spirit in the *preaching of the* gospel of His Son, is my witness *as to* how unceasingly I make mention of you." (Rom 1:1–4; 8–9, emphasis added)

Of first importance, we should note that the term "gospel" appears in a syntactical construction that presents both "God" (v. 1) and "His

Son" as coordinate and parallel agents[13] presenting the "good news" or gospel. As Paul elsewhere observes (Gal 3:8), this gospel has its foundational roots in the Old Testament scriptures. Here the corpus of the prophets contain the promise of God's saving work in Christ. What stands out is that the prophetic promise is not regarding the Messiah, but "concerning His Son." The identity of His Son seems paramount and central to Paul's gospel. After all, this gospel is "the gospel of His Son" (v. 9). While certainly the Son carries a messianic pedigree being a "descendant of David according to the flesh," what Paul wishes to emphasize is the unique filial relationship between the Father and His Son, which was powerfully declared through the resurrection of Jesus from the dead.

CONCLUSION

The present study is by no means complete and really needs to be carried forward throughout the Pauline corpus. From our examination of these key passages that focus on the foundational content of Paul's gospel as it applies to the identity of Jesus Christ, it becomes apparent that familial language is not incidental but essential. Therefore, its presence in the preaching of the gospel is more than important, it is a non-negotiable if we are to be faithful to the Pauline apostolic tradition of the New Testament.

While the ecumenical councils and succeeding generations of church fathers would hammer out the *dual nature* of Christ and His *eternal* relationship to the Father, their theological legacy demonstrates clearly that they grounded their formulations in the witness of the Scriptures and especially the apostolic writings of our canonical New Testament.

---

13. It is also possible to understand "the gospel of His Son" as employing objective genitives, indicating the object or focal point of the gospel—"the gospel concerning His Son." Regardless, the verbal parallelism strikingly identifies the gospel with God's Son.

The issue at hand, then, is much more than a translation strategy with missiological implications. The practice of removing from the text and/or redefining the divine familial terms of Father, Son, and Son of God with the substitution of alternative terms in specialized Scripture translations for Muslims (or non-Muslims) changes the very substructure of the gospel itself.[14]

REFERENCES

Aker, Benny. 2012. "Foundational Issues." Springfield, MO: Assemblies of God Theological Seminary. Unpublished article.

Aland, Barbara and others. 1993. *Nestle-Aland Novum Testamentum Graece.* 27th rev. ed. Munster/Westphalia: Deutsche Bibelgesellschaft, Stuttgart.

Arberry, Arthur J. 1955. *The Koran Interpreted.* New York, NY: Simon and Shuster.

Assemblies of God. 1970. "The Inerrancy of Scripture." *Assemblies of God online.* Beliefs. Position papers. Accessed on April 2012. Available from http://ag.org/top/Beliefs/Position_Papers/pp_downloads/pp_4175_inerrancy.pdf.

Assemblies of God. 2010. "The Scriptures Inspired." *Assemblies of God online.* Beliefs. Our Fundamental Truths. Accessed on April 2012. Available at http://ag.org/top/Beliefs/Statement_of_Fundamental_Truths/sft_full.cfm#1.

Bultmann, Rudolf. 1951. *Theology of the New Testament.* NY: Charles Scribner's Sons.

Collins, Adela Yarbro, and John J. Collins. 2008. *King and Messiah as Son of God: Divine, Human, and Angelic Figures in Biblical and Related Literature.* Grand Rapids, MI: Eerdmans.

Danker, Frederick William, ed. 2001. *A Greek-English Lexicon of the New Testament and Other Early Christian Literature.* 3rd ed. Chicago, IL: University of Chicago Press.

---

14. An expanded edition of this paper is available at FatherSon.ag.org.

Ferguson, Everett. 1993. *Backgrounds of Early Christianity.* 2nd ed. Grand Rapids, MI: Eerdmans.

Hurst, Randy. "Essential Scriptural Integrity." *Pentecostal Evangel,* March 4, 2012, 28–29.

Neufeld, Dietmar. 1997. "And When That One Comes: Aspects of Johannine Messianism." In *Eschatology, Messianism, and the Dead Sea Scrolls,* edited by Craig A. Evans and Peter Flint. Grand Rapids, MI: Eerdmans.

Nock, Arthur Darby. 1964. *Early Christianity and Its Hellenistic Background.* New York: Harper and Row.

Osborne, Grant R. 2002. "Revelation," In *Baker Exegetical Commentary on the New Testament.* Grand Rapids, MI: Baker Academic.

Pearlman, Myer. 1937. *Knowing the Doctrines of the Bible.* Springfield, MO: Gospel Publishing House.

Waltke, Bruce K., and Charles Yu. 2007. *An Old Testament Theology: An Exegetical, Canonical, and Thematic Approach.* Grand Rapids, MI: Zondervan.

Zwemer, Samuel Marinus. 1905. *The Moslem Doctrine of God: An Essay on the Character and Attributes of Allah according to the Koran and Orthodox Tradition.* New York, NY: American Tract Society.

CHAPTER 11

THE WORLD EVANGELICAL ALLIANCE GLOBAL REVIEW PANEL REPORT
A Sympathetic Dissenting Opinion
Kevin Higgins

I write as both a practitioner and an advocate. With more than twenty-five years in active engagement with Muslims in the work of discipleship, church planting, and Bible translation, I have been very involved in face-to-face relationship with Muslims. As director of my organization, I understand the need to explain to churches and partners what we are doing.[1]

I am a sympathetic dissenter relative to the 2013 "Report of the World Evangelical Alliance for Conveyance to Wycliffe Global Alliance and SIL International" regarding the translation of Divine Familial Terms (DFT).[2] I will first list five areas of sympathy with and then six points of dissent from the recommendations of the World Evangelical Alliance (WEA) panel (hereafter the "panel"). I want to begin with the points of affirmation.

FIVE AREAS OF SYMPATHY

First, I am convinced of the panel's fundamental love of the gospel and the Word. I have had the honor to meet several of the panel members personally, including some who disagree with me. I respect them greatly. I know we share a passion for the gospel to be communicated clearly.

---

1. It is important to note that I have never been a member of Wycliffe/SIL and I do not presume to speak for them.

2. Controversy in recent years has focused on the how to render the terms for son and father in Muslim contexts. "Divine familial terms" (DFT) emerged as a sort of shorthand for referring to these words when used for Jesus and God.

Second, I share the panel's sensitivity to the four main contexts in which Bible translation functions and to which a translator needs to pay attention (2013, 4). These are the Old Testament context, the New Testament context, the translator's context, and the new audience's context. All four are critical for translation.[3]

Third, I am in sympathy with the panel in looking to Scripture for translation principles. Page 22 uses scriptural precedent for adding qualifiers such as "in heaven" or "heavenly" to "father" to avoid misunderstanding or to better explain in what way God is father. Mining the Scriptures for more material that speaks directly to how the Scriptures might shape translation approaches or even a theology of translation is important. Surprisingly, the Scriptures are a relatively untapped well of resources for Bible translation approaches.

Fourth, I share the panel's reserve about directives relative to translation decisions coming from outsiders who do not know the audience's context (2013, 4). The panel prefers "overarching principles" and I agree fully.[4]

Fifth, I appreciate the panel's point that Bible translation does not stand alone in evangelism and discipleship. I appreciate that the WEA report cited a number of examples of biblically-based materials that can be adapted for Muslim evangelism and discipleship such as lives of prophets (*qissas* and *sirahs*), and commentaries (*tafsir*).

SIX POINTS OF DISSENT

I will now describe six points of dissent from the conclusions of the panel. The order in which I present them follows the discourse of the WEA document.

---

3. See Shaw and Van Engen (2003) who refer to horizons instead of contexts. The panel did not endorse the book, but did borrow the concept of the four horizons/contexts.

4. Whether the panel limited itself to overarching principles is a debatable point.

"Divine Familial Terms" (DFT) as the Frame of the Discussion

The Panel did not initiate the phrase DFT. These terms emerged from the controversies surrounding Bible translation among Muslims. Yet, framing the discussion with them means that the entire WEA discussion already carries a specific set of theological assumptions: that son is essentially and always a divine term when used in reference to Jesus, and that both terms are primarily "familial" in describing the relationship of son and father.

As such, the terminology already smuggles the conclusion into the discussion. Beginning from the assumption that son and father are divine and familial terms, we should not be surprised that the panel finds that the terms are, well, divine and familial. Surely that is one of the assumptions that must be tested?

The Make-up of the Panel

I affirm that the decision to appoint a panel was prudent. In addition, the panel clearly included highly qualified people who served sincerely and selflessly. I also appreciate the effort that went into the panel's formation: more than eighty people were suggested for inclusion.

However, of the eighty that were suggested, twenty-four were invited, and there were twelve who agreed to serve. The unfortunate result was that the panel exhibits a number of important omissions in its make-up. I do not suggest that this was due to a lack of the intention or design on the part of the panel. Nonetheless there are three significant issues to observe.

First, according to my research, of the twelve panel members: three have translation experience, two worked on translations, and one served as a consultant. The number of translators on the panel seems disproportionate to the other areas of expertise, since the purpose of the panel was to provide recommendations related to the task of *Bible translation*.[5]

---

5. The full list of the panelists can be found at: http://www.worldevangelicals .org/translation-review/. (accessed March 6, 2015).

Second, there were no translators on the panel who support the sort of translation work being criticized. The position being criticized and people who hold it are not represented on the panel. Therefore, the panel's report is greatly weakened in both *content* and also *moral authority*.

Third, there is no representation on the panel from the Muslim background believers who use, appreciate, and value the types of translations being discussed. This renders the report less credible. By credible I do not question whether the panel and its report are honest or learned. But the discussion is one sided, and in a crisis such as this it would seem obvious to include Bible translators and Muslim background believers on *both* sides of this issue.

The Application of the Four Contexts

I have concerns about the actual approach the panel is using relative to the four contexts. While the panel acknowledges the importance of all four contexts, in the end, three of them are largely eclipsed and one of the contexts, that of the translator, in effect gives the final word.

I assume that evangelicals (and the panel) would agree that the main aim of any translation is to communicate the meaning of the original texts in such a way that the new audience can understand the meaning of the original authors as those original authors and their audiences would have understood it.[6] Therefore, the Old Testament and New Testament contexts are the primary voices.

I take it as axiomatic that the primary starting point for understanding the New Testament's usage of Old Testament concepts is the Old Testament understood in its context. Relative to the question of son, this means that the Old Testament background for the term Son of God is the major soil to be mined for understanding the New Testament authors' usage of the phrase. The panel seems to agree when

---

6. I agree there are times when the Holy Spirit inspired authors to write "more than they understood" but, in so doing, this did not eclipse the meaning the authors and their audiences would have understood in their time and culture. I also agree that the primary focus of a Bible translator is to enable new audiences to access that meaning.

it describes two Old Testament uses of Son of God, shaped by near eastern culture: the suzerain treaty in which the suzerain was at times seen as a son of the gods (2013, 21), and the fact that fathers determine the identity of their sons (2013, 22).[7]

But another major Old Testament component is the royal context in which a king is said to become the Son of God. Psalm 2 provides a major text for this theme, "You are my son, this day I have begotten you." This is cited once by the panel but not discussed, except to admit that such a text forms the background for Luke 1:32 (2013, 21). Yet, Psalm 2 mentions specifically the key vocabulary of the entire conversation—son, begetting, "you are My son" (i.e., God's, son)—and sets a good deal of the Old Testament context for the New Testament understanding. The Psalm sets sonship precisely in the messianic and kingly milieu that the panel is relegating to a minimal role. The Old Testament background needs to be given greater voice, as do the varieties of New Testament uses of Son of God. As I will explain below, I see the panel using John's theology as the lens for reading the rest of the biblical material on son.

The fourth context, the context of the audience, fares in a similar way. The panel acknowledges the severe difficulty in communicating the biblical concept Son of God in a Muslim context and agrees that such contexts make "translation of divine familial terms an especially sensitive issue" (2013, 4, 18). However, the way the panel suggests that the audience context should affect translation decisions is open to critique.

Whereas translators, who employ a meaning equivalent approach[8] to the translation of "son" attempt to engage the audience's context

---

7.   In between these two, the panel mentions a third point about the future messianic Kingdom, but as this is much less related to the near eastern background, which is my focus here, I do not refer to it.

8.   I know that translators who favor more dynamic approaches, and translators who favor more literal approaches are *both* focused on the meaning of the text. "Meaning based" versus "literal" translation are not exclusive positions. Both approaches seek to communicate the meaning of the words of the original texts. We differ as to strategies at certain points, but not aims.

through an explanatory translation, the panel states that it is "not permissible" to use less than literal terminology (2013, 19) and recommends literal translation of the key words and the use of paratext and/or modifiers such as "*spiritual* son" or "*kingly* son" (2013, 18, 19, 20, 21, 22).

There are two problems with this recommendation. First, the panel *overestimates* the ability of paratext to overcome misunderstanding. Such material is especially problematic in oral contexts, but even in reading cultures, the effort required to shift attention to a note or look up a glossary reference means that most people just do not do it (especially in group settings). There is also an irony in the panel's insistence that paratext be the solution. If paratext is a sufficient way to overcome the misunderstanding of a literal translation of son, then paratext is a sufficient way to give access to the literal terms in a meaning equivalent translation. In short, the panel overestimates paratext's usefulness.

Second, the panel *underestimates* the connotative meaning of words. Connotative meaning is the meaning we associate with words, while the denotative meaning is the "dictionary" meaning. I agree that the meaning of "Son of God" may be explained using paratext to show that "Son of God" is not physical sexual or polytheistic in nature. But for most Muslims, hearing and understanding, and even *accepting* that explanation intellectually will rarely overcome the deep visceral reaction to the connotative meaning of "Son of God" as implying sex and polytheism.[9]

Suppose I write a book as an American for an American audience. In it, I say that one of my characters is a gay man. I am aware readers will misunderstand, so I proceed to explain in a glossary that the meaning of gay is "happy" or "joyful" and that this is what I mean. The reality is that, for most readers, the connotative association from the words in my text is what will color the reaction. If the reader *does* go to the note or the glossary, the reader may accept my explanation intellectually, and

---

9.   I know Muslims who will not touch a Bible simply because it has this phrase in it. It is a similar reaction to their seeing the word pig in a text like Mark 5. No matter the explanation, there is a deep emotional reaction that this is unclean.

yet, emotionally, still feel the same. In such a case, I am better off to simply use a meaning equivalent translation: happy, glad, joyful.[10]

The panel in my opinion has largely eclipsed the importance of three of the four contexts. In the end, what in fact determines the right translation of son is not context one (the Old Testament background), context two (the various New Testament uses of the word within the varied contexts of the New Testament authors), or context four (the cultural context in which the audience will process whatever is said). As far as I can tell, the final word as to what should govern a translation decision in the view of the panel should be *the translator's context:* a specific theological position relative to the relationship of son and God. My contention is that such an approach undercuts the work of exegesis and sound biblical theology in favor of a particular viewpoint drawn from systematic theology. I am convinced that such an approach may prevent Muslims from having access to the meaning of the biblical authors as those authors and their audiences would have understood the texts.

Assumptions about John's Use of Son

The panel argues that son should be translated literally because it is the term used in the New Testament to show both the similarity and the difference between us and Jesus in our identity as children of God. Jesus "is the unique Son of God, and we become adopted sons (and daughters) through faith" (2013, 14). The section in the report prior to this statement uses John 1:1–3, John 5:26, and John 17:20ff. as the key texts to indicate Jesus' unique, eternal relationship as son to the father. In fact, these verses are used to summarize and explain a list of other New Testament texts.

I agree that adoption is a key theme regarding our relationship to God in the New Testament. In fact, the comparison in John's Gospel is between us as begotten children (John 1:12–13) and Jesus as God's

---

10. Both types of approaches may elect to use paratext. They should not assume that this is sufficient to overcome misunderstanding in the translation itself.

"one of a kind" son (*monogenes*, in both John 1:14–18 and 3:16). The Old Testament echoes in John 3:16 are from Genesis 22 about Isaac the beloved son of Abraham. Both Isaac and Ishmael are begotten. The emphasis relative to Isaac is that he is beloved, unique, and the one elected by God. This certainly does not undermine Jesus' uniqueness, but it is not the uniqueness the panel is describing.[11]

The whole narrative of John's Gospel *does* serve to make clear the eternal nature of Jesus' divinity, but this is shaped by John's use of *logos* found right from the outset of his gospel, preparing the reader's mind to read the rest of the gospel in that light. I am convinced that one valid reading of the first chapter of John is not that Jesus is the "eternally begotten son" but, rather, that the eternally divine Word (1:1–3) becomes flesh in Jesus (1:14), and that it is this Word-made-flesh-Jesus who is God's Son in a unique way (1:14).

The creedal formulas which speak of Jesus as God's eternally begotten Son do so as an appropriate theological extension that brings together multiple scriptural sources into a very compressed statement. However, the panel was asked to make recommendations for how to translate Scripture. Their recommendations seem to me to conflict with the principle that translation should reflect what our best exegesis says the text meant in its original literary and cultural context.

Christian and Muslim Views of Translation

On page 25, the panel makes several comments about Muslim and Christian views of translation:

- For Muslims the Qur'an is untranslatable.
- For Muslims, a translation of the Qur'an is not the word of God, it is the meaning of those words.
- For Christians, a Bible translation *is* the Bible.

At first glance it might seem that nothing further needs to be said. But the reality is much more complex and significant because these

---

11. See Menken (2009) for a thorough analysis of the Johannine use of begetting for believers and the implications of this for translators.

assumptions affect the panels' recommendations about including literal and non-literal translations in one volume. This is an important issue since this is actually the format used or proposed by a number of the projects that have drawn criticism.

First, Muslim views of translation are more complex than what the panel describes. On the one hand, yes, Muslims officially see the Arabic Qur'an as untranslatable. The irony, however, is that they translate and publish a vast number of such "non-translations," including multiple versions in single languages. In Urdu alone there are some 300 different versions (see Moir 2009; Khan 1997). These are not referred to as translations normally, but there are exceptions. Frequently the term *tarjuma* or "translation" is used in the title. I have at my elbow as I write an Urdu Qur'an entitled *Tarjuma-Qur'an-Majid* ("the Translation of the Glorious Qur'an").

The Muslim position would be closer to this: it is impossible for any translation of the Arabic Qur'an to capture all of the richness of meaning and the emotive power of the original text as Muhammad's first hearers would have received it. I suspect that most Christians, especially those with any experience in learning other languages and those with any experience of the biblical languages, would find that statement applicable to the Bible as well: it is impossible for any translation of the Hebrew/Aramaic/Greek Bible to capture all of the richness of meaning and the emotive power of the original text as the Bible's first hearers would have received it. Perhaps Muslim views of translation are not as different from Christian views as the panel states.

Second, the panel states that "a translation of the Bible *is* the Bible" (2013, 25). This is true at one level but, again, it is more complicated than this. I agree with the statement in that, when I am studying a translation of the scriptures I have confidence that it can be used by God to do all that Paul states is the purpose of the inspired text: "for teaching, for reproof, for correction, for training in righteousness" so that I might be "adequate, fully equipped" for ministry and life (2 Tim 3:16–17, NASB). *In this sense, I fully agree that a translation of the Bible is the Bible.*

At the same time, there is a reason why so many different translations in English have been deemed necessary. It is not merely due to changing cultures or changes in the vernacular language, or even the rather modern effort to have translations for every niche of humanity. At least one reason for the variety of translations is precisely because no translation can capture all of the richness of meaning and the emotive power of the original text. Translators know it and so they keep trying. We can conclude, then, that *no single translation of the Bible is able to communicate all that the original biblical text communicates in any given passage. To say that a translation is the Bible is true in what it affirms, but it is not the whole story.*

So, while translations can be said to be the Bible, I would argue this is only true in the limited sense I have described above. This leads to yet a further conclusion, one which is implied in what has already been said but needs to be stated as clearly as possible:

> If it is true that *no single* translation of the Bible is able to communicate *all* that the original biblical text communicates in any given passage, then it is also true that no *single* translation, standing alone, can be said to be *fully* accurate. Nuances and meaning understood by the original authors and audiences will not all be captured in a translation. However, we can say that translations of the Bible (using the plural) can *combine* to be fully accurate.

Accuracy in translation is one of the standards that every translator aims to achieve. It may be time to revisit what constitutes an accurate translation. Ultimately that is what the debate prior to and including the WEA discussion has been about: what is accurate translation? This is not a new debate, and I observe that the variety of viewpoints about what constitutes good or accurate translation has been with us for a long, long time. In fact, in the process of copying the New Testament Scriptures, two major textual traditions emerged.

The Alexandrian text tradition has origins from the early second century and is noted for its brevity and freedom from grammatical and stylistic polishing found in other text traditions. The western textual tradition, common in Italy, Gaul and North Africa from the second century and associated with Irenaeus, Tertullian, and Cyprian, is noted for paraphrase, enrichment of narrative, and harmonization (Metzger 1971). In other words, very early in the process of copying texts, there was an awareness of the need to explain what is implicit in some passages. Very early, there was an instinct in the western tradition to pursue a strategy in copying the texts that resembles closely the strategy of translating the text that would later be known as dynamic equivalent or explanatory.

Biblical scholarship sifts textual material from both of these textual traditions to arrive at the best text. Material from both traditions is incorporated into the Greek text of the New Testament used for translation, exegesis, theology, etc. Every translation, literal in approach or not, depends on both of these textual traditions. It would seem natural to suggest that perhaps our translations for Muslims could make better use of this long tradition.

I mentioned briefly above that this whole discussion about views of translation is important because the panel, based in part on these points, states that translations which contain non-literal translations of the terms son and father are not acceptable even when combined with literal versions, along with the original Greek text. I can guess as to the panel's reasoning here about the interlinear: a translation including non-literal renderings for son and father is assumed to be placed on one page while the literal translation is inserted as an interlinear, along with the Greek (or Hebrew) on the opposite page. One objection to this has been that the interlinear is not readable, and is perhaps worse than paratext material. This makes sense to me as well.

In summary thus far, relative to the other conclusions I have stated, I add this:

> If it is true that *no* single translation of the Bible is able to communicate *all* that the original biblical text communicates in any given passage, and if it is also true that no *single* translation, standing alone, can be said to be *fully* accurate, and if nuances and meaning understood by the original authors and audiences will not all be captured in a translation, and if we can say that translations of the Bible (using the plural) can *combine* to be fully accurate, then we can also say that we need multiple translations in every language, and multiple approaches, if possible, included in one volume to aid understanding.

It is important to mention here one of the panel's concerns about multiple translations for Muslim audiences. The panel mentions that many Muslims are aware that one of the terms used in the Bible for Jesus is Son of God. Thus, the panel suggests that translations which do not render this term literally may lead to Muslim charges of changing the Bible (2013, 15). However, when comparing a few verses from just four Urdu translations of the Qur'an, I am astonished at the variety of word choices, explanatory phrases, and interpretations. Muslims know that these are not changing the Qur'an. In light of this, an approach to Bible translation, such as I am suggesting here, would actually fit with Muslim ideas about the translation of holy books.[12]

Concordance and Consistency

There is an important principle in translation called concordance, which the panel calls consistency (2013, 23). According to this principle, translators seek to render the same Greek or Hebrew term with the same term in the receptor language wherever it is found. However, words almost always have multiple meanings and it may take five

---

12. Muslims also know about different translation approaches. One Urdu example is Maulana Maududi. Introducing his 1948 work, *Tefhim ul Qur'an* Maududi argued for the need for something like a dynamic equivalent approach.

different words to capture in the receptor language the different uses of the same word in, say, Greek. For this reason, translators seek a difficult balance: concordance with comprehension.

Maintaining this balance has been a long-standing best practice in translation: "maintaining concordance as much as possible, but not at the expense of comprehension" (2013, 23, citing SIL Best Practices, statement 3.2). To be fair, the panel appreciates the need for this balance and, with these two words son and father, suggests that it is possible to "preserve both" (2013, 23) but without resorting to non-literal renderings.

This attempt to preserve concordance without sacrificing comprehension is a wonderful idea, but is not the standard required for the translation of other key terms. For example, the Greek word *sarx* is often translated "flesh" in English. It can mean body, but it can also mean our sinful nature (in Paul's use, having nothing to do with the actual body), and it can mean humanity, etc. English translations which want to highlight concordance elect to use "flesh" in each instance in order to help the reader access the fact that in the original, the same word is being used in different ways. This is perfectly acceptable and indeed important. English translations which are more dynamic seek to make the *meaning* transparent. Thus, in one place *sarx* might be translated as body or flesh, and in others, as *sinful nature* or something similar. This is also perfectly acceptable and important.

In the example of *sarx*, Bible translators use both concordance and comprehension emphasizing approaches, but in different translations. The panel suggests that this approach is not appropriate with the words son and father due to the frequency and importance of these terms (2013, 11–15). But surely this is *also* a good rationale for seeking to render their *meaning* as clearly as possible where that meaning is different in a different author? In fact, it is important for a growing movement to be able to do theological reflection on the scriptures aided by translations that *show clearly how the same biblical word is being used in different ways in different places*. This is very true for the phrase Son of God. And, it is important for a growing movement to be able to do theological reflection on the scriptures aided by translations that *show clearly the meaning of the words the original texts used in a particular place and by a particular author.* This is also very true for the phrase Son of God.

One single translation cannot actually do both. We need both types of approach to the difficulties of concordance and comprehension.

Points of Dissent Summary

1. The use of DFT predetermined that the discussion was measured by a certain set of ideas.
2. The make-up of the panel did not represent the viewpoints of those being critiqued or those who find value in these translations.
3. In the end, it is not the biblical material that determines how to translate Son.
4. John's theology seems to be used as a lens to interpret other biblical data and I am not sure John is used correctly at every point.
5. There is an incorrect contrast between Muslim and Christian views of translation which shapes the panel's recommendations in mistaken directions.
6. The decision to favor concordance over comprehension is inadequately defended in the case of son and father.

These factors greatly diminish the degree to which, in my opinion, translators should see the work of the panel as binding or even complete. However, I do not intend that comment to be a final word.

CONCLUSION: HOPES FOR THE FUTURE

In the spirit of sympathetic dissent, I conclude with several hopes for the future. I am aware that a great deal of time, effort, and expense went into the first effort undertaken by the panel and to now suggest there be more work of this nature is, I am sure, something that will be extremely difficult to implement. Nevertheless, I conclude by sharing four hopes for this discussion:

1. *I hope there might be a more representative working group to revisit the issues addressed in the WEA Report and the conclusions drawn.* Such a group could well include members of the original panel. I have already explained one rationale: the lack of full representation for several important constituencies in the original effort. Much more thinking is needed about these issues.

2. *I hope that such a reconstituted working group might engage more in biblical and theological reflection on the task and nature of translation itself than the original effort.* It seems crucial to develop a theology of translation anchored in extensive biblical reflection. There is also a need for a hermeneutic for how we use the Bible to arrive at such a theology.

3. *I hope to see further reflection on what is meant by accuracy in translation.* Further work is needed on the task of refining what we mean by accurate translation.

4. *I hope there might be progress towards an agreed methodology for scriptural primacy in translation.* This may seem an odd statement. How could Scripture not be primary in the task of Bible translation? However, it seems clear to me that there is a pressing need to develop a methodology in all of this which, while taking very seriously the whole tradition of theological development bequeathed to the church by councils and creeds and confessions, allows Scripture its primary place. I believe that the critics of Bibles which make use of explanatory translations of son and father share this commitment to biblical primacy in translation, though there are differences in convictions about the methodology for this.

These are large and complex tasks. If this paper serves to encourage continued work along these lines, then that will be a good beginning.

REFERENCES[13]

Abernathy, David. 2010. "Jesus Is the Eternal Son of God." *St. Francis Magazine* 6, no. 2: 327–394.

Ayoub, Mahmound. 1984. *The Qur'an and its Interpreters.* Vol. 1. Albany, NY: University of New York Press.

Ayoub, Mahmoud, and Omar Irfan Omar, eds. 2007. *A Muslim View of Christianity.* Maryknoll, NY: Orbis.

Brown, Rick, John Penny, and Laith Gray. 2009. "Muslim-Idiom Bible Translations: Claims and Facts." *St. Francis Magazine* 5, no. 6: 87–105.

Carson, D. A. 1991. *The Gospel According to John.* The Pillar New Testament Commentary, Grand Rapids, Eerdmans Publishing Company.

———. 2012. *Jesus the Son of God: A Christological Title often Overlooked, sometimes Misunderstood, and Currently Disputed.* Nottingham, UK: Intervarsity Press.

Davis, Stephen T., Daniel Kendall SJ, and Gerald O'Collins SJ, eds. 2002. *The Trinity: An Interdisciplinary Symposium on the Trinity.* Oxford: Oxford University Press.

Diab, Issa. 2010. "Challenges Facing Bible Translation in the Islamic Context of the Middle East." *The Bible Translator* 61, no. 2: 71–80.

Doty, Stephen, H. 2007. "The Paradigm Shift in Bible Translation in the Modern Era, with Special Focus on Thai," PhD diss., University of Auckland.

Floor, Sebastian. 2007. "Four Bible Translation Types and Some Criteria to Distinguish Them." *Journal of Translation* 3, no. 2: 1–22.

Grudem, Wayne, Leland Ryker, C. John Collins, Vern Poythress, and Bruce Winter. 2005. *Translating Truth: The Case for Essentially Literal Bible Translation.* Wheaton, IL: Crossways Books.

---

13. I have not cited all of these works but include this list as a representative list of resources, from different perspectives, on the issues related to this topic.

Higgins, Kevin S. 2010. "Diverse Voices: Hearing Scripture Speak in a Multi-cultural Environment." *International Journal of Frontier Mission* 27, no. 4: 189–196.

Hill, Harriett, 2003. "Communicating Context in Bible Translation among the Adioukrou of Cote D'Ivoire," PhD diss., Fuller Theological Seminary.

———. 2006. *The Bible at Cultural Crossroads: From Translation to Communication.* Manchester, UK: St. Jerome.

Hill, Harriett, Ernst-August Gutt, Rick Floyd, Margaret Hill, Christoph Unger. 2011. *Bible Translation Basics: Communicating Scripture in a Relevant Way.* Dallas, TX: SIL International.

Khan, Mofakhkhar Hussain, 1997. "An Early History of Urdu Translations of the Holy Qur'ān: A Bio-bibliographic Study." *Islamic Quarterly* 40, no, 1: 211–234.

———. 2001. *The Holy Qur'an in South Asia: A Bio-bibliographic Study of Translations of the Holy Qur'an in 23 South Asian Languages.* Dhaka: Bibi Akhtar Prakasani.

Maududi, Abdul A'la. 1951. *Tarjuma-i-Quran Majeed.* Idara Tarjuman ul Quran (Pvt.) Lahore, Pakistan: Limited.

———. 1988. *Towards Understanding the Qur'an.* Translated and edited by Zafar Ishaq Ansari. Leicester, UK: Islamic Foundation.

McAuliffe, Jane Dammen, ed. 2006. *The Cambridge Companion to the Qur'an.* New York: Cambridge University Press.

Menken, M. J. J. 2009. "'Born of God' or 'Begotten by God?' A Translation Problem in the Johannine Writings." *Novum Testamentum* 51: 352–368.

Metzger, Bruce. 1971. *A Textual Commentary on the Greek New Testament.* 2nd edition. New York: United Bible Societies.

Metzler, Norman. 2003. "The Trinity in Contemporary Theology: Questioning the Social Trinity." *Concordia Theological Quarterly* 67, no. 3–4 (July/October): 270–287.

Moir, Catherine. 2009. "Translational Resonance, Authenticity and Authority in the Bible and the Quran: Translation and Religious Change." *New Voices in Translation Studies* 5. Sheffield, UK: University of Sheffield.

Noss, Philip A., ed. 2007. *A History of Bible Translation.* Rome: Edzioni Di Storia E Letteratura.

"Report of the World Evangelical Alliance for Conveyance to Wycliffe Global Alliance and SIL International," April 26, 2013, Available from: http://www.worldevangelicals.org/translation-review/ (accessed March 2015).

Shaw, R. Daniel, and Charles Van Engen. 2003. *Communicating God's Word in a Complex World: God's Truth or Hocus Pocus?* Lanham, MD: Rowman & Littlefield Publishers.

CHAPTER 12

CONSEQUENCES OF THE DIVINE TERMS CONTROVERSY IN BIBLE TRANSLATION
A Neglected Voice Speaks Out
Mark Naylor

INTRODUCTION

Early in 2012, the Divine Familial Terms (DFT) issue reached an unprecedented crisis point for Wycliffe Bible Translators (WBT).[1] Due to translation choices in some projects, an accusation was made that WBT was taking the term "Son of God" out of Scripture in order to create "Muslim-friendly" Bibles designed to appease Muslims (A Translation Challenge 2012). The outcry was immediate and surfaced on a number of levels: from local believers, fellow translators, denominations, and missions organizations. Some of the responses were harsh and severe, ignoring the commendable work of Wycliffe over the years. Some organizations and denominations cut their ties to Wycliffe, often using rhetoric that was unjust and unkind. Others recognized this as a crisis point and stepped forward to aid Wycliffe and seek to restore and uphold Wycliffe's credibility in the field of Bible translation. Wycliffe Global Alliance and SIL International approached the World Evangelical Alliance (WEA) in March 2012, to independently review their best practice in the translation of "God the Father" and the "Son of God." The WEA responded by forming a panel that presented ten

---

1. This issue was being discussed well before this crisis point, such as in Rick Brown's work found in the *International Journal of Frontier Missiology* (2000, 45,48–49, 2005a, 93–94, 2005b, 138–141). At a gathering in August 2011, Wycliffe adopted, for the first time, a common standard to guide its personnel worldwide, called the "Best Practices for Bible Translation of Divine Familial Terms." By early 2012, however, it was obvious that the crisis would not be resolved by policy actions or by providing "Answers to Commonly Asked questions" (Divine Familial Terms 2012).

recommendations (Final Report of the WEA 2013). Wycliffe's humble response to the recommendations and the transparent way the issue has been addressed seems to have had a calming effect and, to a large measure, has restored the credibility of the organization with respect to the appropriateness of their translation practices.

The translation issue revolves around the divine familial terms, primarily "father" and "son," used in Scripture to refer to the relationship between Jesus and God. The motivation of the translators who provided a rendering with a different but parallel image was to avoid a miscommunication of the terms. The WEA report notes that Muslims "are influenced by qur'anic views, e.g. the belief that for Jesus to be God's Son would require God to have a sexual consort (6:101) or that Christians believe that Jesus and Mary are gods beside God (5:116)" (Final Report of the WEA 2013, 4). These misperceptions by Muslims create a barrier to the acceptance of Scripture and represent a dilemma for the translator: Are familial metaphors integral to the biblical message or, when the receptor audience misconstrues its intent leading to a rejection of Scripture, can equivalent non-familial metaphors be used? In choosing a rendering that did not use divine familial terms, the translators did not anticipate such a strong reaction from Christians who had a history of seeking to clarify and teach Muslims a more appropriate understanding of divine familial language. The presence of a Bible version without such language weakened the teaching of local believers and undermined the support and development of their familial theology.

A BIBLE TRANSLATOR'S PERSPECTIVE

This paper is not about translation principles or the translation task with respect to DFT, which is multi-layered and complex. Scholars have already dealt with this extensively and institutions like CanIL and SIL are better equipped to describe and analyze the controversy so that the many dimensions of Bible translation are adequately considered. I will also not attempt to evaluate the development of the crisis and how it has been handled, nor will I address the process and nature of intercultural communication and its implications for translation.

Instead, I would like to provide a somewhat unique perspective. I have been a Bible translator in a Muslim context for over twenty-five years, yet not associated with Wycliffe, SIL, or CanIL. Although I do not speak for those institutions nor do I represent them in any way, my work on the Sindhi Bible translation, a project of the Pakistan Bible Society, would not have been possible without the support of and collaboration with representatives of these organizations in Pakistan. Also, when it comes to Bible translation, Wycliffe is the elephant and I am but a small donkey walking alongside. So when the elephant stumbles, the donkey gets bumped. I would like to relate the impact of this controversy on my translation ministry and practice, in particular the recognition of the growing influence of what I will refer to as the "fifth context."

THE FIFTH CONTEXT

In their report to the World Evangelical Alliance, the WEA Global Review Panel refers to four "cultural contexts" (Final Report of the WEA 2013, 5) based on the four "horizons" proposed by Shaw and Van Engen (2003, 83) as a "missiological hermeneutic." The WEA report explains that:

> Translators need to consider four primary contexts if the message of the Bible is to be accurately and clearly communicated to an intended audience today. The first context is the Old Testament, focusing on the covenant relationship between God and Israel and the development of the concept of Son of God as Messianic King. The New Testament, the second context, builds on this Old Testament context and focuses on Jesus Christ as the unique Son of God who is the Messianic King, and the fulfillment of the Old Testament covenant relationship in believers, the sons and daughters of God. The translators' own cultures

are the third context, which involves their cultural milieu, the interpretive tradition in which they work, and their methodology for understanding Scripture. The fourth is the context of the intended audience. Good communication will take place only if significant attention is given to understanding the receptor audiences, in this case various Muslim groups, and their cultures. (2013, 4)

Shaw and Van Engen (2003, 91) prefer the term "horizons" allowing for a variety of "contexts" within each horizon; however, I will use the term "cultural context" chosen by the WEA panel to refer to the same dynamic. In chapters 5 and 6 of their book, Shaw and Van Engen describe how this dynamic works, particularly as it applies to Bible translation. They describe "a hermeneutical spiraling of the interaction between the receptors-in-context, and communicator-in-context, and eventually with text-in-context" (Shaw and Van Engen 2003, 91). That is, the meaning of the resulting translation is determined by a dialogue between the translator and the audience as they engage the implications of the original text. Shaw and Van Engen further amplify this dynamic by stating that by "seeking to associate the receptors' questions with deep structural meanings, communicators enable receptors to move towards an understanding [of the text]" (2003, 91).

These descriptions of the "receptors" indicate that the only audience in view, and this is understandable, is the *intended* receptor audience. But even the adjectives "intended" or "primary" used to describe the audience for the translation indicates that there may be others affected by the translation. What the DFT controversy has highlighted is a *secondary* audience,[2] a *fifth context* that is not only *impacted by* but also *impacts* the

---

2. While "secondary audience" may be a sufficient designation to describe those outside of the normal translation process who are influencing the translation, it can be misleading since (1) they are not part of the *intended* recipients, (2) they are not viewing the text as a message *to them* since they have versions in their own language they consider authoritative and (3) the use of the

content of the translation. This fifth context previously had only a limited voice in Bible translation and did not play a significant, if any, role in the dialogue described by Shaw and Van Engen. Instead, it has been viewed as (1) a global Christian framework in which translation occurs (2) supporters, promoters and financers of Bible translation and as (3) secondary audiences with casual, rather than critical interest. However, even though they are not the receptor audience of a particular translation and so do not access God's Word *through* that translation, they are impacted *by* it. That is, they have their own language and preferred Bible translation, but other translations influence the interreligious dynamic and some have been perceived as a threat to their accepted readings and applications. Faced with a perceived threat to their faith, they have joined the translation dialogue that is determining the philosophy, meaning, nature, form, and even content of a translation. Bible translators now face input from the fifth context—those believers in the local or global sphere who are not the primary audience for the translation, but have significant influence on how the translation will be done.

My concern is to underscore one important outcome of the DFT controversy which is that the influence on Bible translation has been broadened to include this fifth context. Believers apart from the primary audience have found their voice and demand a say in how a translation is formed and what is included. Rather than being a minor dialogue partner in the process of translating for unreached people groups (e.g., local Christians) or being encouraging supporters who are content to trust the translator with the task, these secondary audiences have demonstrated an impressive influence over the parameters of Bible translation well beyond the limitations of the four horizons.

It may be that Shaw and Van Engen would argue that this fifth context is actually included in the fourth horizon of the receptor audience. However, the tone of their writing indicates that the focus of

---

term "context" provides a stronger sense of dialectical interaction than the more receptive oriented term "audience." The fifth context is seeking a translation role by influencing the *content* of the translation rather than interacting with the *message* of the translation, which is the role of an audience.

the communication act is on a specific homogeneous group that would use the translation as their primary access to the Scripture. What the DFT controversy has helpfully reinforced is that the homogenous audience is a myth. No people group stands alone without influence from the outside, and no Bible translation stands alone without bearing the weight of interpretation and influence of the global Christian community. The DFT controversy has shattered any illusions we may have had in that regard. It may be that the importance of this fifth context on the actual translation has been downplayed in the past but it cannot be that way any longer.

I am not suggesting that awareness of the fifth context is new, just that we now are called to readjust our thinking about its influence and power because the significance of this group with respect to the act and content of Bible translation has come to the forefront. Even before the DFT controversy, the SIL Best Practice Statement (Final Report of the WEA 2013, 28) had guideline 1.6: "Throughout the process there should be consultation with other local partners, and the translation consultant needs particular sensitivity not to impose his or her own preferences." This guideline is unclear because it does not distinguish between a preference (which I do not want to impose) and a conviction (which I am less inclined to set aside). It also raises the question of whose preference should be decisive and who should be the one to determine that. While the clarity of this guideline is not addressed, the WEA panel (2013, 7–8) does reference it in order to add Recommendation 5 that would enable:

> Translation teams to account not only for the particular audience for whom the translation is being prepared, but also how to consider the impact on local groups with secondary exposure to the translation (overhearers such as existing local churches, close language groups, and so on).

They also addressed the fifth context in Recommendation 8 under issues related to the "ownership" of the translation that includes, besides the "end-users" (the fourth context mentioned above), "believers in local contexts, scholarly and other relevant hermeneutical communities (including existing local church resources), [and] patron donors behind the translation" (2013, 9).

The WEA panel's report itself is an example of the influence of the fifth context. In June 2014, Roy Eyre, President of Wycliffe Canada, wrote an open letter in which he stated that:

> SIL has now incorporated all the panel's ten recommendations into its translation processes. Most recently, SIL implemented a recommendation from the WEA panel report that SIL work with an external group or agency to create policies and procedures for accountability, and review by an external body. SIL asked, and the WEA agreed, to form a Divine Familial Terms Oversight Group. It will provide external review of how SIL implements the panel recommendations. The WEA selected eight evangelical Bible scholars, theologians, and missiologists to the group based on their expertise, experience and personal skills.

This is an expression of taking the fifth context into account. The global Christian community is given authority to establish boundaries and a framework for translation practice and accountability. It establishes a guard at the gate to make sure that people do not step over the line and go where they should not. The role of "evangelical Bible scholars, theologians and missiologists" is to monitor, set parameters, and give guidance. While this is a necessary and appropriate step, I will propose a way forward involving intentional and safe dialogue that suggests that this needed adjustment is insufficient.

THE CONTEXT THAT LED TO THE DFT CONTROVERSY

My first reaction to the DFT controversy was irritation with translators who had not interacted sufficiently with the Christians who would be impacted by their translation, and I was also frustrated with those who reacted defensively with explanations of translation principles to justify their choices. I put the blame for this disruption of the important task of Bible translation on a few that I saw as careless. However, I have come to realize that this was a controversy waiting to happen and not merely the work of a few translators; they were the flashpoint of rumblings that had been going on for a while. The nature of the "carelessness" of which I was accusing others was also evident in my own work.

We have a fireplace insert in our house where we burn wood in the winter months. I have learned that if the fire has burned out leaving only a few live coals, I do not need to try to light a new fire with paper and kindling. Instead I just add a few pieces, shut the door and wait about fifteen minutes. Then, when I throw in a match, the fire starts because the wood is primed by the heat and ignites readily. I propose that the translations at the center of this controversy were simply the match that caused the controversy to explode with wide ranging implications for Bible translation.

What are some of the causes that led to this explosion?

1. The ease of global travel and communication means that translators no longer work in isolation from the sending or surrounding community and Bible translation choices can be easily accessed and shared with wide reaching consequences.

2. The increase of interdisciplinary exchanges means issues affecting Bible translation are more widespread, well-known and debated, and easy access to such scholarship and discussion allows anyone to read and disseminate the content to a wide audience.

3. The cultural forces that have shaped western Christian thinking are different than those that have shaped eastern Christian thinking. Western translation philosophy has produced relevance theory, Skopos theory, and questions about the nature of language and meaning. Believers in the Christian South and East tend to

have a more conservative orientation than many in the western church.[3] They respect tradition and are more suspicious of creativity and experimentation with a tendency to view such thinking as potentially dangerous.

4. These three changes created the possibility of a crisis because of a fourth reality—the fear and discomfort that comes from the perception that something sacred is being threatened. By its nature, Bible translation is vulnerable to this because vernacular language reflects unique categories of thought resulting in creative renderings that can be perceived as a threat to what is comfortable and known. When the contextualization envelope has been pushed too far, as in the case of the DFT crisis, the reaction is—at least in retrospect—inevitable.

IMPACT IN PAKISTAN FROM THE DFT CONTROVERSY

My work is with Sindhi Muslims who are influenced by Sufism and who are familiar with mystical language and metaphorical references to God, such as "lover." Although questions about biological or physical misunderstandings of the divine familial terms do come up, Sindhis can make the shift to a metaphorical understanding of the DFT with little difficulty and so the need to find non-familial equivalents was not considered.

Nonetheless, translation work in Pakistan has suffered because of this controversy. Mr. Anthony Lamuel, president of the Pakistan Bible Society (PBS), wrote an open letter in 2012 dissolving all relationship between PBS and the Language Project (the name of SIL in Pakistan). He writes:

---

3. This is not to deny that many of the more powerful and vocal critics in the DFT issue are located in the West.

> Internationally there has been a big discussion on the matter of translating the Bible using terms and idioms which are rooted in the cultures and religious vocabulary of the target audiences. There have been attempts which have resulted in water downing (sic) the Christian understanding of the terms to make it palatable for the target audiences . . . I am now stating it very clearly that the Pakistan Bible Society has stopped working in Partnership with the Language Project of the Church of Pakistan (KoQ) so any translation of the Bible which appears with terms and idioms which are used for a particular target audience we will have nothing to do with it.

Even though the DFT controversy prompted the letter, the dissolution described was happening before the controversy became public. This provides anecdotal support for the argument that this controversy was the flashpoint of a more widespread concern. This dissolution is still in effect and there continues to be no cooperative translation efforts in Pakistan (Personal communication with S. Kehler 2015).

It is important to acknowledge that a major driver of this decision was politics. PBS is dependent on the support of the churches in Pakistan and because leaders of those churches interpreted the translation as a capitulation to Islamic theology, the credibility of PBS required swift action in order to survive.

One aspect of the letter that made our Sindhi Bible translation team nervous was the formation of a sub-committee to ensure that there would be no "Arabization of Urdu terms." Since the primary audience of the Sindhi translation is Muslim, we use Islamic terminology freely, such as the Arabic *Isa* for Jesus, rather than *Yesou* used by the Christian community. We do, however, use the Persian *Khuda* for God rather than *Allah*. At the same time, we are preparing a translation for a Hindu audience that employs Hindu terminology, such as *Eshvar* for God and *Pavitar Atma* for Holy Spirit. But these choices do not generate the same reaction from PBS or Pakistani Christians. A translation consultant

(Personal communication with S. Kehler 2015) explains why the concern of Pakistani Christians is limited to Muslim sensitive terminology:

> The reaction was more a fear of giving in to the religious majority in the country than translation principles. People agreed that the main difference between attitudes towards Saraiki [Muslim audience] and Sindhi [Hindu audience] was because the majority was seen by the church as the oppressors of the 2 percent Christian minority and so there was a different attitude towards Islamization in comparison to Hinduization.

There is another dimension to this strong reaction against Islamic terminology in Bible translations that supports the suggestion that the fifth context should be accommodated in Bible translation efforts. A Pakistani Christian woman in Canada asked me, "Why are the new translations (in Urdu) using *Allah?*" I explained that the publishers were trying to reach out to the majority community. It was not until later that I realized that by answering her question at face value, I had missed her real concern. She was not asking for an explanation, she was wondering why Pakistani Christians were not being consulted and valued in such decisions. These translations could affect the Christian community negatively if the majority Muslim community was to react against the Christian use of the *Allah*. Bypassing Christians and producing a Bible they will not use makes them feel neglected, disempowered and marginalized by those with power and money. While not justifying this response or joining in an implied criticism of the publishers of such translations, this reaction underscores the need to include such communities in dialogue that considers translation content.

IMPACT OF THE FIFTH CONTEXT ON TRANSLATION IN PAKISTAN

Bible translation into the Sindhi language has been impacted by the fifth context. In the last decade of the twentieth century, the 1979 production of the Jesus film was dubbed into Sindhi using the meaning-based Sindhi translation for a Muslim audience. When we first viewed the film we were surprised to find that instead of the name *Isa*, the common name used among Muslims for Jesus, the Christian community's rendering of *Yesou* was chosen. Such a language choice in Scripture reflects both the Christian community's sensitivity to Islamization of Christian terminology and the influence of outsider Christian communities on the choice of terminology. I have talked to Muslims who watched the film and then asked, "Who is *Yesou?*" When told it was *Isa* they made the connection, but then had to revise some of their understandings of what they saw.

Our philosophy in translating the Old Testament was to follow the Hebrew manuscripts and use the LXX only for help when the Hebrew was unclear. Isaiah 7:14 (NRSV) says, "Therefore the Lord himself will give you a sign. Look, the young woman is with child and shall bear a son, and shall name him Immanuel." The translation "young woman" follows the Hebrew, whereas many versions follow the LXX translation as "virgin" because of the importance of the "virgin" concept to Christ's birth in the Matthew narrative. In Sindhi there is a word (*chokari*) which means unmarried young woman, by implication a virgin, and semantically it closely parallels the Hebrew term. This is the word we originally chose to use. However, we soon received strong negative feedback from the Christian community who were ministering among Sindhi Muslims and referred to the verse as support for the virgin birth. The translation was in danger of being labeled heretical and therefore banned. As a result, we quickly changed the verse to read "virgin" with a footnote indicating that this follows the LXX. Our rationale for the change was that a meaning-based philosophy of translation is receptor oriented and so the perspectives of those impacted by the translation must be taken seriously even if those who make use of the translation are not the intended audience.

In the meaning-based Sindhi translation, our concern was not to provide word for word renderings consistent throughout the translation, but to choose terminology and phrasing that seemed the most natural and fitting to communicate the message to the receptor audience. However, a problem arose when another missionary began translating and publishing Christian books that approached the Old Testament in a more lexical manner. Rather than exploring the meaning of a verse within the discourse of the Old Testament passage, authors of these books selected particular Hebrew words and phrases to support their understanding of New Testament teaching. Meaning-based translations, following the goal of rendering the discourse of a passage in a meaningful fashion, will occasionally not reflect words and phrases in a manner that corresponds to the arguments in the Christian books. Unfortunately, when a translation does not fit that agenda, it may be criticized as wrong. The translation is judged as good or bad based on how it supports a particular hermeneutic and the presence or absence of key terminology.

For example, John 19:37 references Zechariah 12:10 to say, "They will look on the one they have pierced." However, Sindhi does not have a specific word for "pierced" and so, in light of the context, the John passage was rendered, "in whom they have thrust a spear." The Zechariah passage, on the other hand, lacks the context of a spear and was idiomatically translated making the implication of death explicit, "whom they have wounded and killed." While both translations are valid, a complaint was raised because the Sindhi did not provide parallel imagery for the concept of "pierced." Eventually, the New Testament passage was revised to parallel the Old Testament passage of "wounded," but without the explicit mention of "killed."

Another example of an idiomatic rendering that does not match some interpretations is Micah 5:2. The NRSV reads:

> But you, O Bethlehem of Ephrathah,
> who are one of the little clans of Judah,
> from you shall come forth for me
> one who is to rule in Israel,
> whose origin is from of old,
> from ancient days.

Some authors read the phrase "whose origin is from old" as a reference to Jesus' divinity indicating that he has no beginning. However, our Sindhi translation does not permit that understanding since we sought to reflect the idea that this is a reference to the house of David. Our translation reads, "the house of this ruler is established from long ago," where "house" refers to a family line.

As we negotiate these disputes, one possible resolution may be footnotes that give an alternate rendering more consistent with these authors' understanding. Unfortunately, during our conversations, comments were made that questioned the validity of the Sindhi translation and whether or not it could be trusted.

As an example of tensions that have arisen from interactions with the Christian community, the PBS Urdu Bible (1992 [1870]) has translated the word for sour wine (Gk. *oxous*) in John 19:29, a common beverage, as *sirka*, which is considered an acidic substance unsuitable for drinking. As a result, in the churches of Pakistan, the action of the man who relieves Jesus' thirst on the cross with *sirka* is interpreted as inflicting further torture and not as an act intended to bring Jesus some relief. Correcting this misunderstanding is difficult because the commitment to this interpretation is embedded into one of the more formative times in the Christian calendar. The seven sayings of Jesus on the cross are traditionally preached on during the Good Friday service and speakers have commented about the person who tortures Jesus by giving him *sirka*. Our Sindhi translation of common wine creates unintended tensions between the emerging Sindhi believers and Punjabi Christians who rely upon the Urdu translation.

THE WAY FORWARD: DIALOGUE WITH TRANSPARENCY

It seems that there will always be tension between those whose goal is to render Scripture in a way that the primary audience can understand and those who are afraid that creative contextualization leads to miscommunication. One side believes that a loss in one area (such as not reflecting DFT terminology) is made up for in clarity and understanding of the passage, while the other sees this as undermining the nature and purpose of Scripture. Who is right and who is wrong? I suggest that the question of right and wrong in this case is misplaced. Both sides have legitimate concerns. My interest is how to prevent the destructive misrepresentations, accusations, and responses that have been evident in the DFT controversy. These accusations occur not because people are malicious, but because they are afraid. They believe that the foundations of their faith are being attacked, and that the emerging faith of new believers and following generations is in danger of being misguided. They respond strongly in order to protect what is true and precious.

If my thesis is correct and this fifth context has increased influence within the translation task itself, and if fear is a primary motivator for their reaction, then what is the implication for Bible translation and missions? I suggest that the way forward is to generate intentional, safe, and constructive dialogue that transparently and respectfully addresses translation on a number of levels. This goes beyond inviting critics to participate in a process of understanding translation issues and instead creates an environment of mutual discovery. This means enabling people to provide feedback to a translation *in process*, rather than seeking a level of perfection before allowing church and community to interact with the translation.[4] In my own Bible translation experience, I have been forced to think about the importance of interacting well with the fifth context in the translation process and to think more constructively about the positive influence they can have in Bible translation.

From a translator's perspective, I find myself trying to justify certain choices for those who do not have a clear grasp on the nature and

---

4. Comprehension checking with surrounding communities and church as well as the publication of individual books upon completion is a common practice in translation. The point is that the Bible translator's primary passion is for Scriptural accuracy coupled with pressure to generate a publishable text. It can feel like a poor use of time to discuss questions that have already been discussed and resolved by those who have training and knowledge in translation dynamics.

complexity of language, meaning and the translation process. What I have come to realize is that this is the wrong starting point. Until the fears of those challenging certain choices is understood, respected, and attended to by the translator, they cannot hear our reasoning. We need to identify their fears, empathize with their concerns, and address their suspicions by creating safety *before* offering translation principles. The approach is not to argue head-on about a controversial rendering, but to first establish a context of mutual concern so that we can stand side by side and consider the issues as partners in the same mission. By asking for advice *from* them and exploring the controversy *with* them, we can avoid giving the impression that we are being careless in how we render God's Word and we cultivate partners, rather than opponents. We can also avoid a patronizing stance of superior knowledge explaining why we are right and they are wrong as we stubbornly cling to our position. This orientation requires confidence, humility, and a certain amount of skill: confidence that those we deal with are legitimate dialogue partners, humility because we also have something to learn and skill to be able to hear and respond in ways that build common ground rather than entrenching differences.

Rather than analyzing the concerns of the fifth context in order to counter them, we learn to empathize, hear their heart, and set up a *creative* rather than a *confrontational* tension. When conflict occurs, we assume there is a measure of legitimacy to both perspectives. This is not to say that everything about each perspective is correct, nor that the priority of each should be given equal weight. However, when we attack weak points or we argue for the higher priority of a particular stance, the gap between us widens and our interlocutors hear the message, "I am right and you are wrong." By incorporating the concerns of fellow believers into our perspective through such a creative tension, an acceptable way forward may be found.[5]

---

5. One tool to facilitate constructive dialogue is "ABC" from *Crucial Conversations: Tools for Talking when Stakes are High* (Patterson et al., 2012, 170–172). First, identify those aspects within the conflict with which both sides *agree*, then *build* on those aspects with questions that reveal diverging concerns,

The argument for ongoing empathetic dialogue is strengthened by noting that the nature of translation itself is dialogical; there is an intricate network connecting consultants, Bible scholars, translators, insider reviewers, outsider exegetes, and others. Individual decisions are not our prerogative. My role in Sindhi Bible translation is as a "hub," coordinating the work of exegetical analysis with the rendering of the text in the Sindhi language. The rendering looks forward to the audience and readers. The exegesis is a scholarly and rigorous system looking backwards at the original texts to determine an adequate and appropriate meaning that would be as close as possible to the author's intention. My role is to bring these two orientations together and encourage the right questions, so that the interchange generates an appropriate translation.

Another way of phrasing this is to consider that meaning does not reside in the text,[6] but in the meaning-makers who interact with the text, whether it is the author seeking to communicate a message by providing mutually understandable signs, or those deciphering the message from the signs. There is a *covenant* (Vanhoozer 1998, 252–256) between author and reader that the meaning will be communicated and received with integrity and transparency. In this paradigm the translator's work as the "hub" is to facilitate a covenant by supervising a dialogue between the author and those who desire to connect with the author's message. With such an orientation to translation, including the fifth context is not a matter of creating a new and separate task, but of including them as legitimate and active partners within an existing dynamic.

Dialogue is also to be encouraged and promoted over an *extended* period of time because assumptions and beliefs often change slowly. We need to hear something a number of times, relate it to a variety of scenarios and wrestle with it repeatedly in order to own it. Only then

---

and conclude by *contrasting* different perspectives, rather than disagreeing with an opposing perspective.

6. See the philosophical arguments for this in Vanhoozer (1998, 252–256) and Kraft (1991, 82–85).

will we accept what is unfamiliar and be able to change our thinking without undermining what is essential. Thus, the solution to criticism is not to argue our case with the goal of efficiency and immediate agreement, but to allow our critics time to work through new ideas and make adjustments in a process of ongoing dialogue, even as we engage their concerns and make changes ourselves. The power of dialogue is that no interlocutor walks away unchanged.

A friend within SIL is on the board of a parachurch organization dealing with Bible translations and he explained to me that at the time of the DFT crisis, "The main frictions [on our board] were related to literal vs. idiomatic translations but over time they began to see that 'idiomatic' does not mean 'inaccurate' and 'literal' does not mean 'accurate' when it conveys little or no meaning or even the wrong meaning." This, of course, is basic to a Bible translator. All translation is interpretation and the reconstruction of author-intended meaning by the hearer is the determining factor for appropriateness in translation and communication. But if we use "beloved of God" instead of "Son of God" or if we find a non-familial substitute for "father" in order to refer to God when we are dealing with a group that is still grappling with what "accuracy" means in Bible translation, they will be not be able to respond productively. This is not to suggest that they are ignorant or wrong (or, alternatively, that such translation choices are appropriate), but that they are coming to the text from a certain vantage point that has been reinforced over a long period of time. They cannot be convinced by logical arguments. Rather, their fears must be acknowledged and addressed with safety before they can even begin to entertain the translator's dilemma and effectively join in the discussion.

OBJECTIONS AND CONCLUSIONS

Is it legitimate to allow those who have limited understanding of translation principles and an inadequate grasp of the linguistic and cultural challenges of a particular people group, to directly influence a Bible translation? My response is that our answer to this question is irrelevant. The point is that they *do* have influence and they can either support or undermine our efforts. The reality is there and it needs to be managed and leveraged for good.

But is this not adding another time-consuming task to an already time-consuming responsibility? Yes, if we believe that our role is limited to creating a Bible translation. But I believe that this wake-up call is an invitation to be more intimately involved in the *missio Dei*—what God is doing in his mission. It is an opportunity and a challenge. It is a *challenge* because we as Bible translators may fail to respond adequately if we think this controversy is just a bump that is being smoothed out and we can return to our task, back to business as usual. It is an *opportunity* because including others in the translation dialogue means that we can all grow together in our understanding of language, the nature of communication and the function of God's self-revelation through Scripture. Growth in all three areas connects people to what God is doing in bringing about the Kingdom of Heaven in this world. To spend energy in dialogue is an act of humility recognizing that we are not the sole guardians of the Word. We are servants and are required to heed the wisdom and concerns of our brothers and sisters in Christ.

REFERENCES

"A Translation Challenge: The Son of God / Summary of an Ongoing Controversy." n.d. Accessed January 29, 2013. http://www.wycliffe.org/SonofGod.aspx.

Brown, Rick. 2000. "The 'Son of God': Understanding the Messianic Titles of Jesus," *International Journal of Frontier Missions* 17, no. 1:41–52.

———. 2005. "Explaining the Biblical Term 'Son(s) of God' in Muslim Contexts," *International Journal of Frontier Missions* 22, no. 3: 91–96.

———. 2005. "Translating the Biblical Term 'Son(s) of God' in Muslim Contexts," *International Journal of Frontier Missions* 22, no. 4: 135–145.

"Divine Familial Terms: Answers to Commonly Asked Questions." n.d. Accessed December 7, 2015. http://Wycliffe.org.

"Final Report of the WEA Independent Bible Translation Review Panel." n.d. Accessed December 7, 2015. http://www.worldevangelicals.org/translation-review/.

Kraft, Charles H. 1991. *Communication Theory for Christian Witness.* Maryknoll, NY: Orbis.

Lochhead, David. 1988. *The Dialogical Imperative.* Maryknoll, NY: Orbis.

Naylor, Mark. 2013. "Mapping Theological Trajectories that Emerge in Response to a Bible Translation," DTh thesis, University of South Africa.

Patterson, Kerry, Joseph Grenny, Ron McMillan, and Al Switzler. 2013. *Crucial Conversations: Tools for Talking When Stakes Are High.* New York: McGraw-Hill.

Shaw, R. Daniel, and Van Engen, Charles E. 2003. *Communicating God's Word in a Complex World.* New York: Rowan & Littlefield.

Vanhoozer, Kevin J. 1988. *Is There a Meaning in this Text? The Bible, the Reader, and the Morality of Literary Knowledge.* Grand Rapids, MI: Zondervan.

CHAPTER 13

TEACHING BIBLE INTERPRETATION IN INTERCULTURAL CONTEXTS
A Plea for Teaching Bible Interpretation Using Only the Bible
Larry W. Caldwell

INTRODUCTION

Sola Scriptura! This was the rallying cry of the Reformers as they battled against the hierarchy and dogma of the Roman Catholic Church. Sadly, this cry is seldom heard in Protestant circles today. This cry has instead been drowned out by a new hierarchy and dogma, much of it perpetuated in our Bible schools and seminaries. Of course most of us, as Protestants, would quickly give intellectual assent to the idea of *sola Scriptura,* but in reality our teaching and our curricula belay the fact. "The Bible alone" is in our creeds but not necessarily in our practice. We have come to rely instead upon the hierarchy of the critical scholars and the dogma of the historical-critical method. As a result, the cry of "the Bible alone" is seldom heard in our Bible school and seminary classes.

Another rallying cry of the Reformers was the idea of the priesthood of the believer. The Reformers believed that the average Christian did not have to rely upon the Catholic priest to be his/her intermediary or interpreter of Scripture. This is one reason why one of the very first acts of the reformed Luther was to translate the Bible, not into the high German of the intellectuals but rather into the low German of the common people. The Reformers believed that because all Christians were filled with the Holy Spirit they were able to both understand God's Word and interpret God's Word for themselves. Unfortunately, once again, the cry of the priesthood of the believer has largely been lost today as many Protestants rely upon their well-trained pastors, and the Bible scholars, to interpret the Bible for them.

This reliance upon the "experts" is the model perpetuated in most of our Bible college and seminary training programs.

My purpose in writing the above brief, and rather simplistic, summary is to set the stage for where we are now in regard to Bible interpretation, both in the West and the non-West. At least two questions arise. First, do we still really believe in *sola Scriptura* and the priesthood of the believer when it comes to our teaching of Bible interpretation in our Bible colleges and seminaries today? And, secondly, do we merely give "lip service" to these Reformation essentials while instead teaching a variety of things about Bible interpretation but dealing minimally with the Bible itself, alone and in its entirety? The answers to these questions have great implications for all of us who teach the Bible, especially those of us who teach the Bible in intercultural contexts, both in the United States and abroad.[1]

On the whole, Bible colleges and seminaries desire that their students know how to "rightly handle" God's Word (cf. 2 Tim 2:15). As a result, the curricula at most Bible colleges and seminaries worldwide include courses on hermeneutics. Most often, however, these courses focus more on how to "rightly handle" resources found outside the Bible by teaching students how to use (mostly western) commentaries, dictionaries, and language tools. Very little time is spent on actually teaching students how to "rightly handle" the interpretation of the Bible *by itself*—by that I mean studying the Bible primarily on its own—without the use of these outside resources. Though it is seldom talked about, such an emphasis upon the teaching of how to use sources extraneous to the Bible leads to dependency issues on a grand scale, especially for younger non-western churches.

Drawn from my own experience in teaching Bible interpretation courses for over thirty years in both Asian and North American contexts, this article argues for the need to re-examine what is currently taught—and why it is taught—in regards to hermeneutics courses in

---

1. By using the word, "intercultural," I am referring to contexts that assume some movement from one culture to another, as well as contexts that are already multicultural and/or multigenerational.

our Bible colleges and seminaries, especially those found in intercultural contexts in both the West and non-western world. Without such a re-examination, the author contends that we may be training future generations of students who really do not know how to "rightly handle" God's Word. Once this necessary background is given, an alternative teaching model will be proposed and examined at length.

THE CURRENT SITUATION: TEACHING *ABOUT* BIBLE INTERPRETATION

All of us involved in theological education must keep reminding ourselves that the overarching purpose of such theological education is, at its very core, a missiological purpose: to help equip others to better understand and communicate the truths of the Bible to a lost and dying world. In light of this missiological purpose we must continually ask ourselves the following questions: Are we adequately and aggressively training new generations of students to meet the challenges of bringing the gospel to today's world, both locally and globally? Or, are we simply perpetuating old models of theological education that are increasingly irrelevant? (cf. Caldwell and Wan 2012; Caldwell 2013).

While all theological disciplines must take these questions very seriously, I believe that the discipline of hermeneutics is particularly vulnerable to scrutiny. Why do I say this? Because I believe that interpreting God's Word for others, as well as training others to correctly interpret God's Word, is the heart of theological education, whatever the individual discipline. Good Bible interpretation methods should result in the communication of the good news more effectively in any cultural context, especially in our increasingly complex intercultural world. Unfortunately, the Bible interpretation methods of the past two centuries have not adequately equipped the Protestant church for gospel presentation in our world today. My bookshelves, for example, are filled with hundreds of books on Bible interpretation. Most were written during the past three decades. Of these hundreds of books, however, few directly address the complexities of interpreting the Bible in intercultural contexts. Furthermore, these hundreds of resources tell us much *about* the Bible and its interpretation—with various layers of complexity—but not necessarily how to interpret the Bible *without* the use of these, and other, outside sources. In my opinion, these are serious deficiencies.

Examining how we teach Bible interpretation, especially in intercultural contexts, gives us all much to think about. Most of us have had extensive training in Bible interpretation. We have had courses in Old and New Testament backgrounds, Greek and Hebrew, exegesis, and so on. And I dare say that not many of us have seriously questioned the need for all of this extensive training. We bought into the system. We merely assumed that it was the way we should learn to better interpret the Bible. But my point is that it is imperative that we do indeed question the appropriateness of such extensive training, not only for our own lives but for the lives of our students. Yes, some of us will need to be scholars, and some of our students will need to be scholars. And yes, our students will need to be aware of some of the complexities of the biblical text and consequently will need a basic familiarity with the tools that can help answer those complexities. But the bottom line question comes down to this: *how many* and *how much? How many* of our students need to be able to exegete a text in Greek and/or Hebrew? *How much* Greek and Hebrew needs to be required for ministry purposes? *How many* need to be able to write library-based papers comparing and contrasting the views of several commentators on a particular text? *How much* emphasis should be placed on the mastery of the viewpoints of professional scholars? Yes, a small percentage of our students will need to learn a lot of this information, but not everyone; in fact, if we are truly candid, not many at all. What everyone really needs—and this is crucially important—is the necessary training that will equip them to relevantly interpret the Bible in the complicated intercultural contexts of our world today.

At the same time, we usually assume that the Bible interpretation methods that work for us will also work for others. We seldom call into question the possibility that what works for us may not work for others.

We simply take for granted that our way is the correct way. I must hasten to add that this assumption is usually made innocently enough, though at times we consciously refuse to question it since we have so much invested in a particular method. If it works for us, why would we, or should we, question whether or not it will work for others?

Is it possible, however, that the Bible interpretation methods that work so well for us may not work as well for others? In light of the complexities of our intercultural world today it is imperative that we ask this question. We no longer have the luxury to assume that *our* way is the best way or the *only* way.[2] In fact, to make such an assumption today may make our biblical message irrelevant to the very people we are trying to influence with the truths of Scripture. There may, indeed, be other valid interpretation methods available to us that will help the Bible come alive to those individuals who do not share our particular theological heritage, training or worldview. As a result, both western and non-western Christians facing the complexities of making the Bible relevant in their own various contexts need to face this question head on (cf. Caldwell 1999; 2012a; 2012b).

For the past three decades I have been actively seeking how best to interpret the Bible in intercultural situations. What I have discovered, as a result of my quest, is that the western hermeneutical methods in which I have been trained are indeed good methods. Most of these western hermeneutical methods are centered upon historical criticism and the tools of the historical-critical approach. This approach stresses that a biblical passage must be understood in light of at least three factors: (1) the syntax of the words used; (2) the context in which the words are found; and (3) the underlying historical setting behind the

---

2.   Saying this does not mean that I am advocating a pluralistic approach to interpreting the Bible. There are indeed "better" and "worse" interpretation methods. Evangelical scholars are under obligation to point out the strengths and weaknesses of the various methods as well as to advocate the use of methods that are founded upon a high view of Scripture as God's inspired Word to humankind.

words.[3] Bible interpreters who use historical criticism, for the most part, are conscientiously attempting to interpret what the Bible means for us today based upon what it first meant to audiences in its original historical setting. While the end results of western theologians may differ widely, most have genuinely attempted to make the biblical text as relevant for today as it was in its original historical context. I, myself, have been helped by historical criticism, both by the results of others who have used and taught historical-critical methods, as well as by my own use of these tools in my personal Bible study and my Bible teaching.

Hermeneutical methods based upon historical criticism do work. But are they necessarily the *only* ways to interpret the Bible, especially since they tend to teach us more about *how to approach the Bible than how to interpret the Bible itself*? I was a seminary teacher in the Philippines for many years. Before I first came to the Philippines I did not stop to think that perhaps the hermeneutical methods that worked so well in my own cultural context may not work as well in another cultural context. It was only when I was confronted by individuals for whom historical-critical tools were oftentimes irrelevant and/or incomprehensible that I realized that historical-critical tools may not be the "be all and end all" of proper Bible study and that western methods are not necessarily universal. Furthermore, in a more practical vein, historical-critical based hermeneutical methods typically involve the use of expensive books and highly literate advanced training. Our world today—a billion of whom live in oral cultures and another two billion who are only functionally literate—may not be prepared socially or economically for the use of western hermeneutical methods, especially those based upon historical criticism (cf. Chang and Lovejoy 2013). We must, therefore, re-evaluate the appropriateness of

---

3. Historical criticism is also known as the grammatico-historical method. Both phrases, historical-critical and grammatico-historical, fall under the rubric of biblical criticism: "the study which attempts to determine the true meaning of the Bible by using techniques applied to other written documents" (Erickson 1986, 21).

transporting oftentimes expensive and elitist hermeneutical methods into such cultures.[4]

Consequently, for the over thirty years now that I have been teaching hermeneutics, I teach it without allowing my students, whether in western or Asian contexts, to use any source other than the Bible itself. And it works! I still throw in careful handfuls of information based on the historical-critical tools, but in subtle ways that will help my students as they use the Bible as their only source. Such "Bible only" teaching, however, is not without controversy. In fact, at the Philippines seminary where I have taught hermeneutics, the mostly Asian (and western-trained) faculty soon made my "Bible only" hermeneutics course a requirement for all missions and Christian education students (the "practical" majors) while all other students were required to take a very western-based hermeneutics course where they learned lots about Bible interpretation, including, at the time, many readings on the topics of biblical criticism, Barth, Bultmann, and black theology. While not opposed to learning about these topics, I continue to wonder how appropriate such learning is for the training of Asian pastors and church workers in Asia.

All of us need to rethink what theological training is truly appropriate. There is much talk of appropriate technology and of appropriate development; it is time we seriously talk of appropriate theological education, including how we teach the Bible. Do we teach the Bible or do we spend most of our time teaching *about* the Bible, with much of our time spent on the historical-critical tools? For me, it all comes down to the question of "Who says?" Who says that historical criticism is appropriate for serious, and even scholarly, study of the Bible? Who says that it is important for Bible college and/or seminary graduates to master historical criticism? Who says that the historical-critical tools,

---

4.   It should be noted here that historical criticism has come under much scrutiny even in the West and by western theologians over the past forty years. See, for example, Maier (1977); Stuhlmacher (1977); Linnemann (1990) and (2001); Wainwright (1982); Zehr (1986); Harrisville and Sundberg (2002); Sparks (2008); and Hays and Ansberry (2013).

with all of their attendant baggage, are appropriate for those ministering in our world today, especially in non-western contexts? I believe we need more biblical studies courses that will help our students come up with answers from the Bible concerning questions that they themselves face in their current ministry contexts, or will face in future. Are we really training our students for ministry success in our world today? Perhaps it is time to look for alternatives.

AN ALTERNATIVE PROPOSAL FOR *DOING* BIBLE INTERPRETATION: USING *ONLY* THE BIBLE

I began this article with reference to the Protestant Reformers. What follows is an attempt to do Bible interpretation that follows the Reformers by using the Bible only (*sola Scriptura*) and equipping every Christian to do Bible interpretation for him/herself (the priesthood of the believer). The emphasis is upon making the biblical text "come alive" both for the interpreter as well as for his/her ministry audience, whether church, small group, or individual disciple(s). To make this happen, a good interpreter, when studying a Bible passage, will ask the following seven questions. I call these questions the "Seven Steps to Make the Bible Come Alive!"[5]

> Step 1: What kind of literary form is this Bible passage and what are the implications of this?
>
> Step 2: What are the contextual boundaries of the Bible passage?
>
> Step 3: What was God saying through this Bible passage to the original audience back then?
>
> Step 4: What is the general principle that God had in mind through this Bible passage for all peoples and all cultures?

---

5. For more information concerning these "Seven Steps," see my forthcoming book, *Doing Bible Interpretation*.

Step 5: What is God saying through this Bible passage to you today?

Step 6: What is God saying through this Bible passage to your community of believers today?

Step 7: How will you communicate the truths of this Bible passage to your community of believers?

Some will simply look at this "Seven Steps" approach and call it just another way to do inductive Bible study. Typically, inductive Bible study deals with three steps: observation (what does the text say?); interpretation (what does the text mean?); and application (what does the text mean for my life?). On the one hand, this assessment is correct since, like inductive Bible study, the "Seven Steps" deal primarily with the biblical text itself. On the other hand, this assessment is too simplistic since this "Seven Steps" approach takes both the original context and the application process much more seriously than does typical inductive Bible study. I like to think of the "Seven Steps" as a more in-depth and holistic approach.[6]

Note that in these "Seven Steps" the first four steps relate more to the biblical text while the last three steps relate more to the interpreter and his/her particular context or culture. Another way of saying this is that the first four steps relate to exegeting the text while the last three steps relate to exegeting the culture.[7] While the "Seven Steps" draw upon some of the strengths of historical-criticism—especially the emphasis on literary form or genre (Step 1), setting contextual

---

6. I would place the more recent Discovery Bible Study (DBS) process in this same inductive Bible study category. The DBS emphasis upon "read," "obey," and "share" is excellent for both individual and group Bible study, and it can be used in both oral and literate cultures. However, like inductive Bible study, DBS does not give the original context nor the application process the emphasis that they deserve.

7. For more information concerning the distinctions between exegeting the text and exegeting the culture see Caldwell (2013). In this article, I examine Bible interpretation done specifically with the urban and rural poor, especially doing Bible interpretation that considers the social dimensions of the local people using "lower-based" training programs and "border" pedagogies.

boundaries (Step 2), and what the passage meant to its original audience (Step 3)—such historical-critical emphasis is minimal. And even here Steps 2, 3 and 4 are based upon the context of the Bible passage itself and not upon the use of outside resources—like study notes, commentaries, and so on—to help determine answers to these steps. The overall emphasis is to let the Bible text speak for itself first, of course through the guidance of the Holy Spirit.[8]

Steps 5 and 6 relate to what the biblical text is saying today to the interpreter, first in light of the interpreter him/herself (Step 5), as well as in light of the interpreter's community of believers, in other words his/her church or small group (Step 6). Step 5 shows that the heart of all Bible interpretation is personal. If the Bible interpretation does not impact and change the life of the interpreter, then it is incomplete interpretation. And if it impacts the life of the interpreter it will also impact the lives of others in the interpreter's community of believers (Step 6). But what is true for the community of believers should *first* be true for the interpreter. Step 5 builds off the work that has already been done in Steps 1 to 4, especially Steps 3 and 4. Step 6 demonstrates that the Bible interpreter is not learning how to interpret the Bible just for him/herself. Rather, Bible interpretation is being done so that the local community of believers can better understand the Bible passage and how it applies to their daily lives. Here in Step 6, the results of Steps 3, 4 and 5 are applied to the local community of believers. To summarize Steps 5 and 6: good Bible interpretation should change both the life of the interpreter as well as the lives of his/her people.

Step 7 answers the question: How will you communicate the truths of this Bible passage to your community of believers? While Step 6 deals with the actual truth of the Bible passage and what God

---

8. External Bible study tools—like study notes, commentaries, and so on—can be helpful, especially with Step 3. I am not against outside resources *per se*. However, my desire is for the interpreter to exhaust his/her own attempts to understand the Bible passage *first* before going to the external tools. Unfortunately, many Bible interpreters have lost this Bible-first discipline.

is saying to the interpreter's community of believers through that passage, the emphasis of Step 7 is different. Step 7 is where the Bible interpreter tries to best *communicate* those truths. Here the Bible interpreter attempts to pass on the truth of the Bible passage as clearly and relevantly as possible, in ways that the people will best understand. Here is where an understanding of the local community of believers and their local context is so important.

In Step 7 the Bible interpreter tries to answer two questions about the Bible passage: How can the original meaning be best communicated to my modern audience today? How can the original meaning be made relevant using modern words/terms/means/ways of understanding? It is in Step 7 where Bible interpretation is done at the level of the interpreter and the people in their local context. Steps 2 and 3 speak to the importance of the Bible context. At the same time, paying attention to the local context of the local community of believers in Step 7 *is equally important.* Bible interpretation does not occur in a vacuum. Rather, Bible interpretation, if done correctly, is always done *in community* with other believers. All Bible interpretation that is guided by the Holy Spirit should have an effect on the believing community in which the Bible interpretation is occurring, both as individuals and as a group. Step 7 allows this to happen.

It is important, then, that the Bible interpreter understands his/her community well. Among the questions the Bible interpreter should have answers to are these:

- Why do they believe the way they do?
- Why do they think the way they do?
- What are their core values?
- What are those things that shape their worldview (the way they think about the world)?
- What kinds of ideas influence them and their decision-making process?

In connection with the actual Bible passage being studied, here are some questions that should also be asked in Step 7:

- How does the local community of believers understand some of the same concepts/ideas/ways of thinking that are found in the particular Bible passage that is being studied?
- Have there been any recent local events or incidents that have occurred within the local community of believers in the recent past (6 months) that might give insights into how they might interpret a particular passage?
- How will the truths of the Bible passage actually be communicated to the community of believers? What media (movie, TV show, song, indigenous drama or story, and so on) will help explain what the Bible passage is speaking about?

As can be readily seen, there is much to Steps 5 through 7, especially Step 7. Usually something akin to Steps 5 through 7 is left to the so-called "Practical Theology" department and to homiletics courses. This, in my opinion, does a disservice to the entire hermeneutical task of the Bible interpreter. It bifurcates hermeneutics by making a distinction between the exegesis of the biblical text and the exegesis of the culture. Such a distinction puts undo emphasis upon the exegesis of the biblical text in most Bible college and seminary curricula. Instead, if we see the entire hermeneutical process as a holistic continuum from text to community (Steps 1–7), we will be better able to spend the time necessary for both a thorough exegesis of the biblical text as well as a thorough exegesis of the community of believers who will hopefully inculcate that text into their very lives.

CONCLUSION

The Reformation references to *sola Scriptura* and the priesthood of the believer that began this article are an appropriate way to end. How so? Precisely because I believe that we need a new reformation in our approach to hermeneutics and Bible interpretation today if we are to effectively reach the vast numbers of unchurched North Americans, not to mention the billions of unreached and unengaged peoples, who have never heard the good news of Jesus Christ. In fact, I am convinced that until we reform our understanding of how to interpret God's Word—and how to teach others how to interpret God's Word—we will be sending out ministers and missionaries who are only partially trained for ministry.

The dual concepts of *sola Scriptura* and the priesthood of the believer ripped across the European continent five centuries ago and forever changed the course of Christianity. I truly believe that a recapturing of the incredible ramifications of these two concepts can help change the course of Christianity throughout the world in the third millennium. It is imperative that we missiological and theological educators equip our Bible college and seminary graduates to be able to discover and apply the truths of the Bible to their daily lives—and to the daily lives of their congregations and their disciples—without having to rely upon either the interpretational dogma of Protestant scholars and/or upon a scholarly priesthood trained to interpret the Bible for them.

I have raised some difficult questions in this article, but I believe we must ask these questions if we truly desire to make our students the most effective pastors, church workers, and missionaries that they can be. I challenge Bible college and seminary faculty to seriously consider some of the issues I have raised. My overall desire in all of this is that we be as effective as we possibly can be in training our students to "rightly handle" God's Word. The answers we find will help us to better bring the Good News of Jesus Christ to our world in the third millennium.

REFERENCES

Caldwell, Larry W. 1999. "Towards the New Discipline of Ethnohermeneutics: Questioning the Relevancy of Western Hermeneutical Methods in the Asian Context." *Journal of Asian Mission* 1, no. 1: 21–43.

———. 2012a. "Reconsidering Our Biblical Roots: Bible Interpretation, the Apostle Paul and Mission Today. Part 1." *International Journal of Frontier Missiology* 29, no. 2: 91–100. Available from: http://www.ijfm.org/PDFs_IJFM/29_2_PDFs /IJFM_29_2-Caldwell.pdf.

———. 2012b. "Reconsidering Our Biblical Roots: Bible Interpretation, the Apostle Paul and Mission Today. Part 2." *International Journal of Frontier Missiology* 29, no. 2: 113–121. Available from: http://www.ijfm.org/PDFs_IJFM/29_3_PDFs /IJFM_29_3-Caldwell-Pt2.pdf

———. 2013. "Interpreting the Bible with the Poor." In *Social Engagement: The Challenge of the Social in Missiological Education*. The 2013 Proceedings of the Association of Professors of Mission. Wilmore, KY: First Fruits. Available from: http://place .asburyseminary.edu/firstfruitspapers/20.

———. Forthcoming. *Doing Bible Interpretation*. West Palm Beach, FL: Grace Publishing/The Timothy Initiative.

Caldwell, Larry W., and Enoch Wan. 2012. "Riots in the City: Replacing Nineteenth-century Urban Training Models with Relevant 'Urbanized' Training Models for the Twenty-first Century." In *Reaching the City: Reflections on Urban Mission for the Twenty-first Century*, edited by Gary Fujino, Timothy R. Sisk, and Teresa C. Casiño, 97–118. Pasadena, CA: William Carey Library.

Chiang, Samuel E, and Grant Lovejoy, eds. 2013. *Beyond Literate Western Practices: Continuing Conversations in Orality and Theological Education*. Hong Kong: Capstone Enterprises/ International Orality Network.

Erickson, Millard J. 1986. *Concise Dictionary of Christian Theology*. Grand Rapids, MI: Baker Books.

Harrisville, Roy A., and Walter Sundberg. 2002. *The Bible in Modern Culture*. 2nd Ed. Grand Rapids, MI: William B. Eerdmans Publishing Company.

Hays, Christopher M., and Christopher Ansberry, eds. 2013. *Evangelical Faith and the Challenge of Historical Criticism*. Grand Rapids, MI: Baker Academic.

Linnemann, Eta. 2001. *Historical Criticism of the Bible. Methodology or Ideology?* Translated by Robert W. Yarbrough. Grand Rapids, MI: Baker Book House.

———. 2001. *Biblical Criticism on Trial. How Scientific is "Scientific Theology"?* Translated by Robert W. Yarbrough. Grand Rapids, MI: Kregel Publications.

Maier, Gerhard. 1977. *The End of the Historical Critical Method*. Translated by E. W. Leverenz, and R. F. Norden. St. Louis, MO: Concordia Publishing.

Sparks, Kenton L. 2008. *God's Word in Human Words. An Evangelical Appropriation of Critical Biblical Scholarship*. Grand Rapids, MI: Baker Academic.

Stuhlmacher, Peter. 1977. *Historical Criticism and Theological Interpretation of Scripture*. Translated by Roy A. Harrisville. Philadelphia, PA: Fortress Press.

Wainwright, Arthur W. 1982. *Beyond Biblical Criticism. Encountering Jesus in Scripture*. Atlanta, GA: John Knox Press.

Zehr, Paul M. 1986. *Biblical Criticism in the Life of the Church*. Scottdale, PA: Herald Press.

PART FOUR

Historical and
Future Perspectives

CHAPTER 14

SAVING THE FUTURE OF EVANGELICAL MISSIONS

David J. Hesselgrave

*The ultimate measure of a man
is not where he stands
in moments of comfort and convenience
but where he stands
at times of challenge and controversy.*
Martin Luther King

While swimming with a colleague in the Pacific waters of Central Honshu back in 1950, relatively placid surface waters suddenly gave way to a strong undercurrent and then to a threatening undertow. It was the first such experience for both of us and it was scary. Many years later, in 2011, the world watched on television as a giant tsunami in northeastern Honshu destroyed an ultra-modern nuclear power plant and carried entire villages inland or into the depths of the ocean. The landscape will never be the same.

Twentieth-century missions encountered numerous crosscurrents and undertows. In this new century they are also beginning to experience the kind of subterranean tremors that presage a tsunami. How should evangelicals respond so as to preserve the future of evangelical missions? This paper attempts to answer that question.

My objective is to advance Roland Allen's "resubmission" proposal as a way—likely the very best way—for evangelicals to: (a) counter the effects of an approaching missiological tsunami, (b) enable them to discover (or recover) and occupy higher ground, and (c) preserve the future of evangelical missions as we have known them. In attempting this, I intentionally and necessarily deal with the findings and proposals of numerous colleagues. I have endeavored to deal with their ideas candidly, correctly, and courteously. If in some cases I have failed in that attempt, I humbly apologize.

CONCILIAR CHURCHES AND MISSIONS AND THE ECUMENICAL MOVEMENT OF THE TWENTIETH CENTURY

As Latourette's "great century of missions" gave way to the twentieth century, Protestant missions had both reason for hope and cause for concern. The last decades of the nineteenth century witnessed great strides forward in Christian mission. However, those decades also witnessed the inroads of a social gospel, higher criticism, Unitarianism and universalism, as well as an increase in Catholic opposition. Into this milieu the twentieth century ecumenical movement of mainline Protestant denominations was born.

Organizing and Growing the Ecumenical Movement (1910–1960)

When John R. Mott and his colleagues planned the historic World Missionary Conference of Edinburgh 1910, they decided that discussions of a theological nature and of Catholic opposition would not be allowed. This decision was made in order to secure the participation of Randall Davidson, Archbishop of Canterbury, and enhance fellowship and unity. But it was an egregious error. John Stott called it a "fatal flaw" adding, *"In consequence, the theological challenges of the day were not faced. And, during the decades that followed, the poison of theological liberalism seeped into the bloodstream of western universities and seminaries, and largely immobilized the churches' mission"* (Stott 1996, xii, emphasis mine).

Three organizations emerged from Edinburgh: one on missions (the International Missionary Council—IMC), one on Faith and Order, and one on Life and Work. The latter two joined forces to form the World Council of Churches (WCC) in 1948, and the IMC merged with the WCC at the Third Assembly meeting in New Delhi in 1961, becoming its Commission on World Mission and Evangelicalism (CWME). The Third Assembly turned out to be a high point in the history of the WCC. The Eastern Orthodox Church and several small Pentecostal church groups joined the WCC. For the first time in a millennium and a half, eastern and western churches were said to be united in one body. WCC leaders were almost euphoric.

Two aspects of these developments are of special interest here: those having to do with the WCC Statement of Faith and those having to do with WCC missiology. As for the former, the original Statement of Faith of the WCC consisted of but a single affirmation: "The World Council of Churches is a fellowship of churches which confess the Lord Jesus Christ as Lord and Savior." At the Third Assembly in New Delhi the words " . . . according to the Scriptures and therefore seek to fulfill together their common calling to the glory of the one God—Father, Son and Holy Spirit" were added, but as the price exacted by the Eastern Orthodox Church for its participation.

As for Christian mission, James Scherer (1993, 83) notes that the personal conversion view of mission that had predominated in missions previously was replaced by a church-centered view after World War II. However, that church-centered view itself was criticized by Dutch missiologist Johannes Hoekendijk and others. The idea that Christian mission is the mission of God (*missio Dei*), not of the church, was injected into the discussion by Karl Hartenstine in 1952. These and other changes at least signaled that missions and missiology was a central concern of the ecumenical movement. After the merger of the IMC with the WCC in 1961, that interest began to recede.

Decline of the World Council of Churches and Mainline Conciliar Missions (1961–2010)

Early on in the 1960s, much seemed promising from a conciliar point of view. Organizationally, Christian missions were now an important part of the WCC organizationally. Missiologically, in 1961, Georg Vicedom elaborated *missio Dei* in terms of the Kingdom of God and the establishment of shalom in the world. The following year R. Pierce Beaver declared that the " . . . service or relief programs, so closely associated with interchurch aid, *are* mission" (Beaver 1964, 110, emphasis mine). Little wonder, then, that planners of the Fourth

Assembly of the WCC meeting in Uppsala (1968) disregarded Donald McGavran's repeated and penetrating question: "What about the two billion [unevangelized]?" They chose "He makes all things new" as a theme and accompanied it with the motto "Let the world set the agenda" (Hesselgrave 2005, 317–326, esp. 322).

As intimated above, by the early 1990s, the CWME itself had become integrated into the WCC as part of its Programme Unit No. 2 (Churches in Mission, Health, Education and Witness) and disappeared. But just as revealing, or more so, were statistics compiled by A. Scott Moreau and his colleagues. At the beginning of the twentieth century, mainline denominational churches in the U.S. had supplied eighty percent of the North American missionary force. At the end of the century they supplied no more than six percent of it (Moreau et al. 2000, 4, 34)! The church encompassed the world, but ecumenical leaders had failed to take into account the famous dictum of Methodist Bishop Stephen Neill who warned his colleagues that "When everything is mission, nothing is mission" (1959, 81).

CONSERVATIVE CHURCHES AND MISSIONS: THE EVANGELICAL MOVEMENT OF THE TWENTIETH CENTURY

If Edinburgh 1910 conciliar leaders were indifferent to doctrinal distinctives, their conservative Protestant counterparts were not. Conservatives responded to the challenges of liberals and modernists immediately and in two primary ways: first, by forming new alliances, and second, by forging new declarations of faith.

Forming New Alliances—Four Conservative Missionary Associations

Two significant conservative missions associations were organized in the first half of the twentieth century: the Interdenominational Foreign Mission Association of North America (IFMA) and, later, the Evangelical Fellowship of Mission Agencies (EFMA; affiliated with the National Association of Evangelicals). Two others were organized in the last half of the century—the Lausanne Committee for World

Evangelization (LCWE) and the Evangelical Missiological Society (EMS). All four have played major roles in the evangelical movement in the past and, in one form or another and one way or another, all four can be expected to play important roles in its future.

The Interdenominational Foreign Mission Association of North America (IFMA)

In direct response to liberalism and modernism in mainline churches, conservative scholars such as Dyson Hague, James Orr, W. H. Griffith Thomas, B. B. Warfield, James Orr and bishops Handley Moule and J. C. Ryle collaborated on an influential series of twelve books entitled *The Fundamentals*. In response to liberalism, but also to the perceived elitism of Edinburgh leadership, in 1917 eleven leaders of "faith missions" including Charles E. Hurlburt, Henry W. Frost and Roland V. Bingham organized the IFMA.[1] Using *The Fundamentals* as a springboard, one of the first items on their agenda was drawing up a "Doctrinal Basis" or "Declaration of Faith" (both designations appear in the literature) on which fellowship and cooperation was based (Frizen 1992, 119–20, 435–36). It consisted of nine fundamental doctrines—the first having to do with the inerrancy of the autographs of the Bible and the last with the requirements of the Great Commission.

Along with other conservatives, IFMA fundamentalists made a significant contribution to world missions, especially in the first half of the century but also beyond. Joel Carpenter reports:

> The fundamentalists . . . contributed about one out of every seven North American Protestant missionaries in the mid-1930s, and by the early 1950s, the fundamentalists' portion had doubled. Their dynamic missionary movement was an important factor, along with other evangelical missions efforts, in the survival and growth

---

1. IFMA was later called the Interdenominational Fellowship of Mission Associations; still later CrossGlobal Link; and now is part of Missio Nexus.

of the foreign missions enterprise in the twentieth
century. (1990, 93)

The IFMA, however, did not accept charismatic missions agencies into its
membership and left other lacunae to be filled as well. Eventually they were.

The Evangelical Fellowship of Mission Agencies (EFMA)

In 1940, pastor/theologian Harold J. Ockenga and missions specialist,
J. Elwin Wright, assumed leadership roles in the forming of a broad
coalition of evangelicals and churches into the National Association
of Evangelicals (NAE). Among the NAE-affiliated organizations/
ministries formed after 1943, two of the more important were formed
as early as 1945—a missionary arm (the EFMA[2]) and a humanitarian
agency called World Relief.

Several observations are worthy of notice at this point. (1) The
NAE and EFMA were organized in response to a perceived separatism
and divisiveness in the IFMA as well as to liberalism and modernism
in the mainline churches. (2) The NAE adopted a seven-article Statement of Faith that differed from the IFMA Declaration of Faith. Not
only was it shorter, but it employed the word "infallible" in preference
to "inerrant" with respect to the Bible. Also, no article on the Christian mission as such was included (perhaps a byproduct of the fact that
it represented the work of NAE organizers, not EFMA organizers as
such). (3) From the beginning the EFMA was more inclusive than
the IFMA both theologically and ecclesiastically. In fact, at the close
of the century, Wade Coggins wrote, "The EFMA broke new ground
by pulling together evangelicals from various traditions, ranging from
Baptist to Reformed, Mennonite, Holiness and Pentecostal. As a
variety of evangelical denominations, missions and service agencies,
and student ministries joined the association, the EFMA experienced
rapid growth" (Coggins, 2000, 333).

---

2.   It was formed mainly out of the New England Fellowship which had been
initially organized in 1929.

The Lausanne Committee for World Evangelization (LCWE)

The Lausanne movement dates back to the World Congress on Evangelism held in Berlin in 1966. Over the years, the word "evangelism" morphed into "evangelization" and, more recently, into "mission." During those years—and especially since its conference in Lausanne in 1974—the movement has become a global force in evangelical missions. Three major conferences (two in the twentieth century and one in the twenty-first) and their respective declarations mark out the road the LCWE has traveled.

Lausanne I (1974) and its Lausanne Covenant constitute a watershed in the history of evangelical missions. The Covenant mirrored the social concern of some, especially certain Latin American evangelical leaders. It contained only fifteen articles, but it set the Lausanne pattern of (1) widening the scope of Christian mission so as to include social action; (2) opting for the word "infallible" with reference to the authority of Scripture; and, (3) forwarding important declarations that combine theology and missiology, faith and practice.

In at least one respect, the significance of Lausanne II in Manila (1988) and its Manila Manifesto rivaled that of Lausanne I. While Lausanne I enlarged the meaning of "mission," it did so in rather guarded fashion. Lausanne II, on the other hand, expanded the scope of Christian mission greatly and unapologetically. The Manila Manifesto consisted of 221 affirmations!

The most inclusive theologically and expansive missiologically has been the conference at Cape Town, South Africa, in 2010, and its Cape Town Commitment. They will be considered at an appropriate juncture later in this paper.

The Evangelical Missiological Society (EMS)

The EMS was formed in 1991, at the instigation and with the support of Donald A. McGavran. Having traveled a rather circuitous path from conciliar inclinations and associations in the 1920s to a convinced conservatism in his later years, in 1988, McGavran urged the formation of a missiological society whose members would be committed to orthodox faith and whose objective would be the discipling of the *ethne* in obedience to the Great Commission. In a personal letter, McGavran (1988) wrote, "I want to lay before you, David, a very important item . . . I think that the evangelical professors of missions need to establish a nationwide organization called openly and courageously 'The American Society of Christian Missiology.'"

Out of McGavran's urging and with his concerns in mind, an academic society was formed that, unlike its predecessor—the Association of Evangelical Professors of Mission—was open to all leaders and scholars with a special interest in world missions; and, unlike the American Society of Missiology, restricted membership to those who could subscribe either to the Declaration of Faith of the IFMA or to the Statement of Faith of the EFMA.

Stated very generally, the EMS was established in order to foster and further the thinking and doing of evangelical missiology and mission in accord with the teachings of Scripture.

Two Streams of Evangelicalism and Three Areas of Concern

As we have noted, though fundamentalism had arisen in response to liberalism, evangelicalism was as much a response to the "denominational separatism and intellectual and cultural isolationism" of fundamentalists as it was to liberalism (McGee 2000, 338). Nevertheless, major controversies soon surfaced among evangelicals themselves. One had to do with "cooperative evangelism." It was occasioned when Billy Graham crusades welcomed liberal clerics into their committees and on to their platforms. Another—sometimes referred to as the "battle for the Bible"—was precipitated when the dean of Fuller Theological Seminary, Daniel Fuller, proposed that the Bible consists of, not just one, but two types of literature: revelational literature that is without error and non-revelational literature that may contain errors.[3]

---

3. Subsequently, Fuller Seminary substituted "infallible" for "inerrant" in the paragraph on Scripture in its Statement of Faith. "Infallible" in this case basically meant that, since God can neither err nor lie, the revealed portion of

Two streams of evangelicalism emerged out of controversies such as these: a more traditional and exclusive stream and a "neo" or new stream that was more progressive and inclusive. Evangelical seminaries, crusades, student groups and enterprises not only evolved but flourished in spite of controversy and schism—so much so that *Time* Magazine declared 1976 to be the Year of the Evangelical. By the end of the 1980s and the beginning of the 1990s, however, some of evangelicalism's most respected scholars were warning fellow-evangelicals that the movement was traveling too fast and too far in three critical areas: core theology; mission priorities, and ecumenical associations.

The Theological Core: A "Crisis of Christian Belief"

As the 1980s gave way to the decade of the 1990s, one of the foremost evangelical theologians of the twentieth century, Carl F. H. Henry, warned Christians that both the integrity of Scripture and doctrinal orthodoxy were in jeopardy not only in the western world as such but even in its churches. In 1988, Henry authored *Twilight of a Great Civilization: The Drift Toward Neo-Paganism.* The following year he delivered a series of lectures at Rutherford House in Edinburgh, Scotland, that were published under the title *Toward a Recovery of Christian Belief: The Rutherford Lectures* (Henry 1990). According to Henry, in the western world " . . . neo-paganism now routinely leaves its mark on the influential secular centers of western learning" (Henry 1990, ix). In western churches, experiential religion has replaced " . . . clear and credible doctrinal directives" (Henry 1990, xi) and " . . . many popular defenders of the faith have traded their intellectual birthright for a mess of pseudo-intellectual pottage" (Henry 1990, back cover). Henry warned " . . . *Christians must once again stand on the rock of divine revelation, defending it against all comers. Only then will we begin to experience a recovery of Christian belief*" (Henry 1990, back cover, emphasis mine).

Scripture is wholly true. But the unrevealed portion of Scripture is not—not in its entirety at any rate (Hubbard 1979, 18).

Missiological Priorities: The "Lion Facing Missiology"
In his twilight years, the venerable Father of Church Growth, Donald McGavran, looked on as first ecumenists and then evangelicals defined and redefined the mission of the church in terms of education, medicine, relief, interreligious dialogue, community development, social justice, and much else. Deeply concerned, he determined that there was a profound need for the formation of an academic society that would say quite frankly that the purpose of mission/missiology is to carry out the Great Commission; that anything other than that may be a good thing to do, but it is not "missiology" (McGavran 1988). He then published an article entitled "Missiology Faces a Lion" (1989) in which he depicted all-encompassing mission/missiology as a voracious lion ready to gobble up resources desperately needed to carry out the Great Commission task of "discipling the *ethne*." History has proved McGavran to have been a good prophet.[4]

Ecumenical Associations: The Word Evangelical
is "Losing its Descriptive Power"
After carefully examining the evangelical movement that emerged in the late 1940s and became more or less main stream in the 1960s, Indiana State University Professor of History, Richard Pierard, observed that traditionalists, restorationists, Adventists, Pentecostals, Holiness people, fundamentalists and pietists; Episcopalian, Presbyterian and Congregationalist denominations; and, mainline, liberal and ecumenical churches—all were included under the one label "evangelical." Coupled " . . . with the indigenization of mission society operations, the multinational character of relief and evangelistic organizations, and the sending of missionaries by people in third world countries themselves, this broad evangelicalism was a global phenomenon" (Pierard 1991, 313). Pierard concluded that evangelicals " . . . labored to bring together people of like mind from all the various Christian communions, whether or not they

---

4.   Among others, Keith E. Eitel (2010, 30–40) has taken note of the tentative but close relationship between the various meanings ascribed to mission on the one hand, and late-twentieth-century theological liberalism on the other.

had been involved in the earlier struggles for doctrinal purity" (Pierard 1991, 312). And that "As the movement for evangelical ecumenism proceeded apace, *it became increasingly clear that the term [evangelical—ed.] now encompassed so complex a sociological reality that it was losing its description power*" (Pierard 1991, 313, emphasis mine).

EVANGELICALS IN THE TWENTY-FIRST CENTURY: PROBLEMS AND PROSPECTS

As evangelicals entered the twenty-first century, the status of global evangelicalism was mixed. The evangelical movement was growing and, in certain areas of the world, flourishing (Allen 2013; Keesee 2014; Olson 2003). At the same time, there existed a certain ambiguity. A new generation of evangelicals inherited both significant problems and promising proposals; and they managed to create a few of their own and of both types.

Problematic Aspects of the Evangelical Heritage

Although over 1200 delegates had gathered at the great World Missionary Conference in Edinburgh in 1910, no more than 300 gathered at a 2010 Edinburgh conference in commemoration of it! Moreover, the initial draft of the "Common Call" generated at the 2010 conference advanced the idea that the "mission of God" is primarily concerned with liberation and justice. Not until later was the word "evangelism" inserted into the Common Call! (Fox 2011, 89). So, if the 2010 conference constituted a commemoration, it also seems to have been something of a culmination. It signaled the failure, not necessarily of ecumenism/ecumenicity as such, but of the twentieth century conciliar form of it.

As for the evangelical churches and missions of the early twenty-first century, though they have progressed in ways that generally have been applauded and even celebrated, they have not progressed in ways that resolved inherited issues of fundamental concern. In fact, in some ways they have progressed in ways that exacerbated those issues.

1) The Lausanne Committee for World Evangelization has continued to evolve and play an ever larger role in evangelical missions globally. If Lausanne 1974 and the Lausanne Covenant—and Manila 1988 and the Manila Manifesto—were important to twentieth-century missions, Cape Town 2010 and the Cape Town Commitment with its "Confession of Faith and a Call to Action" may well prove to be even more so to twenty-first century missions. The Commitment itself merits careful study for a variety of reasons, but especially because of its ambiguity in defining and describing both Christian faith and Christian mission.

As for the Christian faith, the Commitment sets a record for evangelical declarations of its kind totaling (in Word) 42 pages, 513 paragraphs, 1706 lines, and 22,697 words. Part I is entitled "FOR THE LORD WE LOVE—The Cape Town Confession of Faith" but consists primarily of a series of "love statements" highlighting love for the Lord, love for the word of God, love for God's world, love for the mission of God, and love for much, much more. The Commitment routinely oscillates between confessional objectivity and experiential subjectivity; between "true truth" and "felt love."

As concerns the mission of the church, in Part II entitled, "FOR THE WORLD WE SERVE—A Call to Action," mission is deemed to be "integral mission" and defined as making the gospel known and demonstrating God's Kingdom by striving for justice and peace, caring for all creation; and doing a host of "good Christian things to do" (to use McGavran's phrase).

In short, it is arguable that, if the LCWE has made important contributions to contemporary missions—and it has—it has also contributed to confusion on some of the most fundamental of controversial issues.

2) Recent changes in the Evangelical Missiological Society have not been as noticeable as those in the LCWE, but changes there have been.[5] McGavran would undoubtedly approve of some of them.

---

5. The quotations that follow are taken from materials received by registrants of the annual meeting of the North Central Region of the EMS meeting at

Very possibly he would not approve of others. By way of examples, consider the following.

As relates to purpose and program, "EMS exists to advance the cause of world evangelization." This is done by the ". . . study and evaluation of mission concepts and strategies from a biblical perspective with a view to commending sound mission theory and practice. . . ." Also by facilitating "the discussion of missiological and theological concerns growing out of the mandate of the Church to disciple the nations . . ." McGavran would be most approving of all of this.

As relates to membership, bereft of the faith statements of the old IFMA and EFMA at the time of their merger into the new Missio Nexus, EMS leaders chose to require adherence to the Lausanne Covenant at least on an interim basis. Strictly speaking, however, the Lausanne Covenant is not a statement of faith so much as it is a statement of mission. It is incumbent upon current leaders and members of the EMS to select or construct a more adequate faith statement with an eye to the future. It is well that the Society is ". . .Evangelical that is . . . committed to the doctrinal foundations that salvation is found in Jesus Christ alone and that the Bible is the inspired Word of God." Good as far as it goes, I hardly think that would be sufficient to have satisfied McGavran.

In short, initially the EMS was so constituted as to define and defend an understanding of Christian mission that is conservative and orthodox in contradistinction to and understanding that is liberal and modernistic. To the extent that the EMS is successful overall, it will be successful in those endeavors.

3) Turning to the IFMA/CrossGlobal Link and EFMA/Mission Exchange associations, after two years of discussion, a merger was consummated in 2012 and the new organization was called Missio Nexus. Steve Moore (formerly president of The Mission Exchange) and Marvin Newell (formerly executive director of CrossGlobal Link)

Trinity Evangelical Divinity School, April 25, 2015. See also https://www .emsweb.org/about.

were elected president and senior vice-president respectively and a new statement of faith was adopted. Certain aspects of the merger process are especially germane to our present discussion.

First, though consulted, the NAE as such was not involved in either the merger itself or in the development of the new statement of faith (Newell 2014). EMS leadership was neither consulted nor involved. The involvement of both NAE and EMS leaders—especially those of the NAE—would have been ideal.

Second, the new Missio Nexus statement of faith consists of twelve articles selected from the faith statements of the two associations. Following the text of the old EFMA/Mission Exchange statement of faith, for example, the Missio Nexus statement of faith opts for the word "infallible" in preference to the word "inerrant" with reference to the authority and integrity of Scripture. Following the IFMA/CrossGlobal Link Declaration of Faith, the merged Statement of Faith includes an article on the Great Commission mission. The new Statement of Faith, therefore, represents a compromise between two evangelical organizations. It is not a response to controversial issues posed either by evangelicals within the movement or liberals outside it.

Third, the Preamble to the Missio Nexus Statement of Faith states, "We will continue to develop a Missio Nexus for the largest and most inclusive expression of Great Commission oriented evangelicals in North America that fosters shared learning, opens doors for collaborative action and produces increased effectiveness" (Missio Nexus). In other words, quite matter-of-factly Missio Nexus seems to open the door to an ever-widening evangelical ecumenism. However, without boundaries, evangelicalism cannot remain evangelical.

In short, while the merged Missio Nexus unquestionably lessens duplication and heightens cooperation, it also generates potential for enhancing an evangelical future on the one hand, or for diminishing it on the other.

Hopeful Aspects of the Evangelical Heritage—Positive Precedent and a Promising Proposal

It is apparent that, as the evangelical movement entered the twenty-first century, it was in flux. Moreover, much that was problematic for traditionalists seemed proper to progressives, and vice-versa. What is needed is some way of rising above the fray, examining controversial issues from a higher perspective, and reaching a consensus that will enable evangelicals to discover (or recover) higher ground and occupy it. That way is marked out by historical precedents and a modern proposal.

Church History and Orthodox Doctrine

From the very beginning, Christian churches and missions have formulated truth claims into doctrinal/creedal/faith statements and declarations. For sake of convenience, I often refer to them as "faith statements." But whatever term might be used, the historical record is clear: ecclesiastical and missionary movements and associations of virtually all types have routinely adopted or developed faith statements, more often than not at the expense of significant controversy and great sacrifice. It is with that in mind that Douglas Sweeney has stipulated the meaning of "evangelical." He writes:

> I prefer to describe evangelicalism with more specificity as a movement that is based on historical classical Christian orthodoxy, shaped by a Reformational understanding of the gospel, and distinguished from other such movements in the history of the church by a set of beliefs and behaviors forged in the fires of the eighteenth-century revivals—the so-called "Great Awakening" . . . beliefs and behaviors that had mainly to do with the spread of the gospel abroad. (Sweeney 2008, 2)

Roland Allen's "Resubmission" Proposal

Readers, including scholars, have often missed it, but Lesslie Newbigin did not. In his foreword to the 1961 edition of Allen's celebrated *Missionary Methods: St. Paul's or Ours?* Newbigin maintains that it never was Allen's intention to convince missiologists and missionaries of the rightness of this or that "method of Paul." Rather, Allen's primary objective was to urge " . . . the resubmission in each generation of the traditions of men to the Word and Spirit of God" (Newbigin 1961, ii). Quoting Allen, Newbigin writes, "There are no 'methods' here which will 'work' if they are 'applied.' There is a summons to everyone who will hear to submit inherited patterns of church life to the searching scrutiny of the Spirit" (Newbigin 1961, ii).

In effect, Allen's resubmission approach is fundamentally different than the approach taken by John R. Mott and his colleagues at Edinburgh just two years prior to the publication of Allen's book. In the interest of unity, they proscribed theological discussion. In the interest of truth, Allen prescribed it. Moreover, Allen practiced what he preached. As Newbigin makes clear, Allen's epoch-making book on Paul's missionary methods is not really a manual on missionary methods as much as it is a searching scrutiny into the missionary patterns of Allen's missionary contemporaries.

Using Paul's missionary practices as model and measure, Allen finds the patterns and practices of his contemporaries more "colonial" than "apostolic." Using the "apostolic preaching" of Paul as model and measure, Allen charges his contemporaries with failure to preach "stern doctrine" and a "full gospel." He writes " . . . we have lost two prominent elements of Paul's gospel: the doctrine of judgment at hand, and the doctrine of the wrath of God" (Allen 1961, 72). This loss, Allen goes on to say, resulted in a failure to warn those who reject the gospel of the possibility of imminent judgment on the one hand, and in the devising an "easy doctrine of evangelization" on the other (Allen 1961, 72).

Generational resubmission should be practiced widely and often today, especially among evangelicals and especially among evangelicals involved in Christian mission. Church members—not just church leaders—should discuss mission priorities with a view to determining which candidates and ministries to support, not on the basis of personal preferences and interpersonal relationships, but on the basis of biblical and orthodox teachings. Schools and professional societies would do well to collectively scrutinize controversial issues bearing on the integrity of Scripture and the truth of the gospel—including those issues that arise from even the most popular of patterns and proposals. Early on, EMS conferences, for example, highlighted open discussion and debates on such topics as C. Peter Wagner's territorial spirits and (in conjunction with the Evangelical Theological Society) on Clark Pinnock's incipient open theism. In retrospect, I believe the EMS erred in not responding early on to John Stott's openness to evangelical scrutiny of his "conditional immortality" proposal (Edwards 1988, 320).

At its very beginning, the conciliar ecumenical movement refused to consider even the most fundamental of the Christian faith in order to enhance fellowship and unity. In their very beginnings, conservative evangelical associations, on the other hand, based both faith and fellowship on an authoritative Bible and orthodox doctrine. As made apparent from a reading of *The Changing Face of World Missions* (Pocock, Van Rheenan and McConnell 2005) and much else, changes there have been and changes there will be. But the future evangelical missions—and the evangelical movement as a whole—will depend more on changes that are not made than changes that are made.

PRACTICING RESUBMISSION: THINGS THAT DIFFER AND MAKE A DIFFERENCE

Generational resubmission objectives will most readily be achieved—and higher ground will most readily be discovered and occupied—when certain "tools" are employed. No doubt there are others, but here I make special mention of several that will prove useful. At first blush they may seem commonplace or even trite, but upon reflection it will be clear that—when push comes to shove—defective tools are sometimes employed and effective tools are sometimes overlooked.

"Stakes," "Cords," and "Tethers"

In his dialogue with David Edwards, John Stott says that liberalism resembles a gas-filled balloon that takes off and rises into the air buoyant and free, directed only by its own built-in navigational responses to wind and pressure, but unrestrained by ties to the earth. Evangelical "kites," on the other hand, also travel great distances and soar to great heights, but are "tethered" to earth and held fast by divine revelation. Stott says that evangelical "kites" often need a longer "string" (or "cord") because evangelicals are not renowned for creative thinking. "Nevertheless," he writes, "at least in the ideal, I see evangelicals as finding true freedom under the authority of revealed truth, and combining a radical mind and lifestyle with a conservative commitment to Scripture" (Edwards 1988, 106).

Stott's analogies are indeed insightful. We do well, however, to think of "tethers" more specifically as the faith statements discussed above—those orthodox creeds and confessions that connect churches and missions to the "stake" of Scripture. Concerning these "tethers," Ronald Heine writes:

> By the end of the second century these doctrines about Jesus and God were being summarized in creed-like statements sometimes called the rule of faith . . . The doctrines contained in these statements of faith were considered to go back to the teachings of the apostles and to represent what Jesus Christ himself had taught them . . . *It was this connection with Christ through the teachings of the apostles found in the Scriptures that gave authority to the doctrines accepted by the earliest Christians.* (Heine 2013, 7–8, emphasis mine)

Faith Statements of "Older Churches" and "Younger Churches"

Not often discussed even in missions circles, the formation and adoption of faith statements is of critical importance to churches whether they be older (mother or sending) churches or younger (daughter or receiving) churches. Younger receiving churches around the world immediately and invariably face problems precipitated by local culture and religions. Sooner or later they will also encounter issues that have been confronted by older sending churches as well. It is well to consider the words of J. H. Bavinck and to discuss, decide and work with younger receiving churches in this regard:

> In many instances young churches, at least provisionally, accept the confession of faith of the mother church to which they owe their existence . . . It is equally obvious, however, that gradually they acquire the need for their own confession of faith, in which they can express what they themselves have found in God's Word. Such a confession must be formulated in opposition to the forces opposing them . . . in opposition to the old religions, still followed by many in their environment . . . against Buddhism, Hinduism, Islam, and against the phenomenon of syncretism . . . (Bavinck 1960, 203–204)

Statements of Faith and Statements of Mission

Nancy and Howard Olsen urge church leaders to focus on short- and long-term markers that keep a church moving in the right direction rather than on semantic differences between concepts such as "mission" and "vision," and "objectives" and "goals" (Olsen and Olsen 2009, 22). To a degree we can agree, but only to a degree. The difference between faith/creedal statements on the one hand, and mission/vision statements on the other is not simply semantic or pragmatic; it is quintessential. Mission/vision statements grow out of faith/creedal statements—or, at least, they should. Faith/creedal statements do not grow out of mission/vision statements—or, at least, they should not.

Historian of theology, John Leith, insists that the doing and making of creeds is, in fact, " . . . indispensable to any other service that can be rendered" (1963, 2). Why? For many reasons. Among them, creedal statements: (1) put forth interpretations of Bible teachings that are the result of interaction over time, (2) represent the thinking of broad bodies of orthodox Christian believers, and (3) emanate from the common life of Christians as much as from the study of scholars.

Ad Hoc and Ad Duro Faith Statements

Though Trinity's Tite Tiénou entertains a high regard for the Lausanne Covenant, he nevertheless astutely calls attention to the limitations of all documents engendered at conferences and consultations of the Lausanne variety. Evangelicals need to ponder the truth and implications of Tiénou's words:

> I think that the challenge for evangelicals is that every one of the Lausanne Congresses was actually an ad hoc event. It was organized for the occasion. As a result, continuity between the three is really difficult. Whereas the World Council of Churches or the Roman Catholic Church has an infrastructure behind it, so they have continuity. When evangelicals gather, the people who come are the ones to cause the change when they go home . . . They're not answerable to anyone. We came as individuals, not as delegates of our respective churches. (2011, 13)

Conversational Dialogue and Confrontational Dialogue

Biblical (including Pauline) gospel-related interaction and communication featured dialogue—not just benign conversational dialogue with which we are familiar today, but dialogue/discussion that sometimes involved debate and even disputation. Gottlob Schrenk says that, even when used of lectures, *dialegomai* in the New Testament sometimes refers to " . . . lectures which were likely to end in disputation" (1964, 94). He also notes that "much of New Testament gospel communication was dialogical even though that precise word may not be used" (Schrenk 1964, 94).

Upon examination of the biblical and historical records, it is apparent that Schrenk is correct. Furthermore, dialogical discussion involving debate and disputation was not only prominent in the sending of Paul and his missionary team, it was also important in producing the classical creedal statements of the church; in clarifying justification by faith in the Reformation; in fueling the revival fires of the Great Awakening; and in motivating the early pioneers of modern missions. Historically, discussions/debates had to do with a wide variety of issues essential to a biblical gospel and integral to their resolution.

Biblical Ecumenicity and Sub-Biblical Ecumenicity

The decision of conciliars to rule theological discussion out of order in Edinburgh 1910 was fundamentally flawed because it prized unity at the expense of truth. A generation later and rightly or wrongly (or wrongly and rightly), NAE organizers faulted fundamentalists for bickering over doctrine but failing to show Christian love. These bits of history serve to remind us that the Lord Jesus prayed that his disciples (and we as their followers) be characterized by both true truth (John. 17:17–19) and divine love (John. 17:26).

At least in theory, people on both sides of the conciliar-conservative divide lay claim to both truth and love. In practice, however, either truth or love tends to predominate. Nevertheless, in practice as well as theory, possessing one does not preempt need for the other. Appeals for unity and cooperation that are based on both truth and love are worthy of consideration. Appeals for unity and cooperation based on either one at the expense of the other are not.

THE EVANGELICAL FUTURE: TWO VIEWS

As we have seen, a decade or so before the turn of the century in the late 1980s and early '90s, Carl Henry looked ahead and foresaw the "twilight of western civilization" and the partial eclipse of orthodoxy in the church, including the evangelical church. Donald McGavran looked ahead and foresaw the "lion" of unfettered holism consuming the resources required to "disciple the *ethne*." At the turn of the century, Richard Pierard viewed the evangelical movement as being so theologically and ecclesiastically diverse as to render the very term "evangelical" meaningless.

No doubt readers will have their own opinion as to whether or not—or the degree to which—these scholars were correct. The question today is, "Now that we are well over a decade into the twenty-first century, how do scholars today view the evangelical future?" I can deal here with but two scholars whose views on this question are instructive, if not necessarily representative. The Jordan-Trexler Professor of Religion at Roanoke College, Gerald McDermott, foresees a division in evangelicalism growing out of a controversial issue that has plagued theologians for many, many years. Coalition on Revival head, Jay Grimstead, on the other hand, views the evangelical movement as having divided already over a still larger theological issue. At the same time, he foresees the possibility of an evangelical future that overcomes theological differences of the kind noted by McDermott.

Gerald R. McDermott's "Emerging Divide between Meliorists and Traditionalists"

McDermott maintains that the old division between "Arminian synergism" (i.e., our wills cooperate with God's will in salvation and sanctification) and "Reformed monergism" (i.e., God's will determines ours without making us into robots) has now morphed into a larger and more divisive issue: namely, a division between Meliorists and Traditionalists.

In McDermott's usage of the terms, Meliorist theologians prioritize experience over doctrine: " . . . orthopraxy is 'prior to' orthodoxy;

the main purpose of revelation is transformation 'rather than' information; and doctrine is 'secondary' to evangelical experience" (McDermott 2013, 366). Roger E. Olson, Steve Chalke, Brian McLaren, Clark Pinnock and Tony Campolo are held to be of this persuasion. Traditional theologians prioritize doctrine over experience; place orthodoxy before orthopraxy; and believe the main purpose of revelation to be information. Carl F. H. Henry, Kenneth Kantzer, J. I. Packer, D. A. Carson, Norman Geisler, George Lindbeck, Kevin Vanhoozer, Alister McGrath, and Thomas Oden are held to be of this persuasion. McDermott believes that the division between these scholars and their views is deep and wide enough to be harbinger of a major division yet to come in the evangelicalism movement of the future.

Jay Grimstead's "Global Generic Statement of Faith"

Between 1977 and 2012, Jay Grimstead played a major role in the founding and/or forwarding of three movements—the International Council on Biblical Inerrancy, the Coalition on Revival, and the International Church Council Project. His overarching goal has been " . . . to define and defend traditional doctrines of Christian orthodoxy by creating modern, creed-like position statements through the cooperative work of a consortium of evangelical theologians working together by consensus" (Grimstead and Clingman 2013, 3). With that goal in mind, a consortium of like-minded theologians has produced 42 Articles of " . . . carefully crafted creedal statements which cover a majority of the basic, foundational doctrines of the historic Christian church found in most of the church's various creeds through the past 2000 years" (Grimstead 2015, 2).

Grimstead sees global evangelicalism as divided already. About half of all evangelicals believe that the Bible is part false and part true and about half believe it is wholly true. He does not disparage the sincerity of the former half but, with his mentor Francis Schaeffer, he believes that the inerrancy of the Bible is the watershed of the theological world. Accordingly, he is persuaded that the future of evangelicalism lies with those evangelicals who believe the Bible is wholly true. And in line with this, he reports that the Coalition on Revival is now organizing a "multi-national, multi-denominational, Bible-believing Global Church Council" that will use the 42 Articles "To establish for the 21st century a united, biblical-theological standard of doctrine for the global Body of Christ, which standard is consistent with the mainstream theology of the first twenty centuries" (Grimstead and Clingman 2013, 2). Grimstead believes that it is possible to frame a "Global Generic Statement of Faith" that will support the essentials of Christian doctrine and yet allow for long-standing differences of interpretation in certain areas of theology, eschatology and ecclesiology. The creation of this statement of faith is expected to be one of the first undertakings of Coalition on Revival meetings in Wittenberg in 2017, Zurich in 2019, and Worms in 2021 prior to the 500th anniversaries of three historic events of sixteenth-century Protestant Christianity.

CONCLUSION

Long-term, the future is not in doubt. Short-range, there is every indication that a tsunami is on the way. If so, it will have economic, social, and political dimensions. At its epicenter, however, it will be religious, moral, and theological. For contemporary evangelicals, an inevitable and inescapable question is "How can the evangelical movement survive the coming tsunami and best preserve biblical missions?" There is, of course, no simple answer to that, but whatever else we evangelicals do by way of preparation, we simply must discover and occupy (or rediscover and reoccupy) higher ground both theologically and missiologically. Generational resubmission could be—and should be—part of that process.

The ecumenical and evangelical movements of the last century exhibit certain similarities to be sure. But they are also very different—primarily in the ways in which they have gone about the twin tasks of determining truth and establishing unity. If there is more reason for optimism in evangelical missions today than was warranted among conciliar missions of the last century it is because—like the more traditional evangelicals of the twentieth century—they take biblical authority and orthodox doctrine with utmost seriousness.

There is room for optimism in this regard. It is heartening to hear the reports of colleagues who say that current seminarians are singularly committed to Christ and thoroughly dedicated to his cause. One colleague even compared them favorably to the post-World War II generation that produced the Inca martyrs and the mission scholars and practitioners who, by God's goodness and grace, brought about Ralph Winter's "twenty-five unbelievable years" (Winter 1969). Returning once again to Roland Allen, J. D. Payne (2012) reports that the centennial of the publication of *Missionary Methods* was widely celebrated by evangelicals. Payne adds, "I often hear of how Allen has influenced people's thinking and actions regarding missions in the twenty-first century . . . Even though Allen sleeps, he still speaks—*but this time people are listening*" (2012, 242–243, emphasis mine).

In summary, ultimately this generation of evangelicals will be forced to choose between two options. They will either drift with the tide and hazard the mountainous waves of a coming tsunami, or they will rise to the arduous task of claiming and occupying higher ground. If professors and students—and pastors and missionaries—listen to Allen and listen well, hope for the future of evangelicalism and its missions will be enhanced and enhanced greatly. If, on the other hand, they do not listen, hope for the future will be diminished and diminished greatly. Evangelicals must respond to global changes by aligning (or realigning) missiology with sound theology. Southwestern Baptist Seminary's John Massey states the challenge well:

> Every generation must reform theology, missiology and denominational structures, according to biblical mandates and principles to remain relevant to the needs of a lost world. As evangelicals, in general, and Southern Baptists, in particular, we are facing a critical moment in our collective Christian and denominational life—one that calls for a missiological

alignment with sound biblical theology. In order to do so, evangelicals, and Southern Baptists among them, must critically evaluate and reject the cultural influences of pragmatism, consumerism, and ethnocentrism that are embedded within the structures of culture and adopt instead a radical commitment to the joys and demands of the Great Commission mandate of making disciples of all nations. (2013, 118)

A caution should be conjoined with that challenge: namely, sound biblical theology must be allowed to effect its work in sending as well as receiving churches and missions. Retired pastor of Moody Church, Warren Wiersbe, states the caution well: " . . . doctrine and devotion have been joined together by God and . . . no man dare put them asunder. Our understanding of doctrine ought to lead us into greater devotion to Christ, and our deeper devotion ought to make us better servants and soul-winners" (2011, 121–22).

The church . . . exists
to bear the glory of God's Word
from generation to generation
and from century to century,
until faith will finally be
transformed into light.
J. H. Bavinck (1960, 69)

REFERENCES

Allen, John L., Jr. 2013. *The Global War on Christians: Dispatches from the Front Lines of Anti-Christian Persecution.* New York: Crown Publishing Company.

Allen, Roland. 1961. *Missionary Methods: St. Paul's or Ours?* Grand Rapids, MI: William B. Eerdmans Publishing Company.

Bavinck, J. H. 1960. *An Introduction to the Science of Missions.* Translated by David H. Freeman. Grand Rapids, MI: Baker Books.

Beaver, R. Pierce. 1964. *From Missions to Mission: Protestant World Mission Today and Tomorrow.* New York: Association Press.

Carpenter, Joel. 1990. "Propagating the Faith Once Delivered." In *Earthen Vessels: American Evangelicals and Foreign Missions, 1880–1980,* edited by Joel Carpenter and Wilbert R. Shenk, 92–132. Grand Rapids, MI: William B. Eerdmans Publishing Company.

Coggins, W. T. 2000. "Evangelical Fellowship of Mission Agencies." In *Evangelical Dictionary of World Missions,* edited by A. Scott Moreau, Harold Netland, and Charles Van Engen, 332–333. Grand Rapids, MI: Baker Books.

Edwards, David L., and John R. W. Stott. 1988. *Evangelical Essentials: A Liberal-Evangelical Dialogue.* Downers Grove, IL: Intervarsity Press.

Eitel, Keith E. 2010. "On Becoming Missional: Interacting with Charles Van Engen." In *MissionShift: Global Mission Issues in the Third Millennium,* edited by David J. Hesselgrave and Ed Stetzer, 30–40. Nashville: B&H Publishing Group.

Fox, Frampton F. 2011. "A Participant's Account of Edinburgh 2010." *Evangelical Missions Quarterly,* 47, no. 1: 88–93.

Frizen, Edwin L, Jr. 1992. *75 Years of IFMA 1917–1992: The Nondenominational Missions Movement.* Pasadena, CA: William Carey Library.

Grimstead, Jay, and Eugene Calvin Clingman. 2013. *Rebuilding Civilization on the Bible: Proclaiming the Truth on 24 Controversial Issues.* Ventura, CA: Nordskog.

Grimstead, Jay. 2015. *COR Update for May 2015*. Murphys, CA: P.O. Box 1139.

Heine, Ronald. 2013. *Classical Christian Doctrine: Introducing the Essentials of the Ancient Christian Faith*. Grand Rapids, MI: Baker Books.

Henry, Carl F. H. 1988. *Twilight of a Great Civilization: The Drift Toward Neo-paganism*. Wheaton, IL: Crossway.

———. 1990. *Toward a Recovery of Christian Belief: The Rutherford Lectures*. Wheaton, IL: Crossway.

Hesselgrave, David J. 2005. *Paradigms in Conflict: 10 Key Questions in Christian Missions Today*. Grand Rapids, MI: Kregel Publications.

Hubbard, David Allen. 1979. *What We Evangelicals Believe: Expositions of Christian Doctrine Based on 'The Statement of Faith' of Fuller Theological Seminary*. Pasadena, CA: Fuller Theological Seminary.

Keesee, Tim. 2014. *Dispatches from the Front: Stories of Gospel Advance in the World's Difficult Places*. Wheaton, IL: Crossway.

Leith, John H., ed. 1963. *Creeds of the Churches: A Reader in Christian Doctrine from the Bible to the Present*. Garden City, NY: Doubleday (Anchor Books).

Massey, John D. 2013. "Tracing Contemporary Shifts in the Eschatological Underpinnings of Southern Baptist Missions." *Journal of Evangelism & Missions* 12, no. 2: 107–118.

McDermott, Gerald R. 2013. "The Emerging Divide in Evangelical Theology." *Journal of the Evangelical Theological Society* 56, no. 2 (June): 355–377.

McGavran, Donald A. 1988. Personal letter to David J. Hesselgrave, April 7.

———. 1989. "Missiology Faces a Lion." *Missiology: An International Review* 17, no. 3 (July): 335–341.

McGee, Gary B. 2000. "Evangelical Missions Conferences." In *Evangelical Dictionary of World Missions*, edited by A. Scott Moreau, Harold Netland, and Charles Van Engen, 335–336. Grand Rapids, MI: Baker Books.

Moreau, A. Scott. 2000. "Putting the Survey in Perspective." In *Mission Handbook: U.S. and Canadian Christian Ministries Overseas*, 18th ed., edited by John A. Siewert and Dotsie Tolliver, 33–80, Wheaton, IL: EMIS.

Neill, Stephen. 1959. *Creative Tension: The Duff Lectures, 1958.* London: Edinburgh House Press.

Newbigin, Lesslie. 1961. Foreword to *Missionary Methods: St. Paul's or Ours?* by Roland Allen, i-iii. Grand Rapids, MI: William B. Eerdmans Publishing Company.

Newell, Marvin 2014. Personal letter to David J. Hesselgrave, July 30.

Missio Nexus. 2015. "Statement of Faith." Missio Nexus. Accessed November 6, 2015. http://missionexus.org/statement-of-faith/.

Olsen, Nancy D., and Howard W. Olsen. 2009. "Elements of a Strategic Plan." *NABA Ledger* (Winter): 22–31.

Olson, C. Gordon. 2003. *What in the World is God Doing? The Essentials of Global Mission* Cedar Knolls, NJ: Global Gospel Publishers.

Payne, J. D. 2012. "Roland Allen's Missionary Methods at One Hundred." In *Paul's Missionary Methods: In His Time and Ours,* edited by Robert L. Plummer and John Mark Terry, 235–244. Downers Grove, IL: Intervarsity Press.

Pierard, Richard V. 1991. "Evangelicalism." In *The New 20th Century Encyclopedia of Christian Knowledge,* 2nd ed., general editor J. D. Douglas, 311–313. Grand Rapids, MI: Baker Books.

Pocock, Michael, Gailyn Van Rheenen, and Douglas McConnell. 2005. *The Changing Face of World Missions: Engaging Contemporary Issues and Trends.* Grand Rapids, MI: Baker Academic.

Scherer, James A. 1993. "Church, Kingdom, and *Missio Dei.*" In *The Good News of the Kingdom: Mission Theology for the Third Millennium,* edited by Charles Van Engen, Dean Gilliland, and Paul Pierson, 82–95. Maryknoll, NY: Orbis Books.

Schrenk, Gottlob. 1964. "Dialegomai." In *Theological Dictionary of the New Testament,* Vol 2, edited by Gerhard Kittel and Gerhard Friedrich. Translated by G. W. Bromiley, 93–97. Grand Rapids, MI: William B. Eerdmans Publishing Company.

Sweeney, Douglas A. 2008. "Introduction." In *The Great Commission: Evangelicals and the History of World Mission,* edited by Martin Klauber and Scott Manetsch, 1–9. Nashville, TN: B&H Academic.

Tiénou, Tite. 2011. "Engaging Global Reconciliation." *Trinity Magazine* (Spring): 10–14.

Wiersbe, Warren W. 2001. *10 People Every Christian Should Know.* Grand Rapids, MI: Baker Books.

Winter, Ralph D. 1969. *The Unbelievable Years 1945–1969.* Pasadena, CA: William Carey Library.